Metaprogramming with Pytnon

A programmer's guide to writing reusable code to build
smarter applications

Sulekha AloorRavi

BIRMINGHAM—MUMBAI

Metaprogramming with Python

Associate Group Product Manager: Gebin George

Publishing Product Manager: Shweta Bairoliya

Senior Editor: Nisha Cleetus

Content Development Editor: Yashi Gupta

Technical Editor: Pradeep Sahu

Copy Editor: Safis Editing

Project Coordinator: Deeksha Thakkar

Proofreader: Safis Editing

Indexer: Hemangini Bari

Production Designer: Prashant Ghare

Marketing Coordinator: Sonakshi Bubbar

First published: August 2022
Production reference: 1110822

Published by Packt Publishing Ltd.
Livery Place
35 Livery Street
Birmingham
B3 2PB, UK.

ISBN 978-1-83855-465-1

www.packt.com

To my husband, Dileep V, and to all my family members, for their sacrifices and for exemplifying the power of determination during one of the toughest times of our lives.

– Sulekha AloorRavi

Contributors

About the author

Sulekha AloorRavi is an engineer and data scientist with a wide technical breadth and deep understanding of many technologies and systems. Her background has led her to working on the advanced Python-based application development in the field of artificial intelligence. She enjoys solving real-world business problems with technology and working with data science and business intelligence teams to deliver real value.

She has 15+ years of experience in software engineering and has worked with major IT solution providers and international banks. She graduated with an engineering degree in information technology and later completed a postgraduate program in big data and machine learning. She also enjoys teaching artificial intelligence and machine learning.

I want to thank the people who have been close to me and supported me, especially my husband, Dileep, my nephew, Sathvik, and all my family members.

About the reviewers

Florian Dahlitz has worked in the IT industry together with companies in the insurance, banking, and public industries to realize digitalization and automation as well as AI projects. He received a BSc in applied computer science from the Baden-Württemberg Cooperative State University and will shortly receive his MSc in information systems engineering and management from the **Karlsruhe Institute of Technology** (**KIT**). Florian enjoys teaching others programming in Python and helps them raise their Python skills to the next level. He spends his free time in nature and likes to capture landscapes with his camera.

Sri Manikanta Palakollu is a full-stack web developer with experience in Java, Python, C, C++, databases, AEM, machine learning, and data science. He is a tech reviewer for various tech book publishers. He has published many articles in various fields, such as data science, programming, and cybersecurity, in publications such as HackerNoon, freeCodeCamp, and DDI. He also wrote a book named *Practical System Programming with C, Apress Publications*.

Sri Manikanta has won a national-level hackathon and regularly contributes to various open source projects. He has mentored more than 5,000 students in many national- and international-level coding hackathons hosted by multiple organizations, colleges, and universities.

Dr. Madhavi Vaidya is an experienced and qualified academician and researcher with a demonstrated history of working in the education management industry, skilled in various programming languages.

Dr. Madhavi has an understanding and knowledge of various programming and database technologies, data analytics, information retrieval, software engineering, and project management. She is a strong education professional with a Master of Computer Applications and Doctor of Philosophy in the subject of computer science and engineering. One of the key areas of her research is big data analytics using Hadoop MapReduce and various big data technologies.

Table of Contents

Part 2: Deep Dive – Building Blocks of Metaprogramming I

3

Understanding Decorators and their Applications

4

Working with Metaclasses

5

Understanding Introspection

6

Implementing Reflection on Python Objects

7

Understanding Generics and Typing

8

Defining Templates for Algorithms

Part 3: Deep Dive – Building Blocks of Metaprogramming II

9

Understanding Code through Abstract Syntax Tree

10

Understanding Method Resolution Order of Inheritance

14

Generating Code from AST

15

Implementing a Case Study

16

Following Best Practices

Index

Other Books You May Enjoy

Preface

Effective and reusable code makes your application development process seamless and easily maintainable. With Python, you have access to advanced metaprogramming features that you can use to build high-performing applications.

This book starts by introducing you to the need for and applications of metaprogramming, before navigating the fundamentals of object-oriented programming. As you progress, you will learn about simple decorators, then work with meta classes, and later focus on introspection and reflection.

You will also delve into generics and typing, before defining templates for algorithms.

After that, you will understand your code using abstract syntax trees and explore method resolution order. This book also shows you how to create your own dynamic objects before structuring the objects through design patterns. Finally, you will learn about simple code-generation techniques along with best practices and eventually build your own applications.

By the end of this learning journey, you will have the skills and confidence you need to design and build reusable high-performing applications that can solve real-world problems.

Who this book is for

If you are an intermediate-level Python programmer looking to enhance your coding skills by developing reusable and advanced frameworks, this book is for you. Basic knowledge of Python programming will help you get the most out of this learning journey.

What this book covers

Chapter 1, The Need for and Applications of Metaprogramming, explains the need for one of the most advanced features in Python and its practical applications.

Chapter 2, Refresher of OOP Concepts in Python, gives an overview of the existing OOP concepts, such as classes, methods, and objects, along with examples.

Chapter 3, Understanding Decorators and Their Applications, covers the concept of decorators on functions and classes with the intent to provide you with a detailed overview of decorators, how to code them, and where to use them. This chapter also covers a detailed code walkthrough of the examples.

Chapter 4, Working with Metaclasses, covers the concept of base classes and metaclasses with the intent to provide you with a detailed overview of metaclasses, how to code them, and where to use them. This chapter also covers a detailed code walkthrough of the examples.

Chapter 5, Understanding Introspection, covers the concept of introspection in Python with the intent to provide you with a detailed overview of introspection, how to code it, and where to use it. This chapter also covers a detailed code walkthrough of the examples.

Chapter 6, Implementing Reflection on Python Objects, covers the concept of reflection in Python with the intent to provide you with a detailed overview of reflection, how to code it, and where to use it. This chapter also covers a detailed code walkthrough of the examples.

Chapter 7, Understanding Generics and Typing, covers the concept of generics in Python with the intent to provide you with a detailed overview of generics, how to code them, and where to use them. This chapter also covers a detailed code walkthrough of the examples.

Chapter 8, Defining Templates for Algorithms, covers the concept of templates in Python with the intent to provide you with a detailed overview of templates, how to code them, and where to use them. This chapter also covers a detailed code walkthrough of the examples

Chapter 9, Understanding Code through Abstract Syntax Trees, covers the concept of abstract syntax trees in Python with the intent to provide you with a detailed overview of what abstract syntax trees are, how to code them, and where to use them. This chapter also covers a detailed code walkthrough of the examples.

Chapter 10, Understanding Method Resolution Order of Inheritance, covers the concept of method resolution order in Python with the intent to provide you with a detailed overview of method resolution order, how to code it, and where to use it. This chapter also covers a detailed code walkthrough of the examples.

Chapter 11, Creating Dynamic Objects, covers the concept of dynamic objects in Python with the intent to provide you with a detailed overview of dynamic objects, how to code them, and where to use them. This chapter also covers a detailed code walkthrough of the examples.

Chapter 12, Applying GOF Design Patterns – Part 1, covers the concept of behavioral design patterns in Python with the intent to provide you with a detailed overview of behavioral design patterns and apply them in different applications. This chapter also covers a detailed code walkthrough of the examples.

Chapter 13, Applying GOF Design Patterns – Part 2, covers the concept of structural and creational design patterns in Python with the intent to provide you with a detailed overview of structural and creational design patterns and apply them in different applications. This chapter also covers a detailed code walkthrough of the examples.

Chapter 14, Code Generation, covers the concept of code generation in Python with the intent to provide you with a detailed overview of code generation, how to develop a code generator that generates reusable code, and where to use it. This chapter also covers a detailed code walkthrough of the examples.

Chapter 15, Development of an End-to-End Case Study-Based Application, covers the implementation of all the concepts we have learned so far by developing a case study-based application and a framework to test it. Detailed code with classes and methods along with an explanation of the code is covered in this chapter. Additionally, the steps on how to package and deploy the developed application into a Python library are also covered.

Chapter 16, Following Best Practices, covers the best practices that can be followed while implementing the concepts of metaprogramming and answers questions such as where to use and where not to use these concepts in your Python application development life cycle.

To get the most out of this book

Please install the latest version of Python, preferably Python 3.0 or above, and install the latest version of Anaconda from `https://www.anaconda.com/products/distribution`. Once installed, open Jupyter Notebook to run the examples provided in this book.

Software/hardware covered in the book	Operating system requirements
Python 3 and above	Windows, macOS, or Linux
Anaconda	
Jupyter Notebook	

If you are using the digital version of this book, we advise you to type the code yourself or access the code from the book's GitHub repository (a link is available in the next section). Doing so will help you avoid any potential errors related to the copying and pasting of code.

Download the example code files

You can download the example code files for this book from GitHub at `https://github.com/PacktPublishing/Metaprogramming-with-Python`. If there's an update to the code, it will be updated in the GitHub repository.

We also have other code bundles from our rich catalog of books and videos available at `https://github.com/PacktPublishing/`. Check them out!

Download the color images

We also provide a PDF file that has color images of the screenshots and diagrams used in this book. You can download it here: `https://packt.link/LTQbb`.

Conventions used

There are a number of text conventions used throughout this book.

`Code in text`: Indicates code words in text, database table names, folder names, filenames, file extensions, pathnames, dummy URLs, user input, and Twitter handles. Here is an example: "To explain this further, let us look at an example where we will generate a class named `VegCounter` by parsing a series of strings using the `ast` module."

A block of code is set as follows:

```
actualclass = compile(class_tree, 'vegctr_tree', 'exec')
actualclass
```

When we wish to draw your attention to a particular part of a code block or show the output of a code, the relevant lines or items are set in bold:

```
<code object <module> at 0x0000028AAB0D2A80, file "vegctr_
tree", line 1>
```

> **Tips or Important Notes**
> Appear like this.

Get in touch

Feedback from our readers is always welcome.

General feedback: If you have questions about any aspect of this book, email us at `customercare@ packtpub.com` and mention the book title in the subject of your message.

Errata: Although we have taken every care to ensure the accuracy of our content, mistakes do happen. If you have found a mistake in this book, we would be grateful if you would report this to us. Please visit `www.packtpub.com/support/errata` and fill in the form.

Piracy: If you come across any illegal copies of our works in any form on the internet, we would be grateful if you would provide us with the location address or website name. Please contact us at `copyright@packt.com` with a link to the material.

If you are interested in becoming an author: If there is a topic that you have expertise in and you are interested in either writing or contributing to a book, please visit `authors.packtpub.com`.

Share Your Thoughts

Once you've read Metaprogramming with Python, we'd love to hear your thoughts! Scan the QR code below to go straight to the Amazon review page for this book and share your feedback.

https://packt.link/r/1838554653

Your review is important to us and the tech community and will help us make sure we're delivering excellent quality content.

Part 1: Fundamentals – Introduction to Object-Oriented Python and Metaprogramming

The objective of this section is to give you an overview of the concept of metaprogramming, its usage, and its advantages in building Python-based applications. This section also covers the basics of object-oriented programming in Python, such as the usage of classes, functions, and objects, to help you familiarize yourself with the basic concepts, before deep diving into the complex properties of metaprogramming.

This part contains the following chapters:

- *Chapter 1, The Need for and Applications of Metaprogramming*
- *Chapter 2, Refresher of OOP Concepts in Python*

1

The Need for and Applications of Metaprogramming

Metaprogramming with Python is a practical guide to learning metaprogramming in Python.

In today's programming world, Python is considered one of the easiest languages to learn and use to develop useful applications. Understanding the programming concepts and applying them is easier in Python compared to any other programming language. A Python program can be written simply by adding existing libraries and making use of their inbuilt methods. At the same time, the language also has many powerful features that can help in developing robust libraries and applications.

This book covers the need for one of the most advanced features in Python, called metaprogramming, along with insights into its practical applications. Understanding the concepts of metaprogramming helps in tapping into the advanced features of Python 3 and knowing where to apply them to make Python code more reusable.

Unlike the regular Python-based application development that follows object-oriented programming, metaprogramming covers certain advanced concepts of Python that deal with manipulating the programmable objects of Python, such as its classes, methods, functions, and variables. Throughout this book, we will look at applications and examples that help in understanding these concepts in a user-friendly manner.

In this chapter, we will provide an introduction to metaprogramming and the need to perform metaprogramming using Python 3. We will cover the following topics:

- An overview of metaprogramming
- Understanding why we need metaprogramming
- Exploring the applications of metaprogramming

By the end of this chapter, you will have a high-level understanding of metaprogramming in Python 3, the need for using it, and know of a few practical examples where it can be applied.

Technical requirements

The code examples in this chapter are available on GitHub repository for this chapter at `https://github.com/PacktPublishing/Metaprogramming-with-Python/tree/main/Chapter01`.

An overview of metaprogramming

Metaprogramming is a concept widely heard of in other programming languages such as C++, Java, .NET, and Ruby but not so widely heard of in Python. Python is a programming language that is easy to learn for beginners to programming and efficient to implement for advanced programmers. Therefore, it has an additional advantage in improving efficiency and optimization while developing high-performance applications when techniques such as metaprogramming are blended with the process of application development.

In this book, we will deep dive into the concepts of metaprogramming using Python 3.

The term **meta**, as the name suggests, is a process that references itself or its the high-level information. In the context of programming, metaprogramming also describes the similar concept of a program referencing itself or a program object referencing itself. A program referencing itself or its entity gives data on the program or the programming entity that can be used at various levels to perform activities, such as transformations or manipulations, in a programming language.

To understand the term **meta**, let's consider the term *metadata*. As an example, let's look at a Python DataFrame. For those who are not familiar with the term DataFrame, we can use the term *table*. The one shown in the following screenshot is called *Employee Data*:

Name	Emp ID	Qualification	Experience	Salary
John S	43326	Engineering	5	121163
Sheldon C	44893	Doctorate	7	362531
Alexander D	35942	UnderGrad	3	375620
Howard W	30727	Masters	6	110979
Dileep A	27313	Doctorate	10	328056
Robert W	13214	Engineering	4	122947

Figure 1.1 – Employee Data table

This Employee Data table consists of employee information such as the name of the employee, employee ID, qualification, experience, salary, and so on.

All of this information are attributes of single or multiple employees, and it is the data of employees in an organization. So, what will the metadata be? The **metadata** is the data of how employee data is stored in the Employee Data table.

The metadata for the Employee Data table defines how each column and its values are stored in the table. For example, in the following screenshot, we can see metadata where **Name** is stored as a string with a length of 64 characters, while **Salary** is stored as a **Float** with a length of 12 digits:

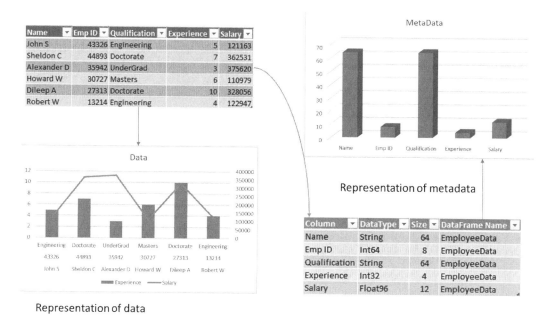

Representation of data

Figure 1.2 – Metadata representation for the Employee Data table

Accessing, modifying, transforming, and updating the Employee Data table using information such as the name or ID of an employee is data manipulation, while accessing, modifying, transforming, and updating the data type or size of the column name or employee ID or salary, is metadata manipulation.

With this understanding, let's look at an example of metaprogramming.

Metaprogramming – a practical introduction

Any programming language that can be used to write code to perform actions consists of a basic unit or piece of code that can be written to perform an action. This is known as a function.

If we have two numbers stored in two variables, a and b, to perform an add action, you can simply add those two numbers by writing a function, as shown in the following code block:

```
def add(a,b):
    c = a + b
    return c
```

Now, if we execute this code, it can go through different scenarios, depending on the input data provided to the add function. Let's take a close look at each of them.

Scenario 1

Running the add function with two integers would result in two numbers being added together, as follows:

```
add(1,3)
4
```

Scenario 2

Running the add function with two strings would result in the concatenation of two words, as follows:

```
add('meta','program')
metaprogram
```

Scenario 3

Let's take a look at running the add function with one string and one integer:

```
add('meta',1)
```

The preceding code would result in the following error:

```
----------------------------------------------------------------
TypeError                            Traceback (most recent call last)
<ipython-input-11-f8ebbea09bb2> in <module>
----> 1 add('meta',1)

<ipython-input-8-1228376a5862> in add(a, b)
      1 def add(a,b):
----> 2     c = a + b
      3     return c

TypeError: can only concatenate str (not "int") to str
```

Figure 1.3 – TypeError

Let's examine this error in detail.

The error in the preceding code snippet denotes a TypeError, which was caused by an attempt to add a meta string with an integer of 1. The question that may occur to you is, *can we resolve this error using metaprogramming?*

The add function in this example denotes a piece of code or program, similar to how the Employee Data table in *Figure 1.1* denotes data. In the same line, can we identify the metadata of the add function and use it to resolve the TypeError object returned by the following code:

```
add('meta',1)
```

Next, we will look at a practical example of metaprogramming. We will be making use of the metadata of the add function to understand this concept.

Metadata of the add function

A function in any programming language is written to perform a set of operations on the input variables; it will return the results as a consequence of the operations performed on them. In this section, we will look at a simple example of a function that adds two variables. This will help us understand that metaprogramming can be applied to functions and manipulate the behavior of the function without modifying the algorithm of the function. We will be adding these two variables by writing an add function. To change the results of the add function, we will be manipulating the metadata of its two input variables, thus getting different results each time a different type of input variable is provided to execute the function. Just like we can manipulate what a function should do by writing lines of code to perform various operations, we can also manipulate the function itself by programming its metadata and setting restrictions on what it should and shouldn't do. Just like a dataset, DataFrame, or table has data and metadata, a program or a function in Python 3 also has data and metadata. In this example, we will be manipulating the actions that are performed by the add function by restricting its behavior – not based on the input data provided to the function but on the *type* of input data provided to the add function instead. Take a look at the following screenshot:

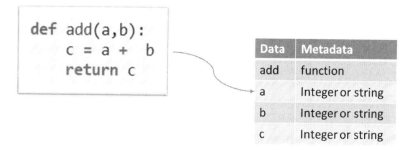

Figure 1.4 – Examining the data and metadata of the add function

The following code helps us identify the metadata for each data item in the add function:

```
def add(a,b):
    c = a + b
    print ("Metadata of add", type(add))
    print ("Metadata of a", type(a))
    print ("Metadata of b", type(b))
    print ("Metadata of c", type(c))
```

A function call to the preceding function will now return the metadata of the add function instead of its result. Now, let's call the add method with an integer as input:

```
add(1,3)
```

We'll get the following output:

```
Metadata of add <class 'function'>
Metadata of a <class 'int'>
Metadata of b <class 'int'>
Metadata of c <class 'int'>
```

Similarly, we can also check the addition of strings, as follows:

```
add('test','string')
```

We'll get the following output:

```
Metadata of add <class 'function'>
Metadata of a <class 'str'>
Metadata of b <class 'str'>
Metadata of c <class 'str'>
```

Python 3 allows us to use the metadata of the code to manipulate it so that it deviates from its actual behavior. This will also provide customized solutions for the problems we are trying to solve.

In the preceding example, we used the type function, a method in Python that returns the class or data type that any object or variable belongs to.

From the preceding output, it is evident that the a and b variables we passed to the add function belong to the integer data type, and its result, c, is an integer too. The add function itself is of the function class/type.

Resolving type errors using metaprogramming

There are many variations on how we can resolve the type error from the add function we saw in the previous section using metaprogramming. We will look at this in this section.

Scenario 1

The following meta-program handles the error and allows the add function to add two strings or two integers. It also suggests that the user enters the input data with the right data types:

```
def add(a,b):
    if (type(a) is str and type(b) is int) or\
        (type(a) is int and type(b) is str):
        return "Please enter both input values as integers or\
          string"
    else:
        c = a + b
        return c
```

In the function definition of add, we have added two conditions – one to check if the type of a is a string and the type of b is an int, or if the type of a is an int and the type of b is a string. We are checking the combination of these input variables to handle the type mismatch error and directing the users to provide the right data type for input variables.

The following table shows the various combinations of input variable data types and their corresponding output or results based on the conditions set on the metadata of the add function, based on **Scenario 1**:

Input a	Input b	Output
integer	integer	integer
string	string	string
integer	string	Message to input both the values as integers or string
string	integer	Message to input both the values as integers or string

Figure 1.5 – Scenario 1 metadata combinations

The following code executes the add function to reinforce the input-output combinations explained in *Figure 1.5*:

```
add(1,3)
4
add('meta','program')
```

```
metaprogram
add('meta',1)
'Please enter both input values as integers or string'
add(1,'meta')
'Please enter both input values as integers or string'
```

Scenario 2

The following meta-program resolves the type mismatch error by converting the mismatching data types into string variables and performing a string concatenation. It is only logical to concatenate a string and an integer using a + operator as we cannot perform arithmetic addition on these two different data types. Take a look at the following program:

```
def add(a,b):
    if type(a) is int and type(b) is int:
        c = a +  b
        return c
    elif type(a) is str and type(b) is int or\
            type(a) is int and type(b) is str or \
            type(a) is str and type(b) is str:
        c = str(a) + str(b)
        return c
    else:
        print("Please enter string or integer")
```

Here, no matter what input we provide for the a and b variables, they both get converted into string variables and are then concatenated using +, whereas if both the input variables are integers, they get added using arithmetic addition.

The following table shows the various combinations of input variable data types and their corresponding output or results based on the conditions set on the metadata of the add function based on **Scenario 2**:

Input a	Input b	Output
integer	integer	integer
string	string	string
integer	string	string
string	integer	string

Figure 1.6 – Scenario 2 metadata combinations

Executing the following code provides the combinations of output values we saw in the preceding table:

```
add(1343,35789)
37132
add('Meta',' Programming')
'MetaProgramming'
add('meta',157676)
'meta157676'
add(65081, 'meta')
'65081meta'
add(True, 'meta')
Please enter string or integer
```

Scenario 3

Now, let's go a step further and restrict the nature of the add function itself to ensure it only performs arithmetic addition and doesn't accept any other data types or combinations of data types.

In the following code block, we have added another condition to perform a data type check on floating-point values, along with data type checks for the string and integer input values.

This function only accepts numeric values as input and will return a message directing users to input numbers so that only arithmetic addition is performed. Let's look at the code:

```
def add(a,b):
    if type(a) is int and type(b) is int or\
        type(a) is float and type(b) is float or\
        type(a) is int and type(b) is float or\
        type(a) is float and type(b) is int:
        c = a + b
        return c
    else:
        return 'Please input numbers'
```

The following table shows the various combinations of input variable data types and their corresponding output or results based on the conditions set on the metadata of the add function based on **Scenario 3**:

Input a	Input b	Output
integer	integer	integer
float	float	float
integer	float	float
float	integer	float
string	string	Message to input both values as numbers
integer	string	Message to input both values as numbers
string	integer	Message to input both values as numbers

Figure 1.7 – Scenario 3 metadata combinations

Executing the following code provides the combination of output values shown in *Figure 1.7*, including the addition of floating-point values:

```
add(15443,675683)
691126
add(54381,3.7876)
54384.7876
add(6.7754,543.76)
550.5354
add(79894,0.6568)
79894.6568
add('meta',14684)
'Please input numbers'
add(6576,'meta')
'Please input numbers'
add('meta','program')
'Please input numbers'
```

These are some of the approaches that can be applied to perform simple metaprogramming on a function. However, these are not the only solutions that solve type errors or manipulate a function. There is more than one way or approach to implementing solutions using metaprogramming.

Understanding why we need metaprogramming

Considering what we've learned about metaprogramming, we may be wondering the following:

"Is it always mandatory to apply metaprogramming techniques or to manipulate the metadata of the code while developing applications using Python 3 or above?"

This is a common question that can be asked not only while developing applications using Python 3 or above, but also when using any programming language that supports the techniques of metaprogramming and gives developers the option to apply them in the application development process.

To answer this question, it is important to understand the flexibility of metaprogramming and the techniques that are supported by Python to handle code manipulation, which will be covered throughout this book.

One of the reasons to apply metaprogramming is to avoid repetition in various aspects of the Python-based application development process. We will look at an example of this in the *Don't Repeat Yourself* section.

In other words, introducing concepts such as code generators at the meta level can save development and execution time in functional- or domain-level programming. Domain-level programming corresponds to writing code for a particular domain, such as finance, networking, social media, and so on.

The other need is to increase the abstraction of your code at the program metadata level rather than at the functional level. **Abstraction** is the concept of information hiding in the literal sense or in terms of object-oriented programming. Implementing abstraction at the meta-program level would help us decide what information to provide to the next level of coding and what not to provide.

For example, developing a function template at the meta-program level would hide the function definition at the domain or functional level, as well as limit the amount of information that goes to the functional-level code.

Metaprogramming allows us to manipulate programs using metadata at the meta level, which helps define how the grammar and semantics of your program should be. For example, in the *Resolving type erors using metaprogramming* section, we looked at controlling the outcome of the data types of a function by manipulating the function's variables.

Don't Repeat Yourself

In any application development process, thousands of lines of code are written. Don't Repeat Yourself is a principle defined by *Andy Hunt and Dave Thomas* in their book *The Pragmatic Programmer*. The principle states that *"Every piece of knowledge must have a single, unambiguous, authoritative representation within a system."*

While writing code, there are very high chances of writing multiple functions or methods that perform similar kinds of repetitive tasks, and the functions or methods, in turn, might be repetitive. This leads to redundancy in application development. The greatest disadvantage of redundancy is that when you make any modifications at one location, the implementation, modification, or code fixing needs to be repeated at multiple locations.

Libraries are developed with classes and methods, including object-oriented programming techniques such as abstraction, inheritance, encapsulation, and so on, to avoid redundancy and maintain coding standards as much as possible. Even then, there are chances of repetitive methods being within a class that can still be simplified.

Metaprogramming can help in handling such instances by implementing approaches such as dynamic code generation, dynamic function creation, and more. Throughout this book, we will be looking at various approaches that help you not to repeat yourself while developing applications.

To get a taste of how we can dynamically generate code and avoid repetitions, let's look at a simple example where arithmetic operations are implemented as repetitive functions.

The following code consists of four basic arithmetic operations that can be performed on two numeric variables. We will be declaring and defining four functions that add, subtract, multiply, and divide two variables, a and b, store the result in a variable, c, and return it while the function is executed:

```
def add(a,b):
    c = a + b
    return c


def sub(a,b):
    c = a - b
    return c


def multiply(a,b):
    c = a * b
    return c


def divide(a,b):
    c = a / b
    return c
```

Each of the preceding functions needs to be called separately and variables need to be provided as input to execute them individually, as follows:

```
add(2,5)
7
sub(2,5)
-3
multiply(2,5)
10
divide(2,5)
0.4
```

In this example, there is only one difference – the arithmetic operator that's used in the function definition. This code can be simplified without implementing metaprogramming, just by declaring a new function that takes in an additional input variable operator.

Let's learn how to avoid this repetitive function definition and simplify the logic. The following code block defines one common function that can be reused to perform all four arithmetic operations. Let's start by importing Python's inbuilt `module` operator, which contains methods that support multiple arithmetic operations:

```
import operator as op
def arithmetic(a, b, operation):
    result = operation(a, b)
    return result
```

In this code snippet, we have declared three variables, including the operation in the function arithmetic. Let's see this in action:

```
arithmetic('2', '5', op.add) '25'
```

Executing this function using input variables would return a concatenated string, 25, that will serve the purpose of creating the common `arithmetic` function to perform multiple operations. We can look at providing various operations as input to see how this one common function serves multiple purposes.

Calling this function with different arithmetic operators would resolve the need for repetitive function definitions:

```
arithmetic(2, 5, op.add)
7
arithmetic(2 , 5, op.sub)
-3
arithmetic(2, 5, op.mul)
10
arithmetic(2 , 5, op.truediv)
0.4
```

This is one approach to resolving code redundancy and avoiding multiple function definitions. But what if we do not want to define the function itself until and unless it is required?

To answer this question, we can implement dynamic function creation using metaprogramming. Dynamic functions are created during the code's runtime as and when they are required.

Although we are still in the introductory chapter, we will discuss an example of dynamic function creation next to get a view of what kind of programming will be covered throughout this book.

Creating dynamic functions

In this section, we'll look at an example of how dynamic functions can be created for the same set of arithmetic operations we discussed earlier in this section.

To create an arithmetic function dynamically, we need to import the library types and the FunctionType type. FunctionType is the type of all user-defined functions created by users during the Python-based application development process:

```
from types import FunctionType
```

To begin this process, we will create a string variable that is a function definition of the arithmetic function:

```
functionstring = '''
def arithmetic(a, b):
    op = __import__('operator')
    result = op.add(a, b)
    return result
    '''
print(functionstring)
```

We'll get the following output:

```
def arithmetic(a, b):
    op = __import__('operator')
    result = op.add(a, b)
    return result
```

Now, we will create another variable, functiontemplate, and compile 'functionstring' into a code object. We will also set the code object to be executed using 'exec'. The compile method is used to convert the string in Python into a code object that can be further executed using the exec method:

```
functiontemplate = compile(functionstring, 'functionstring',
 'exec')
functiontemplate
<code object <module> at 0x000001E20D498660, file
"functionstring", line 1>
```

The code object of the function definition arithmetic will be stored in a tuple in functiontemplate and can be accessed as follows:

```
functiontemplate.co_consts[0]
<code object arithmetic at 0x000001E20D4985B0, file
"functionstring", line 1>
```

The next step involves creating a function object using the functiontemplate code object. This can be done using the FunctionType method, which accepts the code object and global variables as input parameters:

```
dynamicfunction = FunctionType(functiontemplate.co_
consts[0], globals(),"add")
dynamicfunction
<function __main__.arithmetic(a,b)>
```

Upon executing, dynamicfunction, it will behave the same way as the add operation works in the operator module's add method in the arithmetic function:

```
dynamicfunction(2,5)
7
```

Now that we know how to create a function dynamically, we can look at extending it further to create multiple functions, each with a different operation and a different name, dynamically.

To do this, we must create a list of operators and a list of function names:

```
operator = ['op.add','op.sub','op.mul','op.truediv','op.
pow','op.mod', 'op.gt', 'op.lt']
functionname = ['add','sub', 'multiply', 'divide', 'power',\
  'modulus', 'greaterthan', 'lesserthan']
```

Our earlier list of four functions only contained the add, sub, multiply, and divide operations.

The earlier `functionname` list contained eight functions. This is the flexibility we get while creating dynamic functions.

For ease of use, let's also create two input variables, a and b, to be used while executing the function:

```
a = 2
b = 5
```

In the following code, we will be creating a function called `functiongenerator()` that implements metaprogramming to dynamically generate as many arithmetic functions as we want. This function will take four input parameters – that is, the list's `functionname`, `operator`, `a`, and `b`.

Here is the code:

```
def functiongenerator(functionname, operator, a,b):
    from types import FunctionType
    functionstring = []
    for i in operator:
        functionstring.append('''
def arithmetic(a, b):
    op = __import__('operator')
    result = '''+ i + '''(a, b)
    return result
    ''')
        functiontemplate = []
    for i in functionstring:
        functiontemplate.
append(compile(i, 'functionstring', 'exec'))
        dynamicfunction = []
    for i,j in zip(functiontemplate,functionname):
        dynamicfunction.append(FunctionType(i.co_consts[0], \
            globals(), j))
```

```
        functiondict = {}

    for i,j in zip(functionname,dynamicfunction):
        functiondict[i]=j

    for i in dynamicfunction:
        print (i(a,b))

    return functiondict
```

Within `functiongenerator()`, the following occurs:

- A new `functionstring` list is created with a function definition for each arithmetic operator provided in the operator list.

- A new `functiontemplate` list is created with a code object for each function definition.

- A new `dynamicfunction` list is created with a function object for each code object.

- A new `functiondict` dictionary is created with a key-value pair of function name-function objects.

- `Functiongenerator` returns the generated functions as a dictionary.

- Additionally, `functiongenerator` executes the dynamic functions and prints the results.

Executing this function results in the following output:

```
funcdict = functiongenerator(functionname, operator, a,b)
7
-3
10
0.4
32
2
False
True
funcdict
{'add': <function _main_.arithmetic(a,b)>,
 'sub': <function _main_.arithmetic(a,b)>,
 'multiply': <function _main_.arithmetic(a,b)>,
 'divide': <function _main_.arithmetic(a,b)>,
```

```
'power': <function _main_.arithmetic(a,b)>,
'modulus': <function _main_.arithmetic(a,b)>,
'greaterthan': <function _main_.arithmetic(a,b)>,
'lesserthan': <function _main_.arithmetic(a,b)>,}
```

Any specific function from the preceding generated functions can be called individually and used further, as follows:

```
funcdict['divide'](a,b)
0.4
```

The following diagram shows the complete process of metaprogramming to develop these dynamic functions:

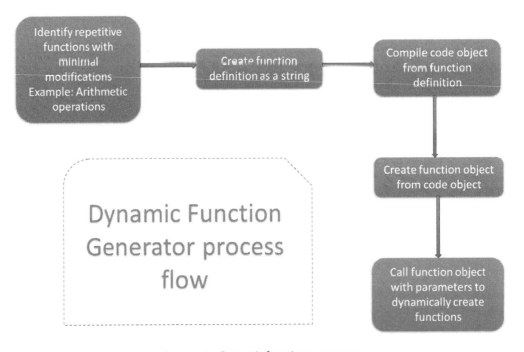

Figure 1.8 – Dynamic function generator

Now that we know about dynamic function generators, let's look at other applications of metaprogramming.

Exploring the applications of metaprogramming

Metaprogramming can be applied to various Python-based application development solutions, such as automated code generators, component-based or flow-based application development, domain-specific language development, and many more.

Any code you develop, be it for a class or a method, internally applies metaprogramming, and its use is inevitable in the Python application development process. However, applying metaprogramming concepts explicitly is a conscious decision-making process and it purely depends on the expected outcome of your application.

In our example of dynamic function creation, we implemented metaprogramming to avoid repetitions and also to ensure the abstraction of the code at the meta-level.

Let's consider a scenario where we want to develop a functional flow-based application for non-programmers to use. For instance, the application can be a domain-specific data transformation tool that works with high levels of abstraction and does not provide too much design or development-based information to the end users. However, it also helps the end users dynamically create modules that can help in their domain-specific problem solving, without the need to write any programs. In such cases, metaprogramming comes in handy for the application development process:

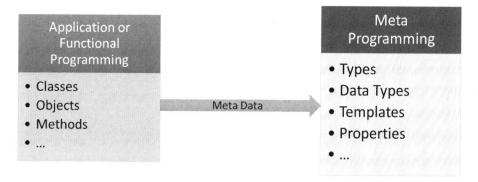

Figure 1.9 – Levels of programming

We will look at the case studies and applications of metaprogramming in more detail throughout this book.

Summary

In this chapter, we provide a quick overview of the programming paradigm of metaprogramming and looked at an example of solving a type error using metaprogramming in Python 3.

We learned why there is a need to apply metaprogramming techniques in the Python application development process. We also learned about the Don't Repeat Yourself concept by looking at a practical approach that explains an example implementation of dynamic function creation using metaprogramming, emphasizing the concepts of avoiding repetition and implementing abstraction at the meta level in the code. Finally, we provided a high-level overview of the applications of metaprogramming that we will look at throughout this book. These skills will help us understand how and why to apply metaprogramming in various applications.

In the next chapter, we will review the object-oriented programming concepts of Python. The next chapter is more of a refresher on object-oriented programming concepts and is optional if you are already familiar with those concepts.

2

Refresher of OOP Concepts in Python

In the previous chapter, we looked at an overview of and discussed the need for metaprogramming and its practical applications, such as using the add function. But before we deep dive into the concepts of metaprogramming, it is important for you to have knowledge of the basic Object-Oriented Programming (OOP) concepts available in Python. This chapter gives an overview of the existing OOP concepts along with examples.

The main topics we will be covering in this chapter are as follows:

- Introducing our core example
- Creating classes
- Understanding objects
- Applying methods
- Implementing inheritance
- Extending to multiple inheritance
- Understanding polymorphism
- Hiding details with abstraction
- Protecting information with encapsulation

By the end of this chapter, you will be able to understand the concepts of OOP in Python along with some practical examples.

> **Note**
> This chapter is completely optional, so if you are already familiar with the concepts of OOP, you can proceed directly learning metaprogramming concepts.

Technical requirements

The code examples shared in this chapter are available on GitHub under the code for this chapter here: `https://github.com/PacktPublishing/Metaprogramming-with-Python/tree/main/Chapter02`.

Introducing our core example

Throughout this chapter, we will be making use of a simulated schema named *ABC Megamart* to explain the concepts of OOP. The availability of an object-oriented approach in a programming language helps with effective reusability and abstraction of the language. Our example, *ABC Megamart*, is a simulated large retail store that sells multiple products across different cities and consists of multiple branches.

Let us give a structure to different entities of this store and look at how they can fit into an organized OOP paradigm. Our store consists of the following:

- Products
- Branches
- Invoices
- Holidays
- Shelves
- Inventory
- Sales
- Promotions/offers
- Exchange counter
- Finance

Each of these entities can have multiple attributes of data or information that are required to perform multiple functions in the smooth and efficient management of the stores.

Let us explore how these entities and their attributes can be structured into a software model developed by applying the concepts of OOP:

- Each of the preceding 10 entities can be connected either directly or indirectly
- Each branch will have sales and each sale will have invoices
- Each branch city will have holidays and sales can happen during holiday seasons
- Each branch (store) can have shelves and products will be placed on shelves
- Each product can have promotions or offers and promotions influence sales

Thus, multiple entities can be linked together to develop software, maintain a database schema, or both, depending on the application being modeled. Here is a representation of how these entities can be linked:

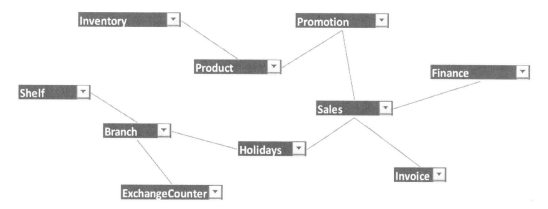

Figure 2.1 – Example of how a simple linkage can be modeled to connect various entities

There is more than one way in which we can structure the previous entity model but we are not covering all of them. This is more of a simple representation of the entity relationship at a higher level.

Using this example as the base, let us now dive into the topic of creating classes in Python.

Creating classes

A **class** is a collection of common attributes and methods that can be reused by creating instances of the class. By creating a class, we define it once and reuse it multiple times, thus avoiding redundancy.

Let us look at what a class can look like. We can consider the Branch entity of *ABC Megamart*. A Branch can have an ID and an Address. Address can further be detailed into Street, City, State, and Zip code. If we consider Branch as a class, ID, Street, City, State, and Zip code would become its attributes. All operations that can be performed by a branch will become its methods.

A branch can sell products, maintain invoices, maintain inventory, and so on. The generic format of a class is as follows:

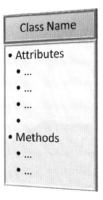

Figure 2.2 – Class

A class can be defined as follows:

```
class ClassName:
    '''attributes...'''
    '''methods...'''
```

The format of the Branch class is as follows:

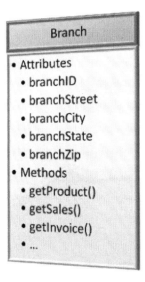

Figure 2.3 – Branch class

Similarly, a `Branch` class can be defined as follows:

```
class Branch:
    '''attributes...'''
    '''methods...'''
```

A `Branch` class can have multiple attributes and methods to perform various operations. These attributes and methods will be initialized as NULLs and added to the class in this example, as shown here:

```
class Branch:
    '''attributes'''
    branch_id = None
    branch_street = None
    branch_city = None
    branch_state = None
    branch_zip = None
    '''methods'''
    def get_product(self):
        return 'product'
    def get_sales(self):
        return 'sales'
    def get_invoice(self):
        return 'invoice'
```

The attributes of the class can be initialized either with a specific value or as NULL and modified later while defining an object for the class and calling it to perform various functions.

Let us look further into utilizing and modifying these class attributes by creating class objects.

Understanding objects

An **object** can be defined as the instance of the class. If we consider a class itself as a data type, then an object can be defined as the variable of a class of type `ClassName`.

A class without an object is practically unusable. All the attributes and methods created for the class can be effectively utilized once we create an object instance, as follows:

```
obj_name = ClassName()
```

Considering the earlier example of a `Branch` class, we can create and utilize its objects as follows:

```
branch_albany - Branch()
```

Now, `branch_albany` is an instance of the`Branch` class and all its attributes can be modified for this instance without impacting the attributes within the class definition of `Branch`. An instance is more like a copy of the class that can be utilized without affecting the class itself. Let's take the following code as an example:

```
branch_albany.branch_id = 123
branch_albany.branch_street = '123 Main Street'
branch_albany.branch_city = 'Albany'
branch_albany.branch_state = 'New York'
branch_albany.branch_zip = 12084
```

Calling the preceding defined attributes returns the following values defined for those attributes:

```
branch_albany.branch_id
123
branch_albany.branch_street
'123 Main Street'
```

We can create another object for the `Branch` class and the class would still remain unaffected. We can then assign a value to `branch_id` that belongs to the newly created `branch` object, as follows:

```
branchNevada = Branch()
branchNevada.branch_id
```

Now, `branchNevada.branch_id` is a variable of the the`branchNevada` object and it returns no value as it can be defined for this instance:

```
branchNevada.branch_id = 456
branchNevada.branch_id

456
```

This is not the only way to define values for class variables using an object. Alternatively, all attributes can be added as parameters to the `init` method in the class definition and all values for those attributes can be initiated while creating an object instance. To make this work, we will have to redefine the `Branch` class, as follows:

```
class Branch:
    def __init__(self, branch_id, branch_street,
```

```
            branch_city, branch_state, branch_zip):
        self.branch_id = branch_id
        self.branch_street = branch_street
        self.branch_city = branch_city
        self.branch_state = branch_state
        self.branch_zip = branch_zip
    def get_product(self):
        return 'product'
    def get_sales(self):
        return 'sales'
    def get_invoice(self):
        return 'invoice'
```

Creating an object instance for the preceding redefined class in the same method as before would lead to an error:

```
object_albany = Branch()
```

The following is the error message we receive:

```
-----------------------------------------------------------------------
TypeError                            Traceback (most recent call last)
<ipython-input-46-349a6b0e68bd> in <module>
----> 1 objectAlbany = Branch()

TypeError: __init__() missing 5 required positional arguments: 'branchID', 'branchStreet', 'branchCity', 'branchState', and 'branchZip'
```

Figure 2.4 – Missing required arguments error

Yes, all the parameters we declared in the init class are missing in the earlier object instantiation. The new object for this class needs to be created with all the values initiated, as follows:

```
object_albany = Branch(101,'123 Main Street',
'Albany','New York', 12084)
print (object_albany.branch_id,
    object_albany.branch_street,
    object_albany.branch_city,
    object_albany.branch_state,
    object_albany.branch_zip)
101 123 Main Street Albany New York 12084
```

With this understanding, let us look at the concept of defining methods inside a class and calling them using objects.

Applying methods

Methods are similar to the user-defined functions we create to perform various operations in a program, the difference being methods are defined inside a class and are governed by the rules of the class. Methods can be utilized only by calling them using an object instance created for that class. User-defined functions, on the other hand, are global and can be called freely anywhere within the program. A method can be as simple as printing a statement or can be a highly complex mathematical calculation that involves a large number of parameters.

Defining methods with simple print statements inside the `Branch` class looks as follows:

```
class Branch:
    def __init__(self, branch_id, branch_street,
      branch_city, branch_state, branch_zip):
        self.branch_id = branch_id
        self.branch_street = branch_street
        self.branch_city = branch_city
        self.branch_state = branch_state
        self.branch_zip = branch_zip
    def get_product(self):
        return 'product'
    def get_sales(self):
        return 'sales'
    def get_invoice(self):
        return 'invoice'
object_albany = Branch(101,'123 Main Street',
'Albany','New York', 12084)
```

By calling the preceding methods from `object_albany`, we will get the following output:

```
object_albany.get_invoice()
'invoice'
object_albany.get_sales()
'sales'
object_albany.get_product()
'product'
```

As a variation, we can look at creating methods with parameters and calculations. For this example, let us consider a scenario where we need to calculate the selling price for a product in a particular branch given the tax rate for the state, the purchase price for the product, and the profit margin. After calculating the selling price of the product, the method should return branch details, product details, selling price, and sales tax.

To write this method, we will create three dictionary variables using Python keyword arguments and name them **branch, **sales, and **product. We will be creating three methods to set values for branch, sales, and product information, as follows:

```python
class Branch:
    def set_branch(self, **branch):
        return branch
    def set_sales(self, **sales):
        return sales
    def set_product(self, **product):
        return product
```

The preceding code takes in all the values that can be included for the branch, sales, and product. We will be creating an object for the Branch class:

```python
branch_nyc = Branch()
```

In the following code, we will make use of the set_branch method to store the values in the branch dictionary variable within the object of Branch:

```python
branch_nyc.branch = branch_nyc.set_branch(branch_id = 202,
branch_street = '234 3rd Main Street',
branch_city = 'New York City',
branch_state = 'New York',
branch_zip = 11005)
```

We will now call the branch attribute on the branch_nyc object, as follows:

```python
branch_nyc.branch
```

Executing the preceding code results in the following output, which is a dictionary of branch_id along with its address:

```python
{'branch_id': 202,
 'branch_street': '234 3rd Main Street',
 'branch_city': 'New York City',
```

```
    'branch_state': 'New York',
    'branch_zip': 11005}
```

Similarly, in the following code, we will make use of the `set_product` method to store the values in the `product` dictionary variable within the object of `Branch`:

```
branch_nyc.product = branch_nyc.set_product(
    product_id = 100001,
    product_name = 'Refrigerator',
    productBrand = 'Whirlpool'  )
```

We will now call the `product` attribute on the `branch_nyc` object, as follows:

```
branch_nyc.product
```

Executing the preceding code results in the following output, which is a dictionary of all product IDs along with their details:

```
{'product_id': 100001,
 'product_name': 'Refrigerator',
 'productBrand': 'Whirlpool'}
```

Similarly, in the following code, we will make use of the `set_sales` method to store the values in the `sales` dictionary variable within the object of `Branch`:

```
branch_nyc.sales = branch_nyc.set_sales(
    purchase_price = 300,
    profit_margin = 0.20,
    tax_rate = 0.452
)
```

We will now call the `sales` attribute on the `branch_nyc` object, as follows:

```
branch_nyc.sales
```

Executing the preceding code results in the following output, which is a dictionary of all sales information:

```
{'purchase_price': 300,
 'profit_margin': 0.2,
 'tax_rate': 0.452,
 'selling_price': 522.72}
```

Calculating the selling price will be done in the following two steps:

1. Calculate the price before tax by adding the purchase price with the product between the purchase price and profit margin percentage.

2. Calculate the selling price by adding the price before tax, with the product between price before tax and sales tax rate.

In the following code, we will include the `calc_tax` method to perform the preceding calculation steps and to return the branch details along with product information and sales data:

```python
class Branch:
    def set_branch(self, **branch):
        return branch
    def set_sales(self, **sales):
        return sales
    def set_product(self, **product):
        return product
    def calc_tax(self):
        branch = self.branch
        product = self.product
        sales = self.sales
        pricebeforetax = sales['purchase_price'] + \
        sales['purchase_price'] * sales['profit_margin']
        finalselling_price = pricebeforetax + \
        (pricebeforetax * sales['tax_rate'])
        sales['selling_price'] = finalselling_price
        return branch, product, sales
```

Calling the preceding function provides the following results:

```python
branch_nyc.calc_tax()
({'branch_id': 202,
  'branch_street': '234 3rd Main Street',
  'branch_city': 'New York City',
  'branch_state': 'New York',
  'branch_zip': 11005},
 {'product_id': 100001,
  'product_name': 'Refrigerator',
  'productBrand': 'Whirlpool'},
```

```
{'purchase_price': 300,
 'profit_margin': 0.2,
 'tax_rate': 0.452,
 'selling_price': 522.72})
```

Now that we know how to apply methods, we can look further into the concept of inheritance.

Implementing inheritance

Inheritance in a literal sense means acquiring the properties of a parent by the child, and it means the same in the case of OOP too. A new class can inherit the attributes and methods of a parent class and it can also have its own properties and methods. The new class that inherits the parent class will be called a child class or a subclass while the parent class can also be called a base class. The following is a simple representation of it:

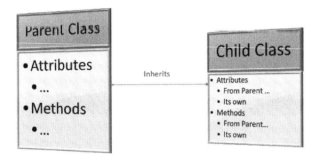

Figure 2.5 – Inheritance

Extending our latest class definition of Branch to have an individual class for NYC—since it has multiple intra-city branches and it also has other properties of its own in addition to the Branch class—we will be applying Inheritance to create a new subclass or child class named NYC. It has propertiessuch as having multiple hierarchies of management. NYC has a regional manager and each branch has its own branch manager. For NYC, we will also add an additional local tax component to the calculation of the selling price, which varies from branch to branch.

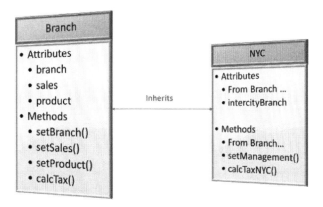

Figure 2.6 – NYC class inherits from Branch class

The general structure of inheritance while defining a child class inheriting from a parent class looks as follows:

```
class Parent:
    '''attributes...'''


    '''methods...'''
class Child(Parent):
    '''attributes...'''


    '''methods...'''
```

Inheriting the NYC child class from the Branch parent class can be defined as follows:

```
class NYC(Branch):
    def set_management(self, **intercitybranch):
        return intercitybranch


    def calc_tax_nyc(self):
        branch = self.branch
        intercitybranch = self.intercitybranch
        product = self.product
        sales = self.sales
        pricebeforetax = sales['purchase_price'] + \
        sales['purchase_price'] * sales['profit_margin']
```

```
finalselling_price = pricebeforetax + \
(pricebeforetax * (sales['tax_rate'] +\
 sales['local_rate']))
sales['selling_price'] = finalselling_price
return branch,intercitybranch, product, sales
```

Let us examine the proceeding code before going any further with object creation. TheNYC subclass has its own additional attribute, `intercitybranch`, introduced as a parameter in its own method, `set_management`. NYC also has its own method to calculate tax, `calc_tax_nyc`. The `calc_tax_nyc` method in NYC includes an additional component, `local_rate`, to calculate the selling price.

Now, let us examinewhether NYC can make use of the methods of the `Branch` class to set the new values for branch, product, and sales:

```
branch_manhattan = NYC()
```

By examining the methods that are available in the `branch_manhattan` object, as shown in the following screenshot, we can see that NYC can make use of the set methods defined in the `Branch` class:

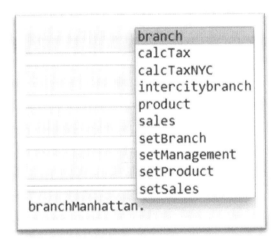

Figure 2.7 – Set methods inherited from Branch

We can proceed further by setting attributes using all of these methods and calculating the selling price after sales tax and local tax rate for the Manhattan branch, as follows:

```
branch_manhattan.branch = branch_manhattan.set_branch(branch_
id = 2021,
branch_street = '40097 5th Main Street',
```

```
branch_borough = 'Manhattan',
branch_city = 'New York City',
branch_state = 'New York',
branch_zip = 11007)
```

We will call the branch attribute on the branch_manhattan object, as follows:

```
branch_manhattan.branch
{'branch_id': 2021,
  'branch_street': '40097 5th Main Street',
  'branch_borough': 'Manhattan',
  'branch_city': 'New York City',
  'branch_state': 'New York',
  'branch_zip': 11007}
```

In the following code, we will make use of the set_management method to store the values in the intercitybranch dictionary variable within the object of NYC:

```
branch_manhattan.intercitybranch = branch_manhattan.set_
management(
      regional_manager = 'John M',
      branch_manager = 'Tom H',
      subBranch_id = '2021-01'
)
```

Let's call the intercitybranch attribute on the branch_manhattan object, as follows:

```
branch_manhattan.intercitybranch
{'regional_manager': 'John M',
  'branch_manager': 'Tom H',
  'subBranch_id': '2021-01'}
```

Similarly, in the following code, we will make use of the set_product method to store the values in the product dictionary variable within the object of NYC:

```
branch_manhattan.product = branch_manhattan.set_product(
      product_id = 100002,
      product_name = 'WashingMachine',
      productBrand = 'Whirlpool'
)
```

We will now call the `product` attribute on the `branch_manhattan` object:

```
branch_manhattan.product
{'product_id': 100002,
 'product_name': 'WashingMachine',
 'productBrand': 'Whirlpool'}
```

Similarly, in the following code, we will make use of the `set_sales` method to store the values in the `sales` dictionary variable within the object of NYC:

```
branch_manhattan.sales = branch_manhattan.set_sales(
    purchase_price = 450,
    profit_margin = 0.19,
    tax_rate = 0.4,
    local_rate = 0.055
)
```

We will further call the `sales` attribute on the `branch_manhattan` object, as follows:

```
branch_manhattan.sales

{'purchase_price': 450,
 'profit_margin': 0.19,
 'tax_rate': 0.4,
 'local_rate': 0.055}
```

With all the preceding attributes and their value assignments, we can calculate tax for the Manhattan branch using the following code:

```
branch_manhattan.calc_tax_nyc()
({'branch_id': 2021,
   'branch_street': '40097 5th Main Street',
   'branch_borough': 'Manhattan',
   'branch_city': 'New York City',
   'branch_state': 'New York',
   'branch_zip': 11007},
 {'regional_manager': 'John M',
   'branch_manager': 'Tom H',
```

```
    'subBranch_id': '2021-01'},
  {'product_id': 100002,
   'product_name': 'WashingMachine',
   'productBrand': 'Whirlpool'},
  {'purchase_price': 450,
   'profit_margin': 0.19,
   'tax_rate': 0.4,
   'local_rate': 0.055,
   'selling_price': 779.1525})
```

We can still make use of the `calc_tax` method available in the `Branch` class if we don't want to calculate the selling price based on the local tax rate:

```
branch_manhattan.calc_tax()
({'branch_id': 2021,
   'branch_street': '40097 5th Main Street',
   'branch_borough': 'Manhattan',
   'branch_city': 'New York City',
   'branch_state': 'New York',
   'branch_zip': 11007},
  {'product_id': 100002,
   'product_name': 'WashingMachine',
   'productBrand': 'Whirlpool'},
  {'purchase_price': 450,
   'profit_margin': 0.19,
   'tax_rate': 0.4,
   'local_rate': 0.055,
   'selling_price': 749.7})
```

The preceding code and its output demonstrate the reusable nature of inheritance in OOP. Now let's look at an extended concept called multiple inheritance.

Extending to multiple inheritance

Python also supports **multiple inheritance**, where we can import a subclass from more than one base class or parent class. In such a scenario, the child class or the subclass inherits all the attributes and methods of the base classes. In this example, we will create two base classes, Product and Branch, and let the Sales class inherit both these base classes. Here is a quick representation of the logic we'd be using:

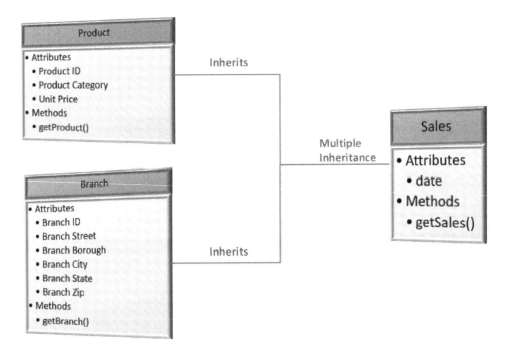

Figure 2.8 – Multiple inheritance example

In the following code, we will be creating a Product class where we will define the attributes for a product and a get_product method to return the product details:

```python
class Product:
    _product_id = 100902
    _product_name = 'Iphone X'
    _product_category = 'Electronics'
    _unit_price = 700

    def get_product(self):
```

```
        return self._product_id, self._product_name,\
            self._product_category, self._unit_price
```

We will also be creating another class, `Branch`, where we will define the attributes for a branch and a `get_branch` method to return the branch details:

```
class Branch:
    _branch_id = 2021
    _branch_street = '40097 5th Main Street'
    _branch_borough = 'Manhattan'
    _branch_city = 'New York City'
    _branch_state = 'New York'
    _branch_zip = 11007

    def get_branch(self):
        return self._branch_id, self._branch_street, \
            self._branch_borough, self._branch_city, \
            self._branch_state, self._branch_zip
```

We will be implementing the concept of multiple inheritance by inheriting two parent classes, `Product` and `Branch`, into the child class, `Sales`:

```
class Sales(Product, Branch):
    date = '08/02/2021'
    def get_sales(self):
        return self.date, Product.get_product(self), \
            Branch.get_branch(self)
```

In the preceding code, the `Sales` class inherited two methods, `get_product`, and `get_branch`, from the `Product` class and the `Branch` class, respectively.

In the following code, we will be creating an object for the `Sales` class:

```
sales = Sales()
```

Calling the `get_sales` method from the `Sales` class results in returning the `date` attribute from the `Sales` class along with the `product` and `branch` attributes from its parent classes:

```
sales.get_sales()
('08/02/2021',
 (100902, 'Iphone X', 'Electronics', 700),
```

```
(2021,
 '40097 5th Main Street',
 'Manhattan',
 'New York City',
 'New York',
 11007))
```

With these examples, we can proceed further to understand the concept of polymorphism, which extends on our earlier examples of inheritance.

Understanding polymorphism

Polymorphism is the concept of the OOP paradigm where we can reuse the name of a function from a parent class either by redefining or overriding an existing function or by creating two different functions for two different classes with the same name and using them separately. In this section, we will look at examples for both variations of polymorphism:

- Polymorphism within inheritance
- Polymorphism in independent classes

Polymorphism within inheritance

Let us look at the earlier example of the child class, NYC, which inherits from Branch. To calculate the selling price along with the local tax rate for the specific branch, we created a new method within the NYC class named calc_tax_nyc. Instead of creating a new method, we can also override the Parent method, calc_tax, with the new calculation in the child class. This concept is polymorphism within inheritance. Here is a representation of it:

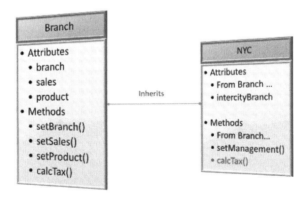

Figure 2.9 – calc_tax method overridden in child class, NYC

To begin with, polymorphism, let us first recall the `calc_tax` method from the `Branch` class, and then we can override it in the child class, `NYC`:

```
class Branch:
    def calc_tax(self):
        branch = self.branch
        product = self.product
        sales = self.sales
        pricebeforetax = sales['purchase_price'] + \
        sales['purchase_price'] * sales['profit_margin']
        finalselling_price = pricebeforetax + \
        (pricebeforetax * sales['tax_rate'])
        sales['selling_price'] = finalselling_price
        return branch, product, sales
```

We will now define the `NYC` class by inheriting the `Branch` class. This class has two methods, `set_management` and `calc_tax`. The `set_management` method returns `intercitybranch` as a dictionary attribute. The `calc_tax` method is now overridden in the child class, `NYC`, and it returns branch details, intercity branch details, product details, and sales details:

```
class NYC(Branch):
    def set_management(self, **intercitybranch):
        return intercitybranch

    def calc_tax(self):
        branch = self.branch
        intercitybranch = self.intercitybranch
        product = self.product
        sales = self.sales
        pricebeforetax = sales['purchase_price'] + \
        sales['purchase_price'] * sales['profit_margin']
        finalselling_price = pricebeforetax + \
        (pricebeforetax * (sales['tax_rate'] + \
        sales['local_rate']))
        sales['selling_price'] = finalselling_price
        return branch,intercitybranch, product, sales
branch_manhattan = NYC()
```

The following is a representation of all the methods supported by the `branch_manhattan` object of the child class, NYC:

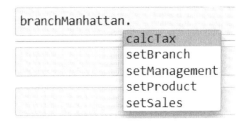

Figure 2.10 – calc_tax after polymorphism

The following code displays the results of calling the `calc_tax` method from `branch_manhattan`, which is the method overridden from its parent class to calculate the selling price after applying the local tax rate:

```
branch_manhattan.calc_tax()
({'branch_id': 2021,
  'branch_street': '40097 5th Main Street',
  'branch_borough': 'Manhattan',
  'branch_city': 'New York City',
  'branch_state': 'New York',
  'branch_zip': 11007},
 {'regional_manager': 'John M',
  'branch_manager': 'Tom H',
  'subBranch_id': '2021-01'},
 {'product_id': 100002,
  'product_name': 'WashingMachine',
  'productBrand': 'Whirlpool'},
 {'purchase_price': 450,
  'profit_margin': 0.19,
  'tax_rate': 0.4,
  'local_rate': 0.055,
  'selling_price': 779.1525})
```

As we can see, the `calc_tax` method returns the output as defined in NYC.

Polymorphism in independent classes

Polymorphism need not always happen in a *parent-childpc* class relationship. We can always have two completely different classes that can have two different function definitions with the same name and the functions can both be utilized by calling them using their class object instances.

For this example, we will be creating two independent classes, `Queens` and `Brooklyn`,, which are two different branches of *ABC Megamart*. We will not associate these branches with the `Branch` parent class in order to explain the concept of polymorphism in independent classes. The Brooklyn branch stocks only **Fast-Moving Consumer Goods** (**FMCG**) products and the Queens branch stocks only electronic products. The maintenance cost for FMCG will be higher compared to electronic products since FMCG products will have an expiry date and they would require cold storage. We will be creating two different functions, one for each class, with the same name, `maintenance_cost`, and defining them according to the requirements of storage for each branch.

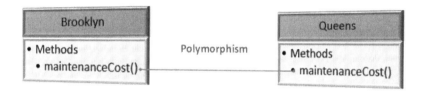

Figure 2.11 – Polymorphism of one method in independent classes

In the following code, for the `Brooklyn` class, we will calculate the maintenance cost only if the product type is FMCG. We will calculate the product of quantity costing 0.25 and add 100 USD for cold storage. If the product type is anything other than FMCG, we will notify you that the product will not be stocked. Let's take a look at the code:

```
class Brooklyn:
    def maintenance_cost(self, product_type, quantity):
        self.product_type = product_type
        self.quantity = quantity
        coldstorage_cost = 100
        if (product_type == 'FMCG'):
            maintenance_cost = self.quantity * 0.25 + \
                coldstorage_cost
            return maintenance_cost
        else:
            return "We don't stock this product"
```

In the following code, for the Queens class, we will calculate maintenance cost only if the product type is Electronics. We will calculate the product of quantity costing 0.05 since the maintenance cost for electronics is lower and there is also no cold storage cost required here. If the product type is anything other than Electronics, we will notify that the product will not be stocked:

```python
class Queens:
    def maintenance_cost(self, product_type, quantity):
        self.product_type = product_type
        self.quantity = quantity
        if (product_type == 'Electronics'):
            maintenance_cost = self.quantity * 0.05
            return maintenance_cost
        else:
            return "We don't stock this product"
```

Please note that we have used the same function names in both the preceding examples. The next step is to call these functions. Each of these functions can be called by creating an object for each class and the functions can be accessed separately to perform different calculations even when they are used within the same program:

```python
object_brooklyn = Brooklyn()
object_queens = Queens()
object_brooklyn.maintenance_cost('FMCG', 2000)
600.0
object_queens.maintenance_cost('Electronics', 2000)
100.0
```

We now have an understanding of the concept of polymorphism within classes. We will next look at abstraction, which behaves along the same lines as polymorphism but with a difference that will be explained further in the coming section.

Hiding details with abstraction

Abstraction is a concept of OOP that helps in hiding internal details of a class or methods by providing a reference class with declarations of classes with empty declarations of methods. These reference classes are called **abstract base** and they are kind of a go-to parent class that holds the skeletal structure of all the methods that need to be implemented if a parent class is inherited. Python has a library called ABC that can be imported to define abstract base classes. Abstraction is more like giving a black box to external users by not revealing all the details of various methods defined inside a class but instead giving a reference class that can help the external users to implement the methods according to their own requirements.

For instance, the users of the Brooklyn branch don't have to know the calculations that are handled by the Queens branch to calculate their maintenance cost. The information that the users of the Brooklyn branch need to know is that they can inherit the `Branch` class and implement the calculations for maintenance costs according to their own books and they need not worry about how the Queens branch is calculating their maintenance costs. At the same time, the `Branch` class, which is their parent class, will not be able to provide one common implementation for calculating maintenance costs since the calculations are going to vary depending on the branch. In this kind of scenario, the `Branch` class can create an abstract method, `maintenance_cost`, and let its subclasses or child classes implement it according to their requirements. The implementation of the `maintenance_cost` method by Brooklyn will not impact the implementation of the same method by Queens; the purpose of the implementation ends within the child class and the parent abstract class is always available for other child classes to define their own implementation.

If this kind of implementation can be done by simply applying polymorphism to a parent class method, then why do we need an abstract class to do the same? Let us first look at this by implementing a parent class and its child classes without actually implementing it as an abstract class:

```python
class Branch():
    def maintenance_cost(self):
        pass


class Brooklyn(Branch):
    def maintenance_cost(self, product_type, quantity):
        self.product_type = product_type
        self.quantity = quantity
        coldstorage_cost = 100
        if (product_type == 'FMCG'):
            maintenance_cost = self.quantity * 0.25 + \
                coldstorage_cost
            return maintenance_cost
        else:
            return "We don't stock this product"


class Queens(Branch):
    def maintenance_cost(self, product_type, quantity):
        self.product_type = product_type
        self.quantity = quantity
        if (product_type == 'Electronics'):
            maintenance_cost = self.quantity * 0.05
```

```
                    return maintenance_cost
        else:
                    return "We don't stock this product"
```

In the preceding implementation, we have two child classes for the Branch class and we have applied polymorphism to override the parent method, but it is still not an abstraction since we will be able to create an object instance for the parent class and the methods of the parent class can be exposed when an object is created.

Instead of the preceding implementation, if we make a slight modification and create Branch as an abstract base class, let us look at what happens then. Here is the representation of what we are going for:

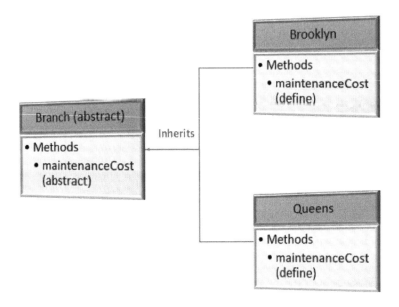

Figure 2.12 -- Abstract class is inherited by two classes and the methods implemented

Here, we will be importing ABC and abstractmethod from the abc library and we will create an abstract class called Branch followed by two child classes, Brooklyn and Queens, which inherit the parent class, Branch:

```
from abc import ABC,abstractmethod
class Branch(ABC):
    @abstractmethod
    def maintenance_cost(self):
        pass
```

```
class Brooklyn(Branch):
    def maintenance_cost(self, product_type, quantity):
        self.product_type = product_type
        self.quantity = quantity
        coldstorage_cost = 100
        if (product_type == 'FMCG'):
            maintenance_cost = self.quantity * 0.25 + \
                coldstorage_cost
            return maintenance_cost
        else:
            return "We don't stock this product"


class Queens(Branch):
    def maintenance_cost(self, product_type, quantity):
        self.product_type = product_type
        self.quantity = quantity
        if (product_type == 'Electronics'):
            maintenance_cost = self.quantity * 0.05
            return maintenance_cost
        else:
            return "We don't stock this product"
```

We imported the ABC library, created Branch as an abstract class, and defined maintenance_cost as an abstract method using the @abstractmethod keyword.

Let us now try to create an object of the Branch class:

```
branch = Branch()
```

It throws the following error:

```
---------------------------------------------------------------------------
TypeError                                 Traceback (most recent call last)
<ipython-input-52-8546e15cc93e> in <module>
----> 1 branch = Branch()
      2 branch.maintenanceCost()

TypeError: Can't instantiate abstract class Branch with abstract methods maintenanceCost
```

Figure 2.13 – Abstract method instantiation error

If an object is instantiated for a class, all the attributes and methods of the class can be accessed through the object. It is possible in regular classes; whereas, in the case of an abstract class, an object cannot be instantiated. This is why it is helpful to hide information that need not be shared with external users.

Abstraction is a method of information protection in Python or any other OOP language. We will now look at encapsulation and more details on how information can be protected in a class.

Protecting information with encapsulation

Encapsulation is the feature of the OOP paradigm that keeps has information protected. A class encapsulates its attributes and methods from being accessed by anyone outside the class. To ensure more protection to the variables and methods inside a class, they can further be declared as private or protected members. **Private** methods or variables can only be accessed within the class, whereas **protected** methods or variables can be accessed by subclasses or child classes that inherit the parent class or the base class. Private variables or methods are prefixed by the special character __ (double underscore) and protected members or variables are prefixed by _ (single underscore). We will look at some examples of private and protected class members.

Private members

In Python, the concept of a private variable does not exist as in other OOP languages. However, we can add two underscore symbols before the name of a variable or method to signify that a specific variable will be used as a private member within the class. It is done so that the developer can understand the naming convention that the program treats the variable as private. Adding two underscores before the name of a variable or method prevents name mangling by the Python interpreter to avoid collisions with the variable during inheritance, and it is not an actual private member as in other languages.

In this example, we will define our familiar Branch class with private variables for product ID, product name, brand, purchase price, and profit margin and create a private method to display the product details. We will also create branch ID, regional manager, and branch manager as class variables that are not private and look at the difference between accessing those using objects outside the class.

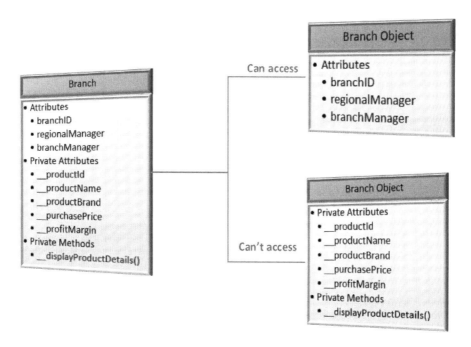

Figure 2.14 – Private members of theBranch class and its accessibility by the Branch object

Let us look at the following code to implement this example:

```python
class Branch():
    branch_id = 2021
    regional_manager = 'John M'
    branch_manager = 'Tom H'
    __product_id = None
    __product_name = None
    __productBrand = None
    __purchase_price = None
    __profit_margin = None

    def __display_product_details(self):
        self.__product_id = 100002
        self.__product_name = 'Washing Machine'
        self.__productBrand = 'Whirlpool'
        self.__purchase_price = 450
        self.__profit_margin = 0.19
```

```
        print('Product ID: ' + str(self.__product_id) + ',\
          Product Name: ' + self.__product_name +
          ', Product Brand: ' + self.__productBrand + ',\
          Purchase Price: ' + str(self.__purchase_price)
          + ', Profit Margin: ' +  str(self.__profit_margin))


    def __init__(self):
        self.__display_product_details()
```

On creating an object instance for the Branch class, we will be able to look at the results of the __display_product_details method since it is called within the class using the default __init__ method:

```
branch = Branch()
```

The output is as follows:

```
Product ID: 100002, Product Name: Washing Machine, Product
Brand: Whirlpool, Purchase Price: 450, Profit Margin: 0.19
```

Let us try to access the branch_id variable, which is not declared as private:

```
branch.branch_id
```

The output is as follows:

```
2021
```

We are able to access this variable. Let us now try to access profit_margin, which is declared with a prefix of double underscore:

```
branch.__profit_margin
```

It gives us the following error:

```
----------------------------------------------------------------
AttributeError                       Traceback (most recent call last)
<ipython-input-48-23ab3c57152f> in <module>
----> 1 branch.__profitMargin

AttributeError: 'Branch' object has no attribute '__profitMargin'
```

Figure 2.15 – Error accessing private variable of a class

We are getting an error since this variable can only be accessed within the class and not by the object of the class due to name mangling. The same applies to the private method created to display product details as well:

```
branch.__display_product_details()
```

We see the following:

```
--------------------------------------------------------------------
AttributeError                         Traceback (most recent call last)
<ipython-input-40-c62854f9e17a> in <module>
----> 1 branch.__displayProductDetails()

AttributeError: 'Branch' object has no attribute '__displayProductDetails'
```

Figure 2.16 – Error accessing private method of a class

The following screenshot shows the list of class members for the Branch class that can be accessed by its object:

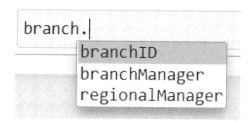

Figure 2.17 – Members accessible by the branch object after including private members

However, these private members can be accessed outside the class by creating an API to do it.

Protected members

In this example, we will recreate the Branch class with protected variables for product ID, product name, brand, purchase price, and profit margin and create a protected method to display the product details. We will create a branch manager as a private variable. We will also create branch ID and regional manager as class variables that are not protected or private and look at the difference in accessing those using objects outside the class. We will also inherit the Branch class further to check which members are accessible.

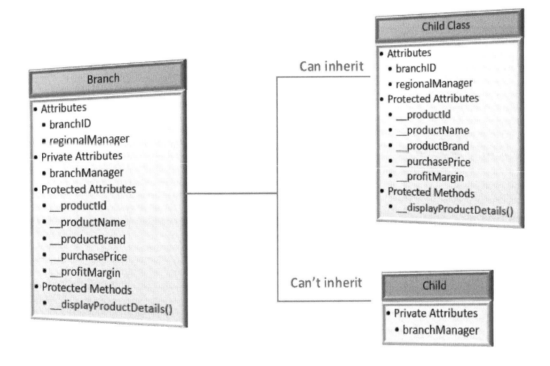

Figure 2.18 – Protected members of the Branch class and its accessibility by inherited subclasses

Let us look at the following code to implement this example:

```python
class Branch():
    branch_id = 2022
    regional_manager = 'Ron D'
    __branch_manager = 'Sam J'
    _product_id = None
    _product_name = None
    _productBrand = None
```

```
    _purchase_price = None
    _profit_margin = None

    def _display_product_details(self):
        self._product_id = 100003
        self._product_name = 'Washing Machine'
        self._productBrand = 'Samsung'
        self._purchase_price = 430
        self._profit_margin = 0.18
        print('Product ID: ' + str(self._product_id) + \
            ', Product Name: ' + self._product_name +
            ', Product Brand: ' + self._productBrand +
            ', Purchase Price: ' + str(self._purchase_price)
            + ', Profit Margin: ' +  str(self._profit_margin))

    def __init__(self):
        self._display_product_details()

branch = Branch()
```

The output is as follows:

```
Product ID: 100003, Product Name: Washing Machine, Product
Brand: Samsung, Purchase Price: 430, Profit Margin: 0.18
```

An object created by Branch cannot access its protected members too similar to the private members, as we see here:

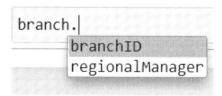

Figure 2.19 – Members accessible by branch object after including protected members

Let us create a child class called `Brooklyn` that inherits the parent class, `Branch`. The child class will inherit all the protected variables and methods from the parent class, whereas it will still not inherit the private members:

```
class Brooklyn(Branch):
    def __init__(self):
        print(self._product_id)
        self._display_product_details()


branch_brooklyn = Brooklyn()
```

The output is as follows:

```
None
Product ID: 100003, Product Name: Washing Machine, Product
Brand: Samsung, Purchase Price: 430, Profit Margin: 0.18
```

The `product_id` variable is a protected member of the parent class and `display_product_details` is also a protected member of the parent class, which is accessible by the init method of the child class, `Brooklyn`.

Let us now include a private member of the parent class and check whether it can be accessed from the child class:

```
class Brooklyn(Branch):
    def __init__(self):
        print(self._product_id)
        self._display_product_details()
        print(self.__branch_manager)


branch_brooklyn = Brooklyn()
```

The output is as follows:

```
None
Product ID: 100003, Product Name: Washing Machine, Product
Brand: Samsung, Purchase Price: 430, Profit Margin: 0.18
```

The following error clarifies that private members will still not be accessible by the child class:

```
----------------------------------------------------------------
AttributeError                          Traceback (most recent call last)
<ipython-input-88-7c2f2e3d9a82> in <module>
----> 1 branchBrooklyn = Brooklyn()

<ipython-input-87-a795a9221f51> in __init__(self)
      3          print(self._productId)
      4          self._displayProductDetails()
----> 5          print(self.__branchManager)

AttributeError: 'Brooklyn' object has no attribute '_Brooklyn__branchManager'
```

Figure 2.20 – Error accessing private attribute of a parent class from its child class

These examples give us an understanding of how encapsulation can be implemented in Python.

Summary

In this chapter, we reviewed the concept of classes and objects and looked at examples of how to create classes and object instances. We also learned the concept of methods and how to create methods inside classes. Along with this, we saw how to apply inheritance and multiple inheritances to classes and apply polymorphism to methods. We then learned how to create abstract classes and methods. Finally, we learned the concept of encapsulation and how to restrict access to methods and variables of a class.

This chapter has provided a review of all the concepts of OOP in Python, which is going to act as the foundation for the main topic of this book, which is metaprogramming.

In the next chapter, we will see in detail the concept of decorators and their implementation with examples.

Part 2: Deep Dive – Building Blocks of Metaprogramming I

The objective of this section is to give you a deeper understanding of the concepts of metaprogramming by looking at each of the building blocks in detail, along with examples of how they can be applied in a practical scenario. This section will have chapters that follow an explanation of the concepts with an implementation-based approach to give hands-on experience along with guided coding knowledge to users while reading this book. The chapters in this section can be read sequentially or independently.

This part contains the following chapters:

- *Chapter 3, Understanding Decorators and Their Applications*

- *Chapter 4, Working with Metaclasses*

- *Chapter 5, Understanding Introspection*

- *Chapter 6, Implementing Reflection on Python Objects*

- *Chapter 7, Understanding Generics and Typing*

- *Chapter 8, Defining Templates for Algorithms*

3

Understanding Decorators and their Applications

From this chapter onwards, we will start looking at various concepts that are part of metaprogramming along with examples of how to apply them. We will first take a look at decorators and how decorators can be implemented in Python 3.

Decorators are one of the metaprogramming concepts that deal with decorating a function without modifying the actual function body. As the name suggests, a decorator adds additional value to a function, a method, or a class by allowing the function to become an argument of another function that *decorates* or gives more information on the function, method, or class being decorated. Decorators can be developed on an individual user-defined function or on a method that is defined inside a class, or they can be defined on a class itself too. Understanding decorators will help us to enhance the reusability of functions, methods, and classes by manipulating them externally without impacting the actual implementation.

In the previous chapter, we reviewed the concept of object-oriented programming, which serves as the base for this chapter and the future chapters in this book.

In this chapter, we will be taking a look at the following main topics:

- Looking into simple function decorators
- Exchanging decorators from one function to another
- Applying multiple decorators to one function
- Exploring class decorators
- Getting to know built-in decorators

By the end of this chapter, you should be able to create your own decorators, implement user-defined decorators on functions/methods and classes, and reuse built-in decorators.

Technical requirements

The code examples shared in this chapter are available on GitHub under the code for this chapter here: `https://github.com/PacktPublishing/Metaprogramming-with-Python/tree/main/Chapter03`.

Looking into simple function decorators

We will now look at different types of function decorators with an example. We will continue using the *ABC Megamart* example we looked at in the previous chapter. Each user-defined function in Python can perform a different operation. But what if we want different functions to show specific additional information, no matter what the functions perform? We can do this simply by defining another function that decorates any function that is provided as an input.

Let's take a look at the following steps to understand this better:

1. A function decorator can be defined as follows:

    ```
    def functiondecorator(inputfunction):
        def decorator():
            print("---Decorate function with this line---
              ")
            return inputfunction()
        return decorator
    ```

    This code defines a simple function decorator that takes in any input function as an argument and adds a line above the function result that prints `---Decorate function with this line---` as the first output line for any input function.

2. This function decorator can be called by a new user-defined function with two different syntaxes. Let us define two simple functions:

    ```
    def userfunction1():
        return "A picture is worth a thousand words "
    ```

    This function returns the phrase `A picture is worth a thousand words`.

3. We will be adding one more function that returns a different phrase: `Actions speak louder than words`:

    ```
    def userfunction2():
        return "Actions speak louder than words"
    ```

4. In the following step, let us add a function decorator to both the preceding user-defined functions and look at the results:

    ```
    decoratedfunction1 = functiondecorator(userfunction1)
    decoratedfunction2 = functiondecorator(userfunction2)
    ```

5. In the preceding code, we have reassigned the functions by adding a decorator function to them. Executing decorated function 1 results in the following:

    ```
    decoratedfunction1()
    ---Decorate function with this line---
    'A picture is worth a thousand words'
    ```

6. Similarly, we can also execute decorated function 2:

    ```
    decoratedfunction2()
    ---Decorate function with this line---
    'Actions speak louder than words'
    ```

    Both of the function results added an additional line, `---Decorate function with this line---`, that was not part of their function definition but was part of the decorator function. These examples show the reusable nature of function decorators.

7. Let us look further into syntax 2, which is the most widely used method of adding decorators to other functions, methods, or classes:

    ```
    @functiondecorator
    def userfunction1():
        return "A picture is worth a thousand words"
    @functiondecorator
    def userfunction2():
        return "Actions speak louder than words"
    ```

    In the preceding code, while defining the user-defined functions, we added an additional line above the definition of `@functiondecorator`. This line signifies that we have added a decorator to the function in the definition stage itself. This decorator can be declared once and reused for any relevant function that is newly defined.

8. Executing the preceding code provides the same results as in the code execution of examples with syntax 1:

```
userfunction1()
---Decorate function with this line---
'A picture is worth a thousand words'
userfunction2()
---Decorate function with this line---
'A picture is worth a thousand words'
```

Now that you understand simple function decorators, we can look into an example that demonstrates its applications.

Understanding function decorators with an application

We can further look into an example of function decorators using a scenario from *ABC Megamart*. In this example, we will create a function to add an email signature for a branch manager in a different format for each branch. We will define two functions, `manager_albany` and `manager_manhattan`, with different font colors and highlights.

Let's look at this first piece of code:

```
def manager_albany(*args):
    BLUE = '\033[94m'
    BOLD = '\33[5m'
    SELECT = '\33[7m'
    for arg in args:
        print(BLUE + BOLD + SELECT + str(arg))


manager_albany('Ron D','ron.d@abcmegamart.
com','123 Main Street','Albany','New York', 12084)
```

The preceding code prints the branch manager's email signature with white, bold, and blue highlighted text:

```
Ron D
ron.d@abcmegamart.com
123 Main Street
Albany
New York
12084
```

Now let's take a quick look at this block of code:

```
def manager_manhattan(*args):
    GREEN = '\033[92m'
    SELECT = '\33[7m'
    for arg in args:
        print(SELECT + GREEN + str(arg))


manager_manhattan('John M',  'john.m@abcmegamart.com', '40097
5th Main Street',   'Manhattan', 'New York City',  'New
York',  11007)
```

This one prints the branch manager's email signature with highlighted text:

```
John M
john.m@abcmegamart.com
40097 5th Main Street
Manhattan
New York City
New York
11007
```

Now, let us add the name of *ABC Megamart* in both the signatures with a yellow highlight and modify the font color of the signature to yellow while keeping the signature highlight colors intact. To do this, we will create a function decorator that takes in the arguments of the preceding functions and add *ABC Megamart* with a black font and yellow highlight:

```
def signature(branch):
    def footnote(*args):
        LOGO = '\33[43m'
        print(LOGO + 'ABC Mega Mart')
        return branch(*args)
    return footnote
```

The following figure is a representation of how an email signature decorator can be implemented on two different signatures.

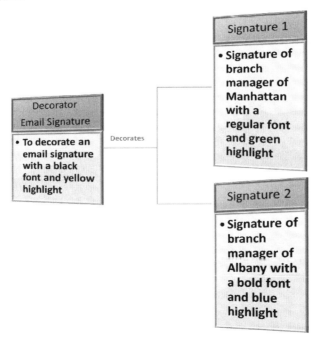

Figure 3.1 – Email signature decorator

The preceding signature decorator adds the name of *ABC Megamart* in both the signatures with a yellow highlight and modifies the font color of the signature to yellow while keeping the signature highlight colors intact.

First, let's add @signature to manager_manhattan:

```
@signature
def manager_manhattan(*args):
    GREEN = '\033[92m'
    SELECT = '\33[7m'
    for arg in args:
        print(SELECT + GREEN + str(arg))


manager_manhattan('John M',  'john.m@abcmegamart.com', '40097
5th Main Street',  'Manhattan', 'New York City',  'New
York',  11007)
```

This code returns the following email signature:

```
ABC Mega Mart
John M
john.m@abcmegamart.com
40097 5th Main Street
Manhattan
New York City
New York
11007
```

Now let's add `@signature` to `manager_albany`:

```
@signature
def manager_albany(*args):
    BLUE = '\033[94m'
    BOLD = '\33[5m'
    SELECT = '\33[7m'
    for arg in args:
        print(BLUE + BOLD + SELECT + str(arg))


manager_albany('Ron D','ron.d@abcmegamart.
com','123 Main Street','Albany','New York', 12084)
```

Doing so returns the following email signature:

```
ABC Mega Mart
Ron D
ron.d@abcmegamart.com
123 Main Street
Albany
New York
12084
```

Adding a function decorator to different functions in the preceding code snippets makes them have common functionality – in this case, the *ABC Megamart* title with a yellow highlight as a common functionality while keeping the individual branch manager signatures. It's a simple example of how reusable decorators can be and the nature of adding metadata or additional information to a function while keeping the actual functionality of the function intact.

Now that we understand what function decorators are and how we can use them, let's look at utilizing decorators for different functions by exchanging them and making them more reusable.

Exchanging decorators from one function to another

We now have an understanding of what a function decorator is and how a function decorator can be used for more than one function. We will look into further exploring the reusability concept of decorators by creating two different decorators to serve two different purposes and later utilizing them by interchanging the decorators between different functions.

To demonstrate this concept, we will be creating Decorator 1 for function 1 and Decorator 2 for function 2, and then we will be exchanging them from one function to another. Let us create two decorators to decorate two different functions.

Decorator 1 will be created to convert a date argument that is provided as a holiday date to the function that sets holidays for the Alabama branch of *ABC Megamart*.

The following figure is a representation of **Decorator 1** and its **Function 1**.

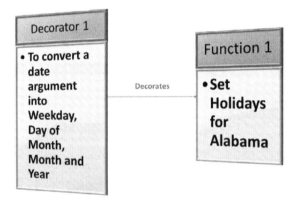

Figure 3.2 – Date converter as a decorator

Let's take a look at the code we'd be using for our desired example:

```
def dateconverter(function):
    import datetime
    def decoratedate(*args):
        newargs = []
        for arg in args:
            if(isinstance(arg,datetime.date)):
                arg = arg.weekday(),arg.day,arg.month,
```

```
            arg.year
        newargs.append(arg)
    return function(*newargs)
return decoratedate
```

The preceding `dateconverter` is a decorator function that takes in another function as an argument. To perform this function, we have imported the `datetime` library that helps us to convert the input date argument into the format of weekday, day of the month, month of the year, and year. This decorator function internally takes in all the arguments passed to the internal function and checks whether any of the function arguments are of the `datetime` data type, and if it finds a `datetime` object, it will be converted to display weekday, day of the month, month of the year, and year.

This decorator also stores the converted format of the `datetime` object along with the rest of the function arguments in a list and passes the list as an argument to the function that is provided as input to this decorator. Let us now create a function to set a holiday calendar for the Alabama branch and decorate it using this decorator function.

Function 1 is to set variables for the Alabama holiday calendar and it takes in the arguments using the `*args` parameter. The first argument of this function will be set as `branch_id`, the second argument as `holiday_type`, the third argument as `holiday_name`, and the fourth argument as `holiday_date`. All of these input arguments are converted into a dictionary variable by the function and it returns the dictionary with its key-value pairs denoting each value.

Here is what the code looks like using the details we just discussed:

```
@dateconverter
def set_holidays_alabama(*args):
    holidaydetails = {}
    holidaydetails['branch_id'] = args[0]
    holidaydetails['holiday_type'] = args[1]
    holidaydetails['holiday_name'] = args[2]
    holidaydetails['holiday_date'] = args[3]
    return holidaydetails
```

In the preceding code, we have started the function definition by adding the decorator `@dateconverter`, which takes care of converting the holiday date into the aforementioned format. Let us now call this function by providing the arguments required to create the holiday details dictionary:

```
from datetime import datetime
holiday =datetime.strptime('2021-01-18', '%Y-%m-%d')
```

In the preceding code, we have created a `datatime` object and stored it in a holiday variable that will be passed as one of the inputs to the `set_holidays_alabama` function:

```
set_holidays_alabama('id1000',
                     'local',
                     'Robert E. Lee's Birthday',
                     holiday)
```

The preceding code gives us the following decorated output:

```
{'branch_id': 'id1000',
 'holiday_type': 'local',
 'holiday_name': 'Robert E. Lee's Birthday',
 'holiday_date': (0, 18, 1, 2021)}
```

We can now go ahead and create another decorator that performs a different manipulation on another function that is provided as input.

Let's now look at **Decorator 2**. The second decorator will be created to check whether the term `id` is present in the input that denotes that the input value is an identifier of any kind and returns the numerical value of the identifier by removing its prefix. This decorator will be added to a function to set promotion details for any input product for the Malibu branch.

The following figure is a representation of **Decorator 2** and **Function 2**:

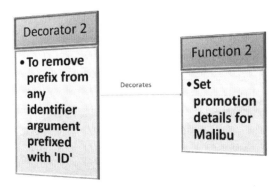

Figure 3.3 – ID identifier as a decorator

Here is the code we'll be using for our decorator:

```
def identifier(function):
    def decorateid(*args):
        newargs = []
        for arg in args:
            if(isinstance(arg,str)):
                arg = arg.lower()
                if 'id' in arg:
                    arg = int(''.join(filter(str.isdigit,
                        arg)))
            newargs.append(arg)
        return function(*newargs)
    return decorateid
```

The preceding identifier is a decorator function that takes in another function as an argument. This decorator function also internally takes in all the arguments passed to its internal function and navigates through each individual argument to check whether it is a string. If the argument is a string, the decorator converts the string into lowercase and checks whether it has a substring ID. If the substring ID is present in the variable, then all strings will be removed from the variable and only digits will be stored in it with the rest of the function arguments in a list, passing the list as an argument to the function that is provided as input to this decorator. Let us now create a function to set promotion details for the Malibu branch and decorate its ID using this decorator function.

Function 2 is to set variables for the product promotion details of the Malibu branch and it takes in the arguments using `*args` similar to the `set_holidays_alabama` function. The first argument of this function will be set as `branch_id`, the second argument as `product_id`, the third argument as `promotion_date`, the fourth as `promotion_type`, and the fifth as `promotion_reason`. All of these input arguments are also converted into a dictionary variable by the function and it returns the dictionary with its key-value pairs denoting each value. There are two `id` arguments in this function that get decorated by the identifier.

Here is what the code looks like using the details we just discussed:

```
@identifier
def set_promotion_malibu(*args):
    promotiondetails = {}
    promotiondetails['branch_id'] = args[0]
    promotiondetails['product_id'] = args[1]
    promotiondetails['product_name'] = args[2]
```

```
    promotiondetails['promotion_date'] = args[3]
    promotiondetails['promotion_type'] = args[4]
    promotiondetails['promotion_reason'] = args[5]
    return promotiondetails
```

In the preceding code, we have started the function definition by adding the decorator `@identifier`, which takes care of removing the prefixes from the `id` variable. Let us now call this function by providing the arguments required to create the product promotion details dictionary:

```
from datetime import datetime
promotion_date = datetime.strptime('2020-12-23', '%Y-%m-%d')
```

Here, we have created a `datatime` object and stored it in a promotion date, which will be passed as one of the inputs to the `set_promotion_malibu` function, but this date variable will stay in the same format as defined:

```
set_promotion
malibu('Id23400','ProdID201','PlumCake',promotion_
date,'Buy1Get1','Christmas')
```

The preceding code gives us the decorated output that follows:

```
{'branch_id': 23400,
 'product_id': 201,
 'product_name': 'plumcake',
 'promotion_date': datetime.datetime(2020, 12, 23, 0, 0),
 'promotion_type': 'buy1get1',
 'promotion_reason': 'christmas'}
```

We now have two decorators and two different functions decorated by them. To check whether these decorators can be exchanged, let us now redefine these functions by swapping the decorators using the following code:

```
@identifier

def set_holidays_alabama(*args):
    holidaydetails = {}
    holidaydetails['branch_id'] = args[0]
    holidaydetails['holiday_type'] = args[1]
    holidaydetails['holiday_name'] = args[2]
```

```
        holidaydetails['holiday_date'] = args[3]
        return holidaydetails


@dateconverter

def set_promotion_malibu(*args):
        promotiondetails = {}
        promotiondetails['branch_id'] = args[0]
        promotiondetails['product_id'] = args[1]
        promotiondetails['product_name'] = args[2]
        promotiondetails['promotion_date'] = args[3]
        promotiondetails['promotion_type'] = args[4]
        promotiondetails['promotion_reason'] = args[5]
        return promotiondetails
```

Let us input the required arguments and execute the preceding function, `set_holidays_alabama`:

```
from datetime import datetime
holiday =datetime.strptime('2021-01-18', '%Y-%m-%d')
set_holidays_alabama('id1000',
                    'local',
                    'Robert E. Lee's Birthday',
                    holiday)
```

This code gives us the decorated output as follows:

```
{'branch_id': 1000,
 'holiday_type': 'local',
 'holiday_name': 'robert e. lee's birthday',
 'holiday_date': datetime.datetime(2021, 1, 18, 0, 0)}
```

In the preceding output, the identifier is applied on the branch ID and there is no change to the holiday date. Similarly, let us execute the following code:

```
promotion_date = datetime.strptime('2020-12-23', '%Y-%m-%d')
set_promotion_
malibu('Id23400','ProdID201','PlumCake',promotion_
date,'Buy1Get1','Christmas')
```

This code gives us the decorated output that follows:

```
{'branch_id': 'Id23400',
  'product_id': 'ProdID201',
  'product_name': 'PlumCake',
  'promotion_date': (2, 23, 12, 2020),
  'promotion_type': 'Buy1Get1',
  'promotion_reason': 'Christmas'}
```

The following figure is a representation of how the two decorators will be exchanged or swapped between their functions:

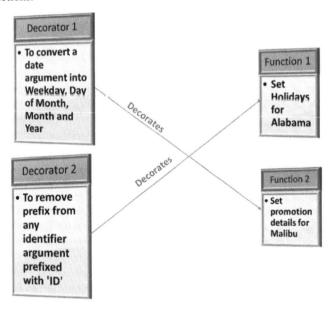

Figure 3.4 – Exchange decorators

Let us reuse the previous examples to look further into the concept of applying multiple decorators to one function.

Applying multiple decorators to one function

So far, we have understood that decorators can be created and added to functions to perform metaprogramming on the functions. We also understand that decorators can be reused and exchanged for different functions. We have also understood that decorators add decoration or value to a function from outside of the function body and help in altering the function with additional information. What if we want the function to perform two different actions through decorators and at the same time do not want the decorators to become more specific? Can we create two or more different decorators and apply them to a single function? Yes, we can. We will now look at decorating a function with more than one decorator and understand how it works.

For this example, let us reuse the decorators `dateconverter` and `identifier`. To understand this concept, we can reuse one of the previously declared functions, `set_promotion_malibu`, which has both a `datetime` object as an input argument – promotion date – and two ID values as input arguments – `branch_id` and `product_id`.

The following figure is a representation of adding two decorators to a function:

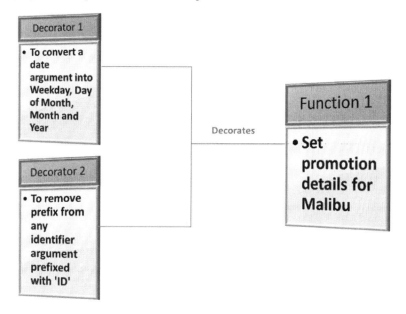

Figure 3.5 – Multiple decorators for one function

The following code puts our example into action:

```
@identifier
@dateconverter

def set_promotion_malibu(*args):
    promotiondetails = {}
    promotiondetails['branch_id'] = args[0]
    promotiondetails['product_id'] = args[1]
    promotiondetails['product_name'] = args[2]
    promotiondetails['promotion_date'] = args[3]
    promotiondetails['promotion_type'] = args[4]
    promotiondetails['promotion_reason'] = args[5]
    return promotiondetails
```

In this code, we have added both decorators to the set_promotion_malibu function:

```
promotion_date = datetime.strptime('2021-01-01', '%Y-%m-%d')

set_promotion_
malibu('Id23400','ProdID203','Walnut Cake',promotion_
date,'Buy3Get1','New Year')
```

Executing the preceding code results in the application of both decorators on the input values:

```
{'branch_id': 23400,
 'product_id': 203,
 'product_name': 'walnut cake',
 'promotion_date': (4, 1, 1, 2021),
 'promotion_type': 'buy3get1',
 'promotion_reason': 'new year'}
```

From the preceding output, we can see that @identifier is applied on branch_id and product_id. At the same time, @dateconverter is applied on the promotion_date. Let us now explore other variants of decorators.

Exploring class decorators

A **class decorator** is similar to the function decorator that we discussed earlier. Class decorators can be used to decorate, modify behavior, or debug a function, similar to a function decorator, which adds behavior to a function without actually modifying the function itself. A class decorator can be defined as a class by using two of its default or built-in methods: __init__ and __call__. Any variable initialized as part of the __init__ function of a class while creating an object instance of the class becomes a variable of the class itself. Similarly, the __call__ function of a class returns a function object. If we want to use a class as a decorator, we need to make use of the combination of these two built-in methods.

Let us look at what happens if we don't use the call method. Look at the following piece of code:

```
class classdecorator:
    def __init__(self,inputfunction):
        self.inputfunction = inputfunction

    def decorator(self):
        result = self.inputfunction()
        resultdecorator = ' decorated by a class decorator'
        return result + resultdecorator
```

Here, we have created a class named classdecorator and have added the init method to take a function as input. We have also created a decorator method that stores the result of the initialized function variable and adds a decorator string decorated by a class decorator to the input function result.

Let us now create an input function to test the preceding classdecorator:

```
@classdecorator

def inputfunction():
    return 'This is input function'
```

Adding this class decorator should decorate the input function. Let us check what happens when we call this input function:

```
inputfunction()
```

We get the following type error, which states `classdecorator` is not callable:

```
------------------------------------------------------------------------
TypeError                                Traceback (most recent call last)
<ipython-input-6-769efba848f3> in <module>
----> 1 inputfunction()

TypeError: 'classdecorator' object is not callable
```

Figure 3.6 – Error due to an incorrect definition of the class decorator

We are receiving this error since we did not use the right method to make the class behave as a decorator. The `decorator` method in the preceding code returns a variable but not a function. To make this class work as a decorator, we need to redefine the class as follows:

```
class classdecorator:
    def __init__(self,inputfunction):
        self.inputfunction = inputfunction

    def __call__(self):
        result = self.inputfunction()
        resultdecorator = ' decorated by a class decorator'
        return result + resultdecorator
```

Here, we have replaced the `decorator` method with the built-in method `__call__`. Let us now redefine the input function and see what happens:

```
@classdecorator
def inputfunction():
    return 'This is input function'
```

We can call the preceding function and check the behavior of this class decorator:

```
inputfunction()
```

```
'This is input function decorated by a class decorator'
```

The following figure is a simple representation that shows an incorrect way of creating a class decorator:

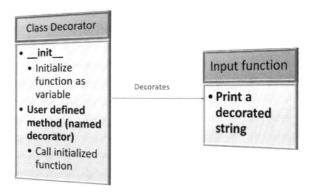

Figure 3.7 – Wrong method for creating a class decorator

Here is the correct way of creating it:

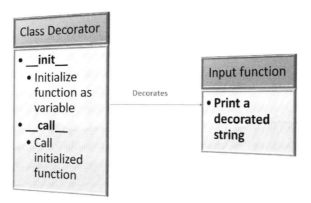

Figure 3.8 – Correct method for creating a class decorator

Now that you have a better understanding of class decorator, we can proceed to analyze the application of class decorator on *ABC Megamart*.

Understanding class decorators with an application

We will look into a detailed example of the class decorator by applying it to a scenario on *ABC Megamart*. Let us consider a scenario where *ABC Megamart* has a separate class created for each branch. Let us also assume each class has its own method, `buy_product`, to calculate a product's sales price by specifically applying the sales tax rate for the specific branch and product being purchased. When the mart wants to apply seasonal promotions that involve eight generic promotion types. Each branch class need not have a promotion calculation method to be applied to its calculated sales price. Instead, we can create a class decorator that can be applied to the `buy_product` method of each branch and the class decorator will, in turn, calculate the final sales price by applying promotion discounts on the actual sales price calculated by the branch.

We will create two classes and add the `buy_product` method to each class to calculate the sales price without adding a class decorator. This is to understand the return values of the actual methods:

```
class Alabama():

    def buy_product(self,product,unitprice,quantity,
        promotion_type):
            alabamataxrate = 0.0522
            initialprice = unitprice*quantity
            salesprice = initialprice +
                initialprice*alabamataxrate
            return salesprice, product,promotion_type
```

Creating an object instance for the previous class and calling the method with its arguments returns the following result:

```
alb1 = Alabama()
alb1.buy_product('Samsung-Refrigerator',200,1,'20%Off')


(210.44, 'Samsung-Refrigerator', '20%Off')
```

Similarly, we can define the class `Arizona` and add the method `buy_product` and execute the following code to verify its return value without a decorator:

```
class Arizona():

    def buy_product(self,product,unitprice,quantity,
        promotion_type):
            arizonataxrate = 0.028
```

```
        initialprice = unitprice*quantity
        salesprice = initialprice +
          initialprice*arizonataxrate
        return salesprice, product,promotion_type

arz1 = Arizona()
arz1.buy_product('Oreo-Cookies',0.5,250,'Buy2Get1')
```

(128.5, 'Oreo-Cookies', 'Buy2Get1')

The preceding buy_product method takes in product name, unit price, quantity, and promotion type as input and calculates the initial price by multiplying the unit price by the quantity of a product. It further calculates the sales price by adding the product of the initial price to the state tax rate along with the initial price calculated in the previous step. Finally, the method returns the sales price, product name, and promotion type. The sales tax rates are different for each state and the sales price calculation differs according to the sales tax rates.

We can now create a class decorator to apply a promotional discount on the sales price and calculate the final sales price for a product by including the offer rate or discount rate.

In the following code, let us define the class applypromotion and add two built-in methods required to make the class behave as a decorator:

- The __init__ **method**: This is a function or method as an input variable in this scenario

- The __call__ **method**: This method accepts multiple input arguments, which are also the arguments of the function or method being decorated

The input arguments are applied to the function or method being decorated and it further applies various discount rates to the sales price resulting from the input function by checking for eight different promotion types, recalculating the sales price, and storing it as the final sales price, as follows:

```
class applypromotion:
    def __init__(self, inputfunction):
        self.inputfunction = inputfunction

    def __call__(self,*arg):
        salesprice, product,promotion_type =
          self.inputfunction(arg[0],arg[1],arg[2],arg[3])
        if (promotion_type == 'Buy1Get1'):
            finalsalesprice = salesprice * 1/2
```

```
        elif (promotion_type == 'Buy2Get1'):
            finalsalesprice = salesprice * 2/3
        elif (promotion_type == 'Buy3Get1'):
            finalsalesprice = salesprice * 3/4
        elif (promotion_type == '20%Off'):
            finalsalesprice = salesprice - salesprice * 0.2
        elif (promotion_type == '30%Off'):
            finalsalesprice = salesprice - salesprice * 0.3
        elif (promotion_type == '40%Off'):
            finalsalesprice = salesprice - salesprice * 0.4
        elif (promotion_type == '50%Off'):
            finalsalesprice = salesprice - salesprice * 0.5
        else:
            finalsalesprice = salesprice
        return "Price of   " + product + ": " +
'$' + str(finalsalesprice)
```

The class decorator to @applypromotion is now ready to be further used by other functions or methods. We can now apply this decorator to the buy_product method from the class Alabama:

```
class Alabama():
    @applypromotion
    def buy_product(product,unitprice,quantity,promotion_type):
        alabamataxrate = 0.0522
        initialprice = unitprice*quantity
        salesprice = initialprice + initialprice*alabamataxrate
        return salesprice, product,promotion_type
```

Creating an object instance for the preceding code and calling its method works as follows:

```
alb = Alabama()
alb.buy_product('Samsung-Refrigerator',200,1,'20%Off')

'Price of - Samsung-Refrigerator: $168.352'
```

Similarly, we can also redefine the class `Arizona` and its method `buy_product` by adding the class decorator as follows:

```
class Arizona():
    @applypromotion
    def buy_product(product,unitprice,quantity,
      promotion_type):
        arizonataxrate = 0.028
        initialprice = unitprice*quantity
        salesprice = initialprice +
          initialprice*arizonataxrate
        return salesprice, product,promotion_type
```

Creating an object instance for the preceding code and calling its method works as follows:

```
arz = Arizona()
arz.buy_product('Oreo-Cookies',0.5,250,'Buy2Get1')

'Price of - Oreo-Cookies: $85.66666666666667'
```

Let us review the results of `buy_product` methods from Arizona before adding the decorator and after adding the decorator. The preceding code has the output after adding the decorator and the following code has the output before adding the decorator:

```
arz1.buy_product('Oreo-Cookies',0.5,250,'Buy2Get1')

(128.5, 'Oreo-Cookies', 'Buy2Get1')
```

After adding the `applypromotion` decorator, the sales price for 250 packs of cookies is at a discounted rate of $85.66 compared to the price of $128.50 before applying the promotion. The store need not always add a promotion on a product and the `buy_product` method can reuse the `applypromotion` decorator only when it needs to sell a product on promotion, thus making the decorator externally alter the behavior of the class while keeping the `buy_product` method's actual functionality intact.

The simple representation of this example is as follows:

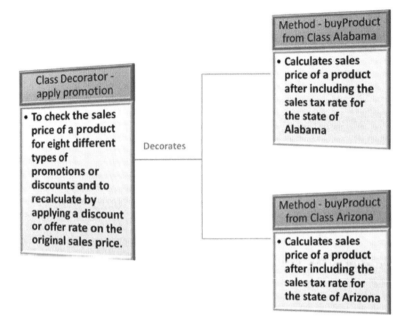

Figure 3.9 – Class decorator to apply promotional discounts on products

Having learned how to apply class decorators to methods or functions from other classes, we will proceed further to look at some of the built-in decorators available in Python.

Getting to know built-in decorators

Now, the question is, do we have to always create user-defined or custom decorators to be applied to classes and methods, or do we have some pre-defined decorators that can be used for specific purposes.

In addition to the user-defined decorators that we've looked at throughout this chapter, Python has its own built-in decorators, such as @staticmethod and @classmethod, that can be directly applied to methods. These decorators add certain important functionalities to methods and classes during the process of the class definition itself. We will be looking at these two decorators in detail, as follows.

The static method

The **static method** – @staticmethod – is a decorator that takes in a regular Python function as an input argument and converts it into a static method. Static methods can be created inside a class but will not use the implicit first argument of the class object instance usually denoted as an argument named self like the other instance-based methods.

To understand this concept, let us first create the class Alabama and add a function to the class buy_product without self as an argument and without the static method decorator and check its behavior:

```python
class Alabama:
    def buy_product(product,unitprice,quantity,promotion_type):
        alabamataxrate = 0.0522
        initialprice = unitprice*quantity
        salesprice = initialprice +
            initialprice*alabamataxrate
        return salesprice, product,promotion_type
```

Here we have defined the class Alabama with the function buy_product. Let us now create an object instance and call the function inside the class to check its behavior:

```python
alb = Alabama()
alb.buy_product('Samsung-Refrigerator',200,1,'20%Off')
```

Executing this code leads to the following error:

```
---------------------------------------------------------------
TypeError                                Traceback (most recent call last)
<ipython-input-351-32f04240a8b7> in <module>
----> 1 alb.buyProduct('Samsung-Refrigerator',200,1,'20%Off')

TypeError: buyProduct() takes 4 positional arguments but 5 were given
```

Figure 3.10 – Error on calling a function without static method and self

Rerunning the preceding function without creating an object works as follows:

```python
Alabama.buy_product('Samsung-Refrigerator',200,1,'20%Off')
(210.44, 'Samsung-Refrigerator', '20%Off')
```

To avoid the preceding error and to call a function inside a class with or without creating an object, we can convert the function into a static method by adding the @staticmethod decorator to it. We can now look at how it works:

```
class Alabama:
    @staticmethod
    def buy_product(product,unitprice,quantity,
        promotion_type):
        alabamataxrate = 0.0522
        initialprice = unitprice*quantity
        salesprice = initialprice +
            initialprice*alabamataxrate
        return salesprice, product,promotion_type


    def another_method(self):
        return "This method needs an object"
```

We have added an additional method named another_method, which can only be called using an object instance. Let us now create an object for the class and call both the preceding methods:

```
albstatic = Alabama()
albstatic.buy_product('Samsung-Refrigerator',200,1,'20%Off')


(210.44, 'Samsung-Refrigerator', '20%Off')


albstatic.another_method()


'This method needs an object'
```

Both the methods, static and instance, can be called using the object of the class. At the same time, the static method can also be called using the class itself without creating an object:

```
Alabama.buy_product('Samsung-Refrigerator',200,1,'20%Off')
(210.44, 'Samsung-Refrigerator', '20%Off')


Alabama.another_method()
```

Executing this code leads to the following error:

```
---------------------------------------------------------------------
TypeError                                 Traceback (most recent call last)
<ipython-input-347-cd717ea651b5> in <module>
----> 1 Alabama.anotherMethod()

TypeError: anotherMethod() missing 1 required positional argument: 'self'
```

Figure 3.11 – Error on calling an instance method using its class

The static method generated the expected output when called using its class, while the instance method did not run. This is the advantage of using a static method to convert a function into a method inside a class.

The class method

The **class method** – @classmethod – is also a built-in decorator similar to @staticmethod, and this decorator also converts a function into a static method inside a class. @staticmethod does not have an implicit argument of the object to a class whereas @classmethod has an implicit argument, cls, which gets added to the function, while the @classmethod decorator is added to it as seen in the following code block:

```
class Alabama:
    @classmethod
    def buy_product(cls,product,unitprice,quantity,
      promotion_type):
        alabamataxrate = 0.0522
        initialprice = unitprice*quantity
        salesprice = initialprice +
          initialprice*alabamataxrate
        return cls,salesprice, product,promotion_type
```

This function can be called either with or without creating a class instance. We can look at both in the following code:

```
Alabama.buy_product('Samsung-Refrigerator',200,1,'20%Off')
(__main__.Alabama, 210.44, 'Samsung-Refrigerator', '20%Off')


alb = Alabama()
alb.buy_product('Samsung-Refrigerator',200,1,'20%Off')
(__main__.Alabama, 210.44, 'Samsung-Refrigerator', '20%Off')
```

In the preceding code, we can see that a function converted by `@classmethod` into a class method can be called directly using the class or by creating an object of the class.

These are a few of the built-in decorators and there are more such decorators available in Python 3 that can be explored and reused.

Summary

In this chapter, we have learned how to create simple decorators and how to apply decorators with examples. We saw how to exchange decorators from one function to another along with how to add multiple decorators to one function.

We now understand the concept of class decorators and have looked at an example of how to apply them. And finally, we learned how to use some built-in decorators such as `@staticmethod` and `@classmethod`.

All of these concepts are part of Python metaprogramming and they are used to change the behavior of a function or a method externally and without impacting the internal functionalities of the function or method.

In the next chapter, we will be looking at the concept of meta classes with different examples.

4

Working with Metaclasses

Metaclasses, the focal point of this chapter, can manipulate the way a new class is created by decorating the arguments without impacting the actual class definition itself. Metaclasses are not very frequently used in Python application development unless there is a need for more advanced implementations of frameworks or APIs that need features such as manipulation of classes or dynamic class generation and so on.

In the previous chapter, we looked at the concept of decorators with some examples. Understanding decorators helps in following metaclasses with more ease since both decorators and metaclasses deal with metaprogramming on Python 3 program objects by manipulating them externally.

In this chapter, we will cover the following main topics:

- Overview of metaclasses
- The structure of a metaclass
- The application of metaclasses
- Switching metaclasses
- Inheritance in metaclasses
- Manipulating class variables

By the end of this chapter, you should be able to create your own metaclasses, implement inheritance on metaclasses, and reuse ones that are already created.

Technical requirements

The code examples shared in this chapter are available on GitHub under the code for this chapter here: `https://github.com/PacktPublishing/Metaprogramming-with-Python/tree/main/Chapter04`.

Overview of metaclasses

Mctaclasses are classes that can be created separately with certain features that can alter the behavior of other classes or can help in dynamically manufacturing new classes. The base class of all metaclasses is the `type` class and the object or instance of a metaclass will be a class. Any custom metaclass that we create will be inherited from the `type` class. `type` is the class of all data types in Python as well and everything else in Python 3 is an object of the `type` class. We can test this statement by checking the type of different program objects in Python, as follows:

```
class TestForType:
    pass

type(TestForType)
type

type(int)
type

type(str)
type

type(object)
type

type(float)
type

type(list)
type
```

In this chapter, we will look at some examples of how to use these metaclasses, how to implement them, and how to reuse them. We will continue with our *ABC Megamart* examples to proceed further with the understanding of metaclasses.

The structure of a metaclass

A metaclass is like any other class, but it has the ability to alter the behavior of other classes that take it as their metaclass. Understanding the structure of a metaclass helps us create our own customized metaclasses, which can be used further in manipulating new classes. The superclass of a metaclass is the type itself. When we create a class with `type` as its superclass and override the __new__ method to manipulate the metadata of a class it returns, then we have created a metaclass. Let's take a closer look with the help of some simple examples.

The __new__ method takes `cls` as its first argument, which is the class itself. The members of the class that has `cls` as its first argument can be accessed by the class name and the rest of the arguments as other metadata of the class, as seen here:

```
class ExampleMetaClass1(type):
    def __new__(classitself, *args):
        print('class itself: ', classitself)
        print('Others: ', args)
        return type.__new__(classitself, *args)
```

In the preceding code, we have created the class `ExampleMetaClass1`, which inherits the class `type` and overrides the __new__ method to print the class instance and its other arguments.

Let's now create the class `ExampleClass1` and add the preceding metaclass to it:

```
class ExampleClass1(metaclass = ExampleMetaClass1):
    int1 = 123
    str1 = 'test'


    def test():
        print('test')
```

Running the preceding code displays the following result:

```
class itself:  <class '__main__.ExampleMetaClass1'>
Others:  ('ExampleClass1', (), {'__module__': '__main__',
'__qualname__': 'ExampleClass1', 'int1': 123, 'str1': 'test',
'test': <function ExampleClass1.test at 0x00000194A377E1F0>})
```

The first part of this output is the class instance `<class '__main__.ExampleMetaClass1'>` and the remaining arguments are the class name and the arguments of the class. A simple representation of the metaclass definition is as follows:

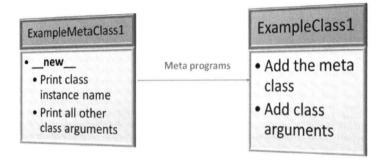

Figure 4.1 – Example metaclass definition

Let's dive into a little more detail with another example in our next subsection.

Analyzing the arguments

We now will dig deeper into the arguments of the `__new__` method of a metaclass. Analyzing the arguments of a metaclass will provide clarity on what information of a class can be customized using a metaclass. The data that can be manipulated in the classes that adds a metaclass while defining is represented in the following figure:

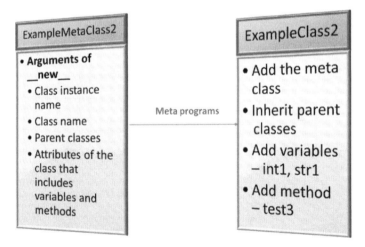

Figure 4.2 – Example metaclass with more arguments

Let's now follow these steps to see how the behavior of arguments affects classes:

1. First, look at the following code where we have all arguments of a metaclass segregated—class instance; class name; all parent classes, superclasses, or base classes of the class; and all variables and methods created within the class:

```
class ExampleMetaClass2(type):
    def __new__(classitself, classname, baseclasses,
                attributes):
        print('class itself: ', classitself)
        print('class name: ', classname)
        print('parent class list: ', baseclasses)
        print('attribute list: ', attributes)
        return type.__new__(classitself, classname,
            baseclasses, attributes)
```

2. Next, we will be creating two parent classes—`ExampleParentClass1` and `ExampleParentClass2`:

```
class ExampleParentClass1():
    def test1():
        print('parent1 - test1')


class ExampleParentClass2():
    def test2():
        print('parent2 - test2')
```

3. Now, we will create the class `ExampleClass2` where we will be inheriting both of the preceding parent classes and adding the metaclass as `ExampleMetaClass2`:

```
class ExampleClass2(ExampleParentClass1,
ExampleParentClass2, metaclass = ExampleMetaClass2):
    int1 = 123
    str1 = 'test'

    def test3():
        print('child1 - test3')
```

4. Executing the preceding code results in the following output:

```
class itself:  <class '__main__.ExampleMetaClass2'>
class name:  ExampleClass2
parent class:  (<class '__main__.ExampleParentClass1'>,
<class '__main__.ExampleParentClass2'>)
attributes:  {'__module__': '__main__', '__qualname__':
'ExampleClass2', 'int1': 123, 'str1': 'test', 'test3':
<function ExampleClass2.test3 at 0x00000194A3994E50>}
```

This example shows us the highlighted arguments that are returned by the metaclass and gives an overview of which values can possibly be manipulated from a class using metaprogramming.

5. Let us look at the type of each of the classes created in this example:

```
type(ExampleParentClass1)
type
type(ExampleParentClass2)
type
type(ExampleMetaClass2)
type
type(ExampleClass2)
__main__.ExampleMetaClass2
```

As we can see, the type of all other classes is the type itself whereas the type of `ExampleClass2` is `ExampleMetaClass2`.

Now that you understand the structure of a metaclass, we can look further into applications of metaclasses on our *ABC Megamart* example.

The application of metaclasses

In this section, we will look at an example where we will create a metaclass that can automatically modify the user-defined method attributes of any branch class that is newly created. To test this, let us follow these steps:

1. Create a metaclass with the name `BranchMetaclass`:

```
class BranchMetaclass(type):
```

2. Create a __new__ method with class instance, class name, base classes, and attributes as its arguments. In the __new__ method, import the `inspect` library, which can help inspect the input attributes:

```
def __new__(classitself, classname, baseclasses,
    attributes):
    import inspect
```

3. Create a new dictionary, `newattributes`:

```
newattributes = {}
```

Iterate over the class attributes, check that the attributes start with __, and don't change the value.

4. Continue iterating over the other attributes and check if the attributes are functions. If they are functions, prefix `branch` to the class method and convert the method name into title case:

```
for attribute, value in attributes.items():
        if attribute.startswith("__"):
            newattributes[attribute] = value
        elif inspect.isfunction(value):
            newattributes['branch' +
                attribute.title()] = value for a
                attribute, value in
                attributes.items():
        if attribute.startswith("__"):
            newattributes[attribute] = value
        elif inspect.isfunction(value):
            newattributes['branch' +
                attribute.title()] = value
```

5. If the preceding conditions are not met, save the value of the attribute as it is:

```
else:
            newattributes[attribute] = value
```

6. Return the new method with new attributes:

```
return type.__new__(classitself,
                classname, baseclasses,
                newattributes)
```

7. Within the metaclass, also create a regular user-defined method, `buy_product`, to calculate the sales price of a product:

```
def buy_product(product,unit_price,quantity,statetax_
rate,promotiontype):
        statetax_rate = statetax_rate
        initialprice = unit_price*quantity
        sales_price = initialprice +
            initialprice*statetax_rate
        return sales_price, product,promotiontype
```

8. Next, we will create another new class, `Brooklyn`, and add this metaclass to the class. By adding the metaclass, we want the methods in the class `Brooklyn` to have a prefix branch and change the methods to title case while creating the methods of `Brooklyn`.

    The `Brooklyn` class has four variables, `product_id`, `product_name`, `product_category`, and `unit_price`. We will also create a method to calculate the maintenance cost and this method should be converted from `maintenance_cost` to `branchMaintenance_cost` due to the metaclass that alters the behavior of the newly created class. Here's the new class:

```
class Brooklyn(metaclass = BranchMetaclass):
    product_id = 100902
    product_name = 'Iphone X'
    product_category = 'Electronics'
    unit_price = 700


    def maintenance_cost(self,product_type, quantity):
        self.product_type = product_type
        self.quantity = quantity
        cold_storage_cost = 100
        if (product_type == 'Electronics'):
            maintenance_cost = self.quantity * 0.25 +
                cold_storage_cost
            return maintenance_cost
        else:
            return "We don't stock this product"
```

9. We can list all the arguments of the class `Brooklyn` and check if the metaclass has altered its behavior:

```
dir(Brooklyn)
['__class__',
 '__delattr__',
 '__dict__',
 ,__dir__',
 ,__doc__',
 ,__eq__',
 ,__format__',
 ,__ge__',
 ,__getattribute__',
 ,__gt__',
 ,__hash__',
 ,__init__',
 ,__init_subclass__',
 ,__le__',
 ,__lt__',
 ,__module__',
 ,__ne__',
 ,__new__',
 ,__reduce__',
 ,__reduce_ex__',
 ,__repr__',
 ,__setattr__',
 ,__sizeof__',
 ,__str__',
 ,__subclasshook__',
 ,__weakref__',
 'branchMaintenance_cost',
 'product_category',
 'product_id',
 'product_name',
 'unit_price']
```

10. Let us now create an object and look at its methods and variables, as follows:

```
brooklyn = Brooklyn()
brooklyn.branchMaintenance_Cost('Electronics',10)
102.5
brooklyn.product_id
100902
brooklyn.product_name
'Iphone X'
brooklyn.product_type
'Electronics'
```

A simple representation of this example is as follows:

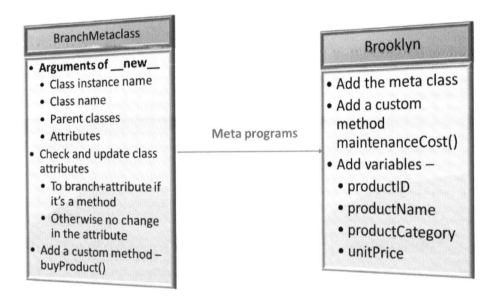

Figure 4.3 – Application of metaclass on ABC Megamart – Branch example

So far, we've looked at an overview of a metaclass, understood its structure, performed an analysis of its arguments, and applied our understanding by creating a custom metaclass on our core example. We will look at a few more applications in the following section.

Inheriting the metaclass

In this section, we will walk through an example where we will inherit the metaclass to check whether it can be inherited as a regular parent class without altering the behavior of the new class that is being created. Take a look at the following code:

```
class Queens(BranchMetaclass):
    def maintenance_cost(product_type, quantity):
        product_type = product_type
        quantity = quantity
        if (product_type == <FMCG>):
            maintenance_cost = quantity * 0.05
            return maintenance_cost
        else:
            return "We don't stock this product"
```

Let's now create an object for the preceding class to check if an object can be created:

```
queens = Queens()
```

We get the following `TypeError`:

```
--------------------------------------------------------------------------
TypeError                               Traceback (most recent call last)
<ipython-input-214-bfc347d19820> in <module>
----> 1 queens = Queens()

TypeError: __new__() missing 3 required positional arguments: 'classname', 'baseclasses', and 'attrib
utes'
```

Figure 4.4 – Error while creating an object for the class inheriting a metaclass

This error occurred as __new__ is a static method that is called to create a new instance for the class and it expects three arguments of the class, which are not provided while creating the class object. However, there is another way of calling the newly created class, `Queens`. The class can be called directly, and its methods can be used without having to create an object:

```
Queens.maintenance_cost('FMCG',120)
6.0
```

The `maintenance_cost` method did not get modified into `branchMaintenance_cost` since the metaclass is not used as a metaclass but as a parent class. Since the metaclass is inherited, Queens also inherits the user-defined methods of `BranchMetaclass` as follows:

```
Queens.buy_product('Iphone',1000,1,0.04,None)
(1040.0, 'Iphone', None)
```

Inheriting as a parent and metaclass

Let's now look at what happens when we inherit a class as a parent and also add it as a metaclass while creating a new class:

```
class Queens(BranchMetaclass, metaclass = BranchMetaclass):
    def maintenance_cost(product_type, quantity):
        product_type = product_type
        quantity = quantity
        if (product_type == 'FMCG'):
            maintenance_cost = quantity * 0.05
            return maintenance_cost
        else:
            return "We don't stock this product"
```

In the preceding code, we have added `BranchMetaclass` as the parent class for the class `Queens` and we have also added it as a metaclass. This definition should make the class `Queens` inherit the custom methods from `BranchMetaclass` and also change the `maintenance_cost` method into `branchMaintenance_cost`. Let's see if it does:

```
Queens.branchMaintenance_Cost('FMCG',2340)
117.0
```

In the preceding code execution and output, the `maintenance_cost` method is converted into the `branchMaintenance_cost` method as expected. Now run the following command:

```
Queens.buy_product('Iphone',1500,1,0.043,None)
(1564.5, 'Iphone', None)
```

The `buy_product` method, which is a custom method from `BranchMetaclass`, is also inherited since it is a parent class.

Here is a simple representation of this example:

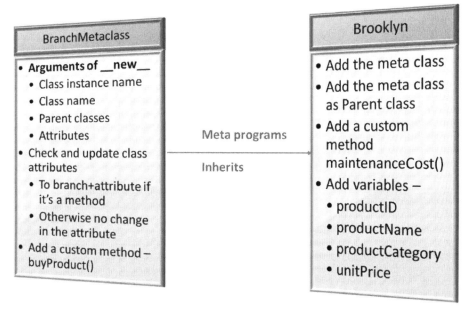

Figure 4.5 – Application of metaclass and also inheriting it on ABC Megamart branch example

Let us look further into examples of switching metaclasses from one class to another.

Switching metaclasses

We can now look into the concept of switching metaclasses for a class. You may think, *why do we need to switch metaclasses?* Switching metaclasses reinforces the reusability concept of metaprogramming and in this case, it helps in understanding how a metaclass created for use on one class can also be used for a different class without impacting the class definition.

In the example for this section, we will be creating two meta classes – `IncomeStatementMetaClass` and `BalanceSheetMetaClass`. For the Malibu branch of *ABC Megamart*, we will create a class to capture the information required for its financial statements. The two financial statements relevant for this example are Income Statement attributes and Balance Sheet attributes for the Malibu branch. To differentiate where a particular attribute or method of a class should go, we will be creating two metaclasses that look at the names of the attributes and tag them under Income Statement or Balance Sheet accordingly.

The following is a simple representation of the attributes that will be manipulated by the aforementioned metaclasses:

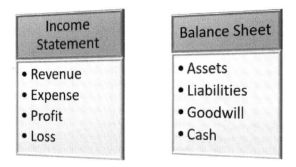

Figure 4.6 – Finance attributes used in this metaclass example

Take a look at the following code snippet:

```
class IncomeStatementMetaClass(type):
    def __new__(classitself, classname, baseclasses,
            attributes):

        newattributes = {}
        for attribute, value in attributes.items():
            if attribute.startswith("__"):
                newattributes[attribute] = value
            elif («revenue» in attribute) or \
            ("expense" in attribute) or \
            ("profit" in attribute) or \
            ("loss" in attribute):
                newattributes['IncomeStatement_' +
                    attribute.title()] = value
            else:
                newattributes[attribute] = value
        return type.__new__(classitself, classname,
            baseclasses, newattributes)
```

Here, the new method is modified to check for attributes that have the key as one of the parameters that belong to an income statement such as revenue, expense, profit, or loss. If any of this terminology occurs in the method name or variable name, we will add a prefix of IncomeStatement to segregate those methods and variables.

To test this metaclass, we will be creating a new class, Malibu, with four variables and four methods, as follows:

```python
class Malibu(metaclass = IncomeStatementMetaClass):
    profit = 4354365
    loss = 43000
    assets = 15000
    liabilities = 4000
    def calc_revenue(quantity,unitsales_price):
        totalrevenue = quantity * unitsales_price
        return totalrevenue

    def calc_expense(totalrevenue,netincome, netloss):
        totalexpense = totalrevenue - (netincome + netloss)
        return totalexpense

    def calc_totalassets(cash,inventory,accountsreceivable):
        totalassets = cash + inventory + accountsreceivable
        return totalassets

    def calc_totalliabilities(debt,accruedexpense,
        accountspayable):
        totalliabilities = debt + accruedexpense +
            accountspayable
        return totalliabilities
```

In the preceding code, we have added the metaclass `IncomeStatementMetaClass` and we see that the attributes of the class `Malibu` modify the behavior of variables and methods as follows:

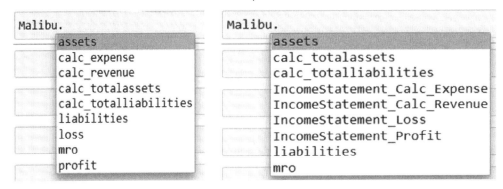

Figure 4.7 – Malibu without metaclass (left) and Malibu with metaclass (right)

We will further add another metaclass, `BalanceSheetMetaClass`, to deal with the balance sheet-related attributes in the class `Malibu`. In the following metaclass, the new method is modified to check for attributes that have the key as one of the parameters that belong to a balance sheet such as `assets`, `liabilities`, `goodwill`, and `cash`. If any of these terms occur in the method name or variable name, we will add a prefix of `BalanceSheet` to segregate those methods and variables:

```python
class BalanceSheetMetaClass(type):
    def __new__(classitself, classname, baseclasses,
                attributes):
        newattributes = {}
        for attribute, value in attributes.items():
            if attribute.startswith("__"):
                newattributes[attribute] = value
            elif («assets» in attribute) or \
            ("liabilities" in attribute) or \
            ("goodwill" in attribute) or \
            ("cash" in attribute):
                newattributes['BalanceSheet_' +
                    attribute.title()] = value
            else:
                newattributes[attribute] = value
        return type.__new__(classitself, classname,
            baseclasses, newattributes)
```

In the preceding code, we have added the metaclass `BalanceSheetMetaClass` and we see that the attributes of the class `Malibu` modify the behavior of variables and methods as follows:

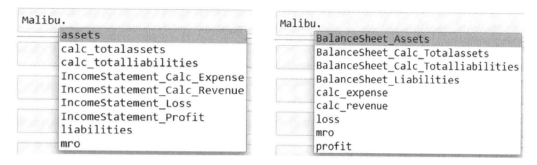

Figure 4.8 – Malibu with IncomeStatementMetaClass (left) and Malibu with BalanceSheetMetaClass (right)

Now that you know why we need to switch metaclasses, let us look at the application of metaclasses in inheritance.

Inheritance in metaclasses

Inheritance, in a literal sense, means a child acquiring the properties of a parent and it means the same in the case of object-oriented programming too. A new class can inherit the attributes and methods of a parent class and it can also have its own properties and methods.

In this example, we will look at how inheritance works on metaclasses by creating two classes, `California` and `Pasadena` – `California` being the parent class and `Pasadena` the child class.

Let's check these steps out to understand inheritance better:

1. In the previous section, we already created two metaclasses that inherited type as their parent class – `IncomeStatementMetaClass` and `BalanceSheetMetaClass`. We will start by creating the class `California` with the `IncomeStatement` metaclass:

    ```
    class California(metaclass = IncomeStatementMetaClass):
        profit = 4354365
        loss = 43000
        def calc_revenue(quantity,unitsales_price):
            totalrevenue = quantity * unitsaleprice
            return totalrevenue

        def calc_expense(totalrevenue,netincome, netloss):
    ```

```
        totalexpense = totalrevenue -
    (netincome + netloss)
        return totalexpense
```

Here, we have defined only those attributes that can be modified by the `IncomeStatement` metaclass.

2. Next, we will create another class, `Pasadena`, with the `BalanceSheet` metaclass:

```
class Pasadena(California,metaclass =
BalanceSheetMetaClass):
    assets = 18000
    liabilities = 5000
    def calc_totalassets(cash,inventory,
        accountsreceivable):
        totalassets = cash + inventory +
            accountsreceivable
        return totalassets


    def calc_totalliabilities(debt,accruedexpense,
        accountspayable):
        totalliabilities = debt + accruedexpense +
            accountspayable
        return totalliabilities
```

We have defined here only those attributes that can be modified by the `BalanceSheet` metaclass.

3. Executing the code of the `Pasadena` class results in the following error:

```
---------------------------------------------------------------
TypeError                          Traceback (most recent call last)
<ipython-input-47-a1dffb78fdd6> in <module>
----> 1 class Pasadena(California,metaclass = BalanceSheetMetaClass):
      2     assets = 18000
      3     liabilities = 5000
      4     def calc_totalassets(cash,inventory,accountsreceivable):
      5         totalassets = cash + inventory + accountsreceivable

TypeError: metaclass conflict: the metaclass of a derived class must be a (non-strict) subclass of th
e metaclasses of all its bases
```

Figure 4.9 – Error while executing a child class that has a different metaclass

This error was thrown since Pasadena inherited the parent class California, which has a different metaclass, IncomeStatementMetaClass, which is inherited from type, and Pasadena's metaclass BalanceSheetMetaClass is also inherited from type.

4. To resolve this error, we can redefine the BalanceSheetMetaClass with the parent class as IncomeStatementMetaClass instead of the type class, as follows:

```python
class BalanceSheetMetaClass(IncomeStatementMetaClass):
    def __new__(classitself, classname, baseclasses,
                attributes):
        newattributes = {}
        for attribute, value in attributes.items():
            if attribute.startswith("__"):
                newattributes[attribute] = value
            elif («assets» in attribute) or \
            ("liabilities" in attribute) or \
            ("goodwill" in attribute) or \
            ("cash" in attribute):
                newattributes['BalanceSheet_' +
                    attribute.title()] = value
            else:
                newattributes[attribute] = value
        return type.__new__(classitself, classname,
            baseclasses, newattributes)
```

5. Let's now rerun the California parent class and also the Pasadena child class to check if the behavior modification of both the metaclasses is implemented in the Pasadena class:

```python
class California(metaclass = IncomeStatementMetaClass):
    profit = 4354365
    loss = 43000
    def calc_revenue(quantity,unitsales_price):
        totalrevenue = quantity * unitsaleprice
        return totalrevenue
    def calc_expense(totalrevenue,netincome, netloss):
        totalexpense = totalrevenue - (netincome +
            netloss)
        return totalexpense
```

```
class Pasadena(California,metaclass =
BalanceSheetMetaClass):
    assets = 18000
    liabilities = 5000
    def calc_totalassets(cash,inventory,
        accountsreceivable):
        totalassets = cash + inventory +
            accountsreceivable
        return totalassets
    def calc_totalliabilities(debt,accruedexpense,
        accountspayable):
        totalliabilities = debt + accruedexpense +
            accountspayable
        return totalliabilities
```

6. Here is the output from the Pasadena class, and as we can see, both the BalanceSheet and IncomeStatement attributes are modified as per their metaclasses:

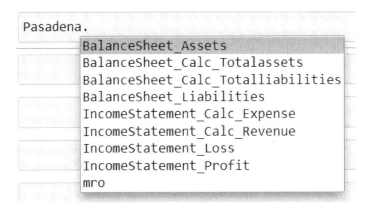

Figure 4.10 – Pasadena class with inheritance

A simple representation of this application is as follows:

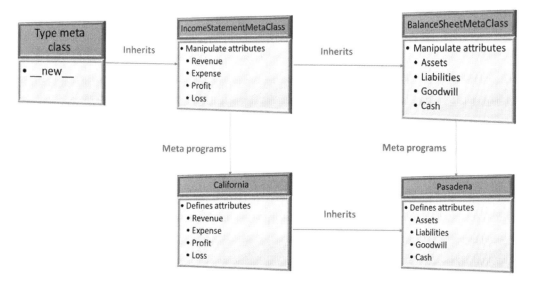

Figure 4.11 – Inheritance in metaclasses

In this case, we have redefined the parent class of BalanceSheetMetaClass to be IncomeStatementMetaClass since Python does not automatically resolve their parent classes while they were both inherited by type and instead throws a metaclass conflict. Redefining the parent class of BalanceSheetMetaClass not only resolves the error but will also not impact the overall functionality of the class since IncomeStatementMetaClass is in turn inherited from type.

Let us look at another example where we will be adding additional information to class attributes.

Manipulating class variables

In this section, we will take an example to look at manipulating class variables further using metaclasses. We will be creating a metaclass named SchemaMetaClass and will define the __new__ method to manipulate attributes of a class if they are variables of data types that belong to integer, float, string, or boolean. Let's go through the steps real quick:

1. We will now create the SchemaMetaClass with the parent class as type and have modified the new method to check the following conditions:

    ```
    class SchemaMetaClass(type):
    ```

2. Create the dictionary object `newattributes`. If the `class` attribute is a built-in `class` method that starts with ___, then the attribute's value is stored as such in `newattributes`:

```
def __new__(classitself, classname, baseclasses,
            attributes):

    newattributes = {}

    for attribute, value in attributes.items():
        if attribute.startswith("__"):
            newattributes[attribute] = value
```

3. If the `class` attribute is an integer or float variable, then the class returns a dictionary item with the attribute name as `ColumnName`, the value as `Value`, Type as `NUMERIC`, and `Length` as the length of the value:

```
elif type(value)==int or type(value)==float:
    newattributes[attribute] = {}
    newattributes[attribute]['ColumnName']
        = attribute.title()
    newattributes[attribute]['Value']
        = value
    newattributes[attribute]['Type']
        = 'NUMERIC'
    newattributes[attribute]
['Length'] = len(str(value))
```

4. If the `class` attribute is a string variable, then the class returns a similar dictionary item with Type as `VARCHAR`:

```
elif type(value)==str:
    newattributes[attribute] = {}
    newattributes[attribute]['ColumnName']
        = attribute.title()
    newattributes[attribute]['Value']
        = value
    newattributes[attribute]['Type']
        = 'VARCHAR'
    newattributes[attribute]['Length']
        = len(value)
```

5. Similarly, if the `class` attribute is a boolean object, a similar kind of dictionary item with Type as BOOLEAN is returned:

```
elif type(value)==bool:
    newattributes[attribute] = {}
    newattributes[attribute]['ColumnName']
        = attribute.title()
    newattributes[attribute]['Value']
        = value
    newattributes[attribute]['Type']
        = 'BOOLEAN'
    newattributes[attribute]['Length']
        = None
```

6. Any other variable or method is stored like so in `newattributes`:

```
else:
    newattributes[attribute] = value
return type.__new__(classitself, classname,
    baseclasses, newattributes)
```

7. We will now create the class `Arizona` with the metaclass as `SchemaMetaClass`, define all the variables for a product, and define a method that creates a schema out of the metaprogrammed class attributes:

```
class Arizona(metaclass = SchemaMetaClass):
    product_id = 200443
    product_name = 'Iphone'
    product_category = 'Electronics'
    sales_quantity = 2
    tax_rate = 0.05
    sales_price = 1200
    profit = 70
    loss = 0
    sales_margin = 0.1
    promotion = '20%Off'
    promotion_reason = 'New Year'
    in_stock = True
```

```
    def create_schema(self):
        import pandas as pd
        tableschema = pd.DataFrame([self.product_id,
                                    self.product_name,
                                  self.product_category,
                                   self.sales_quantity,
                                       self.tax_rate,
                                     self.sales_price,
                                        self.profit,
                                         self.loss,
                                    self.sales_margin,
                                      self.promotion,
                                  self.promotion_reason,
                                      self.in_stock])
        tableschema.drop(labels = ['Value'], axis = 1,
                            inplace = True)
        return tableschema
```

We have added product details of an example product (in this case, an iPhone) and the variables are a combination of different data types – `string`, `integer`, `float`, and `bool`. We will define the method `create_schema`, which imports the pandas library to create a DataFrame that gives a table-like structure to the variables and returns the data frame as a table schema.

8. Now, consider a scenario where the metaclass is not added to the preceding code. Calling the `product_name` variable would have resulted in the following:

```
objarizona = Arizona()
objarizona.product_name
```

```
'Iphone'
```

9. Since we have added the metaclass in the preceding `Arizona` class definition, calling the `product_name` results in the following:

```
objarizona = Arizona()
objarizona.product_name

{'ColumnName': 'Product_name',
 'Value': 'Iphone',
 'Type': 'VARCHAR',
 'Length': 6}
```

10. Similarly, we can look at the results of a few other variables as follows:

```
objarizona.product_category

{'ColumnName': 'Product_category',
 'Value': 'Electronics',
 'Type': 'VARCHAR',
 'Length': 11}

objarizona.sales_quantity
{'ColumnName': 'Sales_
quantity', 'Value': 2, 'Type': 'NUMERIC', 'Length': 1}

objarizona.tax_rate
{'ColumnName': 'Tax_
rate', 'Value': 0.05, 'Type': 'NUMERIC', 'Length': 4}
```

11. Using the metaprogrammed class variables further, we have defined the method `create_schema` to return a table schema:

```
objarizona.create_schema()
```

We get the following table, which includes all of the variables defined in the class:

	ColumnName	Type	Length
0	Productid	NUMERIC	6.0
1	Productname	VARCHAR	6.0
2	Productcategory	VARCHAR	11.0
3	Salesquantity	NUMERIC	1.0
4	Taxrate	NUMERIC	4.0
5	Salesprice	NUMERIC	4.0
6	Profit	NUMERIC	2.0
7	Loss	NUMERIC	1.0
8	Salesmargin	NUMERIC	3.0
9	Promotion	VARCHAR	6.0
10	Promotionreason	VARCHAR	8.0
11	Instock	BOOLEAN	NaN

Figure 4.12 – Output of the method create_schema

These are some examples of how metaclasses can be used in developing applications. Metaclasses can further be used in more complex scenarios such as automated code generation and framework development.

Summary

In this chapter, we have learned how to create metaclasses and some applications of metaclasses.

We then saw how to switch metaclasses, reuse the functionalities, and how to implement inheritance on classes that use metaclasses. Finally, we also saw how to manipulate the variables of metaclasses further.

All of these concepts are part of Python metaprogramming and they are used to change the behavior of a class externally and without impacting the internal functionalities of the class itself.

In the next chapter, we will be looking at the concept of reflection with different examples.

5
Understanding Introspection

In this chapter, we will look at introspection in Python 3 and understand how it is useful in metaprogramming. **Introspection** is a concept where we can learn about the properties or attributes of objects in Python during runtime using a suite of Python's built-in methods.

Why introspection? Introspection is an information-gathering process for Python objects, and the information thus gathered can help in utilizing the objects to perform generic operations by manipulating them externally and, in turn, can help us in writing metaprograms.

Before we understand how to implement introspection, we will have a look at the built-in functions of Python that help in performing introspection. Throughout this chapter, we will look at each function that helps us introspect and understand the objects we use in our programs.

In this chapter, we will be taking a look at the following main topics:

- Introducing built-in functions
- Using the built-in `id` function
- Debugging unintentional assignments using `id`
- Finding out whether an object is callable
- Checking whether an object has an attribute
- Checking whether an object is an instance
- Checking whether an object is a subclass
- Understanding the usage of property
- Using property as a decorator

By the end of this chapter, you should be able to apply built-in functions to introspect Python objects, apply them to examples, and use them to debug code.

Technical requirements

The code examples shared in this chapter are available on GitHub under the code for this chapter here: `https://github.com/PacktPublishing/Metaprogramming-with-Python/tree/main/Chapter05`.

Introducing built-in functions

To understand introspection and the usage of Python's built-in functions to perform introspection, we will continue making use of our core example of *ABC Megamart* throughout this chapter.

We will be covering the usage of the following built-in functions to introspect Python objects:

- `id()`
- `eval()`
- `callable()`
- `hastattr()`
- `getattr()`
- `isinstance()`
- `issubclass()`
- `property()`

Introspecting Python objects helps in understanding the properties of objects, which in turn, helps in metaprogramming these objects and using them to debug the objects, which we will be looking at in further chapters as well.

With this understanding, let's look further into the concept of how to use these built-in functions and introspect objects.

Using the built-in id function

Understanding the characteristics of a Python object helps in writing metaprograms on the object. The memory address of an object is one of its characteristics or properties that can be manipulated using metaprogramming. The `id` function in Python 3 can be called to identify an object using the object's memory address. Identifying an object through its memory address helps in analyzing objects to find out whether there are multiple assignments or copies of an object created unintentionally during the process of code development.

To understand this further, here is how we will work:

1. We will be creating a class named `Billing`, which calculates and prints a simple bill for any product that is provided as input. Refer to the following code:

```
class Billing:
    def __init__(self,product_name,unit_
price,quantity,tax):
        self.product_name = product_name
        self.unit_price = unit_price
        self.quantity = quantity
        self.tax = tax

    def generate_bill(self):
        total = self.unit_price * self.quantity
        final_total = total + total*self.tax
        print('***********-------------------
            **************')
        print('Product:', self.product_name)
        print('Total:',final_total)
        print('***********-------------------
            **************')
```

2. Let's now create an object for the `Billing` class:

```
billing = Billing('Delmonte Cheese',6,4,0.054)
```

3. Let's now call the `generate_bill` method to print the bill:

```
billing.generate_bill()
```

This code gives the following output:

```
***********-------------------**************
Product: Delmonte Cheese
Total: 25.296
***********-------------------**************
```

4. In the next step, let's create a separate `generate_bill` function that performs the same set of operations as the `generate_bill` method that was created inside the `Billing` class. The function will take in four parameters (`product_name`, `unit_price`, `quantity`, and `tax`):

```
def generate_bill(product_name,unit_price,quantity,tax):
    total = unit_price * quantity
    final_total = total + total*tax
    print('**********-----------------
          **************')
    print('Product:', product_name)
    print('Total:',final_total)
    print('**********-----------------
          **************')
```

5. In the next step, we will be copying the `Billing` class into another variable named `Invoicing`:

```
Invoicing = Billing
```

So far, we have three objects:

- A class named `Billing`

- A function named `generate_bill`

- A variable that assigned the `Billing` class to a variable called `Invoicing`

6. Now, let's apply Python's built-in `id` function to get the memory address of each of these objects:

```
id(Billing)
2015859835472
id(Invoicing)
2015859835472
id(generate_bill)
2015871203792
```

In the preceding output, we can notice that both `Billing` and `Invoicing` have the same memory address since `Invoicing` is a copy of the `Billing` class. The following figure is a simple representation of this example:

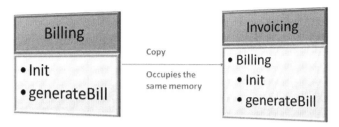

Figure 5.1 – The Billing class copied to Invoicing

With this understanding, we can further look into how we can use the id function in implementing metaprogramming.

Debugging unintentional assignments using id

In this section, we will be discussing what happens when we make unintentional references or assignments to an object while defining an attribute, a method, or a function, and how to resolve such incorrect assignments using the built-in id function. When a reference is made unintentionally, the memory address of the object is shared between the actual object and the reference object. In this example, we will be making use of id to debug the Python objects created in the preceding section and identify duplicate assignments or references of an object that might have been created unintentionally while developing an application. Here is how it works:

1. To begin with, let's create a dictionary item, class_id_count, to capture the number of occurrences of the memory address of each class:

    ```
    class_id_count = {}
    ```

2. In the next step, we will be creating the following four lists:

    ```
    duplicates = []
    ids = []
    classes = []
    classnames = []
    ```

    Here, we capture duplicate memory addresses with duplicates, capture results of the id function with ids, capture the class details with classes, and capture the names of classes with classnames.

3. In this step, we will be iterating over the directory of Python objects and checking whether the type of the object is type since the type of class is type in Python. This step helps in identifying all the objects that are classes and then updating the lists created with ids, classes, and classnames. Refer to the following code block:

```
for obj in dir():
    if type(eval(obj)) == type:
        ids.append(id(eval(obj)))
        classes.append(eval(obj))
        classnames.append(obj)
```

4. We will now iterate over the `ids` list and check that the `id` is not in `class_id_count`, and then add it; if it is already in `class_id_count`, we will add it to the `duplicates` list:

```
for i in ids:
    if i not in class_id_count:
        class_id_count[i] = 1
    elif (class_id_count[i] == 1):
        duplicates.append(i)
        class_id_count[i] += 1
```

5. We will further iterate over the `classes` and `classnames` lists and check whether there are duplicates. Then, we will print the classes that have duplicates:

```
for cls,clsname in zip(classes,classnames):
    for clsid in duplicates:
        if (id(cls)==clsid):
            print(clsname,cls)
```

The output of the preceding code is as follows:

```
Billing <class '__main__.Billing'>
Invoicing <class '__main__.Billing'>
```

6. Executing the preceding code results in the following output:

```
class_id_count
{2196689735984: 2}
duplicates
[2196689735984]
ids
[2196689735984, 2196689735984]
classes
[__main__.Billing, __main__.Billing]
classnames
['Billing', 'Invoicing']
```

In the preceding output, we can see that both the `Billing` and `Invoicing` classes have the same memory address and they are duplicates. There can be scenarios where we might have intentionally referenced a class, and there can also be scenarios where multiple variable assignments to the same memory address might have happened by mistake. In such intentional scenarios, `id` can be used to check duplicate assignments to a memory address.

The following figure is a simple representation of this example:

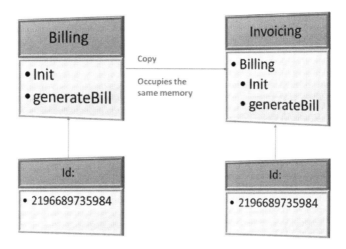

Figure 5.2 – Two classes with one memory address

With this understanding, we will look further into another built-in function, `callable`.

Finding out whether an object is callable

In this section, we will look at another built-in function named `callable`. As the name implies, this function helps in identifying whether a Python object can be called. Functions and methods can be called to enable various operations to be performed on the input parameters. Not all Python objects are callable. For example, a string variable or a numeric variable stores information but will not perform any action when executed. The `callable` function helps in verifying such objects that can be called and those that cannot be called in a function.

Why do we need to check whether an object is callable? Python is an object-oriented programming language where we can write libraries and write classes within the libraries that are encapsulated. The end user of classes or libraries need not always have access to the class definition or method definitions. While importing the Python libraries, we might sometimes want to know whether the imported object is just a variable that stores a value or whether it is a function that can be reused. The simplest way of checking this is to see whether the object is callable, as functions or methods are usually callable. This comes in handy, especially when the developer of a library did not provide any documentation for its methods and attributes.

Let's make use of `callable` in the following example:

1. Let's create a new Python file and save it as `product.py`. Go to `https://github.com/PacktPublishing/Metaprogramming-with-Python/blob/main/Chapter05/product.py` and add the following code, which creates a class named `Product`. Add the following four attributes to it: `Product ID`, `Product Name`, `Product Category`, and `Unit Price`. We will now assign values to these four attributes, as follows:

```
class Product:
    _product_id = 100902
    _product_name = 'Iphone X'
    _product_category = 'Electronics'
    _unit_price = 700
```

2. Now, let's add a method named `get_product` within the `Product` class. This method would simply return the four attributes created in the preceding step:

```
def get_product(self):
    return self._product_id, self._product_name,
        self._product_category, self._unit_price
```

3. In this step, we will import the `Product` class from `product.py` and create an object for it:

```
import product
prodobj = product.Product()
```

4. Let's now check whether the class is callable by using the built-in `callable` function. The class is callable and so the function returns `True`:

```
callable(product.Product)
True
```

5. In this step, we can also check whether a class object is callable. The object is not callable since we did not overwrite the `__call__` method of the class to make it callable, and so the function returns `False`:

```
callable(prodobj)
False
```

6. We can now check whether a Python object is callable and then get its attributes:

```
if callable(prodobj.get_product):
    print(prodobj.get_product())
```

```
    else:
        print("This object is not callable")
```

7. Similarly, we can also check whether a Python object is callable and then print the details of the object if it returns `True`:

```
if callable(prodobj):
    print(prodobj)
else:
    print('This is not a method')
```

With this example, we can look further into the next function, `hasattr`.

Checking whether an object has an attribute

While using a method or a function object defined in a framework or library by importing the library into another program, we might not always know all the attributes of the object. In such cases, we have a built-in `hasattr` function that can be used to introspect if a Python object has a specific attribute.

This function checks whether a given object has attributes. To test this function, we will create a class for the inventory of *ABC Megamart*, add the required attributes for the products stored in the inventory, and also include the price of the products along with the tax component. The price will be calculated both before and after tax for the products stored in the inventory. The following are the steps for it:

1. We will create a class called `Inventory` and initiate it with the variables required for an inventory, such as `product_id`, `product_name`, `date` (of purchase), `unit_price`, `quantity`, `unit_discount`, and `tax`, as shown in the following code:

```
class Inventory:
    def __init__(self,product_id,product_name,date,unit_
price,quantity,unit_discount,tax):
        self.product_id = product_id
        self.product_name = product_name
        self.date = date
        self.unit_price = unit_price
        self.quantity = quantity
        self.unit_discount = unit_discount
        self.tax = tax
```

2. In this step, we will add a method to `Inventory` to calculate the amount before tax and, in this method, we will have three input parameters: `quantity`, `unit_price`, and `unit_ discount`. If these three variables are `None`, then this method will use the same variables initiated during the instantiation of the `Inventory` class to calculate the amount before tax:

```python
def calc_amount_before_tax(self,quantity=None,unit_
price=None, unit_discount=None):
        if quantity is None:
            self.quantity = self.quantity
        else:
            self.quantity = quantity

        if unit_price is None:
            self.unit_price = self.unit_price
        else:
            self.unit_price = unit_price

        if unit_discount is None:
            self.unit_discount = self.unit_discount
        else:
            self.unit_discount = unit_discount
        amount_before_tax = self.quantity *
            (self.unit_price - self.unit_discount)
        return amount_before_tax
```

3. We will also add another method to the `Inventory` class to calculate the amount after tax. This method is also defined in a similar pattern as `calc_amount_before_tax`:

```python
def calc_amount_after_tax(self, quantity=None,unit_
price=None,unit_discount=None,tax=None):
        if quantity is None:
            self.quantity = self.quantity
        else:
            self.quantity = quantity

        if unit_price is None:
            self.unit_price = self.unit_price
        else:
            self.unit_price = unit_price
```

```
        if unit_discount is None:
            self.unit_discount = self.unit_discount
        else:
            self.unit_discount = unit_discount

        if tax is None:
            self.tax = self.tax
        else:
            self.tax = tax
        amount_after_tax =
            self.calc_amount_before_tax(
            self.quantity,self.unit_price,
            self.unit_discount) + self.tax
        return amount_after_tax
```

4. We will now create the last method for this class, which returns the consolidated inventory details, creates a DataFrame, and returns the DataFrame:

```
    def return_inventory(self):
        import pandas as pd
        inventory_schema = pd.DataFrame([
                        self.product_id,
                        self.product_name,
                        self.date,
                        self.unit_price,
                        self.quantity,
                        self.unit_discount,
                        self.tax,
                        self.calc_unt_before_tax(),
            self.calc_amount_after_tax()]).transpose()
        inventory_schema.columns = ["Product_id",
            "Product_name","Date","Unit_price",
            "Quantity","Unit_discount","Tax",
            "Amount Before Tax", "Amount After Tax"]
        return inventory_schema
```

5. Then, create an object for the `Inventory` class and initialize its attributes:

```
inventory = Inventory(300021,
                'Samsung-Refrigerator',
                '08/04/2021',
                200,
                25,
                10,
                0.0522)
```

6. Check whether the object returns the attributes:

```
inventory.product_id
300021
inventory.product_name
'Samsung-Refrigerator'
inventory.date
'08/04/2021'
inventory.unit_price
200
inventory.quantity
25
inventory.unit_discount
10
inventory.tax
0.0522
inventory.calc_amount_before_tax()
4750
inventory.calc_amount_after_tax()
4750.0522
inventory.return_inventory()
```

The output of the preceding code is as follows:

	ProductID	ProductName	Date	UnitPrice	Quantity	UnitDiscount	Tax	Amount Before Tax	Amount After Tax
0	300021	Samsung-Refrigerator	08/04/2021	200	25	10	0.0522	4750	4750.0522

Figure 5.3 – The output – Inventory details

7. Next, let's make use of `dir` to list down all the names of arguments in the `Inventory` class:

```
dir(Inventory)
['__class__',
 '__delattr__',
 '__dict__',
 ,__dir__',
 ,__doc__',
 ,__eq__',
 ,__format__',
 ,__ge__',
 ,__getattribute__',
 ,__gt__',
 ,__hash__',
 ,__init__',
 ,__init_subclass__',
 ,__le__',
 ,__lt__',
 ,__module__',
 ,__ne__',
 ,__new__',
 ,__reduce__',
 ,__reduce_ex__',
 ,__repr__',
 ,__setattr__',
 ,__sizeof__',
 ,__str__',
 ,__subclasshook__',
 ,__weakref__',
 ,calc_amount_after_tax',
 ,calc_amount_before_tax',
 ,return_inventory']
```

8. Now, let's make use of `hasattr` to check whether the class has attributes. If the type of attribute is a method, then use `getattr` to get the attributes. Executing the following loop results in the list of all the attributes of `Inventory`:

```
for i in dir(Inventory):
    if (hasattr(Inventory,i)):
        if type(getattr(inventory, i)) is
type(getattr(inventory,  '__init__')):
            print(getattr(Inventory,i))<class 'type'>


<function Inventory.__init__ at 0x000001C9BBB46CA0>
<function Inventory.calc_amount_after_tax at
0x000001C9BBB46DC0>
<function Inventory.calc_amount_before_tax at
0x000001C9BBB46D30>
<function Inventory.return_inventory at
0x000001C9BBB46E50>
```

With this understanding, we can further look into another built-in function, `isinstance`.

Checking whether an object is an instance

In this section, we will look at another function named `isinstance`, which can be used to check whether an object is an instance of a particular class. As we are covering introspection in this chapter, we are more focused on what functions are available to introspect an object rather than how these functions can be used further to manipulate or debug a piece of code. *Chapter 6*, will cover the usage of these functions on metaprogramming along with examples.

In the preceding section, we created a class named `Inventory`. In this section, we can continue using the same class and create another object for the class. This is shown as follows:

```
inventory_fmcg = Inventory(100011,
                'Delmonte Ketchup',
                '09/04/2021',
                5,
                0.25,
                0.10,
                0.0522)
inventory_fmcg.product_id
100011
```

```
inventory_fmcg.calc_amount_before_tax()
1.225
inventory_fmcg.calc_amount_after_tax()
1.2772000000000001
inventory_fmcg.return_inventory()
```

The output of the preceding code is as follows:

	ProductID	ProductName	Date	UnitPrice	Quantity	UnitDiscount	Tax	Amount Before Tax	Amount After Tax
0	100011	Delmont Ketchup	09/04/2021	5	0.25	0.1	0.0522	1.225	1.2772

Figure 5.4 – The output – Inventory details of inventory_fmcg

Now, let's check whether `inventory_fmcg` is an object of the `Inventory` class using `isinstance`:

```
isinstance(inventory_fmcg, Inventory)
```

True

Similarly, we can also check whether the previously created `inventory` object is still an instance of the `Inventory` class:

```
isinstance(inventory, Inventory)
```

True

Let's consider a scenario where we have reallocated the object inventory to another value by mistake while writing the code, and we might still need to make use of the object and call its methods to return the inventory details. To test this scenario using `isinstance`, we can look at the following steps:

1. Check whether an object is an instance of the `Inventory` class and call a method of the function. If the object is not an instance of the class, check the type of variable to which it has been reallocated:

    ```
    if isinstance(inventory, Inventory):
        display(inventory.return_inventory())
    else:
        print("Object reallocated to", type(inventory),
            ", please correct it")
    ```

2. The preceding code results in the following output since `inventory` is still an object of the `Inventory` class:

	ProductID	ProductName	Date	UnitPrice	Quantity	UnitDiscount	Tax	Amount Before Tax	Amount After Tax
0	300021	Samsung-Refrigerator	08/04/2021	200	25	10	0.0522	4750	4750.0522

Figure 5.5 – The output – Inventory details

3. Now, let's reallocate the `inventory` variable to some other string value and call the `return_inventory` method on it:

```
inventory = "test"
```

4. Calling the `return_inventory` method for the `inventory` object will result in the following error:

```
---------------------------------            -------------------------------------
AttributeError                                       Traceback (most recent call last)
<ipython-input-88-36f88e397ab9> in <module>
----> 1 inventory.returnInventory()

AttributeError: 'str' object has no attribute 'returnInventory'
```

Figure 5.6 – Error on calling the return_inventory method on a reallocated object

5. To avoid the preceding error and to let the code handle this error gracefully and, at the same time, provide more information to the developer, we can modify the code as follows using the `isinstance` method:

```
if isinstance(inventory, Inventory):
    print(inventory.return_inventory())
else:
    print("Object reallocated to", type(inventory),
        ", please correct it")
```

The output of the preceding code is as follows:

```
Object reallocated to <class 'str'> , please correct it
```

With this understanding, we can look further into another in-built function, `issubclass`.

Checking whether an object is a subclass

In this section, we will look at the issubclass function. This function is used to check whether a given input class is actually a child class or a subclass of a specific parent class. To introspect a class using this function, let's look at the following steps:

1. Create an FMCG class by initializing variables for supplier information such as supplier_name, supplier_code, supplier_address, supplier_contract_start_date, supplier_contract_end_date, and supplier_quality_code, shown as follows:

```
class FMCG:
    def __init__(self, supplier_name, supplier_code,
        supplier_address, supplier_contract_start_date,\
    supplier_contract_end_date, supplier_quality_code):
        self.supplier_name = supplier_name
        self.supplier_code = supplier_code
        self.supplier_address = supplier_address
        self.supplier_contract_start_date =
            supplier_contract_start_date
        self.supplier_contract_end_date =
            supplier_contract_end_date
        self.supplier_quality_code =
            supplier_quality_code
```

2. Add a method in the class to simply get the supplier details initialized in the class and return it as a dictionary object with a key and a value:

```
def get_supplier_details(self):
    supplier_details = {
        'Supplier_name': self.supplier_name,
        'Supplier_code': self.supplier_code,
        'Supplier_address': self.supplier_address,
        'ContractStartDate':
                self.supplier_contract_start_date,
        'ContractEndDate':
                self.supplier_contract_end_date,
        'QualityCode': self.supplier_quality_code
    }
    return supplier_details
```

3. Create an object for the FMCG class and initialize the variables with supplier data and then display the supplier details by calling the preceding method:

```
fmcg = FMCG('Test Supplier','a0015','5093 9th Main
Street, Pasadena,California, 91001', '05/04/2020',
'05/04/2025',1)
fmcg.get_supplier_details()
{'Supplier_name': 'Test Supplier',
 'Supplier_code': 'a0015',
 'Supplier_address': '5093 9th Main Street,
    Pasadena,California, 91001',
 'ContractStartDate': '05/04/2020',
 'ContractEndDate': '05/04/2025',
 'QualityCode': 1}
```

4. Here, we can then create another class for condiments that covers both inventory details and FMCG supplier details by inheriting this class from both the FMCC class and the Inventory class. This class will be initialized with all the product-level inventory variables and the supplier-level variables:

```
class Condiments(FMCG,Inventory):
    def __init__(self,*inventory):
        self.product_id = inventory[0]
        self.product_name = inventory[1]
        self.date = inventory[2]
        self.unit_price = inventory[3]
        self.quantity = inventory[4]
        self.unit_discount = inventory[5]
        self.tax = inventory[6]
        self.supplier_name = inventory[7]
        self.supplier_code = inventory[8]
        self.supplier_address = inventory[9]
        self.supplier_contract_start_date =
                                inventory[10]
        self.supplier_contract_end_date =
                                inventory[11]
        self.supplier_quality_code = inventory[12]
```

5. Then, let's add a method to simply return all the variables initialized in the `Condiments` class by storing them as a DataFrame or table:

```
def return_condiment_inventory(self):
    import pandas as pd
    inventory_schema = pd.DataFrame([
                    self.product_id,
                    self.date,
                    self.unit_price,
                    self.quantity,
                    self.unit_discount,
                    self.tax,
                    self.calc_amount_before_tax(),
                    self.calc_amount_after_tax(),
                    self.get_supplier_details()
                            ]).transpose()
    inventory_schema.columns = ["Product_id",
        "Date","Unit_price","Quantity",
        "Unit_discount","Tax","Amount Before Tax",
        "Amount After Tax",'Supplier_details']
    return inventory_schema
```

6. We can now create an object for this class and call its method:

```
ketchup = Condiments(100011,'Delmonte
Ketchup','09/04/2021',5,0.25,0.10,0.0522,'Test
Supplier','a0015','5093 9th Main Street,
Pasadena,California, 91001', '05/04/2020',
'05/04/2025',1)


ketchup.return_condiment_inventory()
```

7. Executing the preceding code results in the following output:

	ProductID	Date	UnitPrice	Quantity	UnitDiscount	Tax	Amount Before Tax	Amount Before Tax	SupplierDetails
0	100011	09/04/2021	5	0.25	0.1	0.0522	1.225	1.2772	{'SupplierName': 'Test Supplier', 'SupplierCod...

Figure 5.7 – The output – Condiment inventory details

8. Now let's check whether the FMCG class is a subclass of `Inventory`. It will return as `False` since FMCG is not a subclass of `Inventory`:

```
issubclass(FMCG,Inventory)
False
```

9. In this step, we will check whether `Condiments` is a subclass of FMCG and also whether it is a subclass of `Inventory`. Both should return as `True` since `Condiments` is inherited from both of these classes:

```
issubclass(Condiments,FMCG)
True
```

```
issubclass(Condiments,Inventory)
True
```

10. Next, we will be creating an object for a class by, first, checking whether a class is a subclass of a specific parent class, then creating an object accordingly, and then calling a method on the newly created object:

```
if issubclass(Condiments,FMCG):
    fmcg = Condiments(100011,'Delmonte
        Ketchup','09/04/2021',5,0.25,0.10,0.0522,
        'Test Supplier','a0015','5093 9th Main Street,
        Pasadena,California, 91001', '05/04/2020',
        '05/04/2025',1)
else:
    fmcg = FMCG('Test Supplier','a0015','5093 9th Main
        Street, Pasadena,California, 91001',
        '05/04/2020', '05/04/2025',1)
display(fmcg.get_supplier_details())
```

11. Executing the preceding code results in the following output:

```
{'Supplier_name': 'Test Supplier',
 'Supplier_code': 'a0015',
 'Supplier_address': '5093 9th Main Street,
    Pasadena,California, 91001',
 'ContractStartDate': '05/04/2020',
 'ContractEndDate': '05/04/2025',
 'QualityCode': 1}
```

With this understanding, we can look further into the last topic of this chapter.

Understanding the usage of property

In this section, we will look at the last built-in function covered in this chapter, `property`. This function is used to initialize, set, get, or delete methods of attributes in Python. These values are called the properties of an object. Let's first understand how `property` works on Python objects by creating an example.

We can create a property by simply calling the `property` function and storing it as a variable. Refer to the following code:

```
test_property = property()
test_property
<property at 0x1c9c9335950>
```

We still did not answer the question of how this function creates a property. The `property` function takes in four variables to get, set, delete, and document the properties of an attribute. To examine it further, let's look at it in a little more detail. The steps are as follows:

1. Create a class named `TestPropertyClass`.

2. Initialize it with a `test` attribute and set it as `None`.

3. We will then add three methods to perform the functions of getting, setting, and deleting the initialized `test` attribute.

4. We will then create another variable within the class named `test_attr` and assign the `property` function to it with the `get`, `set`, and `delete` methods created in this class.

The code for this example is as follows:

```
class TestPropertyClass:
    def __init__(self):
        self._test_attr = None
    def get_test_attr(self):
        print("get test_attr")
        return self._test_attr
    def set_test_attr(self, value):
        print("set test_attr")
        self._test_attr = value
    def del_test_attr(self):
        print("del test_attr")
```

```
        del self._test_attr
    test_attr = property(get_test_attr, set_test_attr,
        del_test_attr, "test_attr is a property")
```

In the preceding code, `get_test_attr` simply returns the `test` attribute, `set_test_attr` sets a value to the `test` attribute, and `del_test_attr` deletes the `test` attribute.

Let's now create an object for this class and check how `property` works on it:

```
test_property_object = TestPropertyClass()
test_property_object.test_attr
get test_attr
```

In the preceding code, calling the `test` attribute has, in turn, invoked the `get_test_attr` method since it is provided as the `get` method to the `property` function. Let's confirm this understanding further by setting a value to `test_attr`:

```
test_property_object.test_attr = 1980
set test_attr
```

Assigning a value to the `test_attr` variable has now invoked the `set_test_attr` method since it is provided as a `set` method to the `property` function. Calling the `test_attr` attribute again returns the value set in the preceding step:

```
test_property_object.test_attr
get test_attr
1980
```

Similarly, deleting the attribute, in turn, invokes the `del_test_attr` method since it is provided as a `delete` method to the `property` function:

```
del test_property_object.test_attr
del test_attr
```

Once the attribute is deleted, the `get` method will still be invoked while calling the attribute, but it will not return the value previously assigned since it is deleted:

```
test_property_object.test_attr
```

The output of the preceding code would now look as follows:

```
get testAttr
```

```
-------------------------------------------------------------------------
AttributeError                              Traceback (most recent call last)
<ipython-input-148-b983341ece3a> in <module>
----> 1 testPropertyObject.testAttr

<ipython-input-142-ad7fa9f7c228> in get_testAttr(self)
      5         def get_testAttr(self):
      6             print("get testAttr")
----> 7             return self._testAttr
      8
      9         def set_testAttr(self, value):

AttributeError: 'testPropertyClass' object has no attribute '_testAttr'
```

Figure 5.8 – The get method invoked on a deleted attribute

By modifying the behavior of the getter, setter, or deleter methods, we can modify the properties of the attribute itself. We will look at this statement in detail in *Chapter 6*.

With this understanding of assigning the property function to a variable and then invoking its getter, setter, and deleter methods, we will further look into another variation of implementing property.

Using property as a decorator

In the preceding section, we looked at how to use property as a function to modify the properties of an attribute in a class. In this section, we will look at how to use property as a decorator. Let's consider the same TestPropertyClass as in the preceding example and modify the class definition to use the @property decorator statement instead of the property() function statement. Refer to the following code:

```
class TestPropertyClass:
    def __init__(self):
        self._test_attr = None
    @property
    def test_attr(self):
        return self.test_attr
    @test_attr.getter
    def test_attr(self):
        print("get test_attr")
        return self._test_attr
```

```
    @test_attr.setter
    def test_attr(self, value):
        print("set test_attr")
        self._test_attr = value
    @test_attr.deleter
    def test_attr(self):
        print("del test_attr")
        del self._test_attr
```

In the preceding code, we have added `@property` as the decorator for `test_attr`, and we have also added `@test_attr.setter` for the `set` method, `@test_attr.getter` for the `get` method, and `@test_attr.deleter` for the `delete` method.

Let's proceed with executing the code further to check whether `getter`, `setter`, and `deleter` are working as expected:

```
test_property_object = TestPropertyClass()
test_property_object.test_attr
get test_attr
```

In the preceding code, calling the attribute invoked the `getter` method. Similarly, `setter` and `deleter` also invoked the `set` and `delete` methods, respectively:

```
test_property_object.test_attr = 1982
set test_attr
test_property_object.test_attr
get test_attr
1982
del test_property_object.test_attr
del test_attr
```

These are some of the examples of how introspection can be applied to Python objects using Python's built-in functions.

Summary

In this chapter, we have learned how to introspect Python objects using built-in functions.

We then saw how to use the `id` function, and how to debug code using `id`. We also looked at how to check whether an object is callable, how to check whether an object has an attribute, how to check whether an object is an instance, how to check whether an object is a subclass, and finally, we looked at how to get, set, and delete properties on attributes. From all of these concepts, we learned how to inspect Python objects such as classes, methods, and functions. From the examples covered under each topic, we also learned how to apply introspection in practical use cases.

In the next chapter, we will be extending the learning from introspection and applying it further to understand reflection on Python objects.

6

Implementing Reflection on Python Objects

In this chapter, we will look at reflection in Python 3 and understand how it is useful in metaprogramming. **Reflection** is a continuation of introspection, or it can be looked upon as a concept where we can make use of the information we learn from the introspection of properties or attributes of objects in Python and apply them to manipulate the objects, and so perform metaprogramming.

Why reflection? As we know from the previous chapter, introspection is an information-gathering process for Python objects. Reflection is the process of utilizing the information gathered from objects through introspection, and in turn, performing generic operations on them by manipulating them externally to perform metaprogramming.

Throughout this chapter, we will look at implementing reflection using each function that helped us introspect objects in the previous chapter and perform metaprogramming on the objects we use in our programs.

In this chapter, we will take a look at the following main topics:

- Introducing built-in functions used in reflection
- Using `id` to delete duplicates
- Using `callable` to dynamically check and generate methods
- Using `hasattr` to set values
- Using `isinstance` to modify an object
- Using `issubclass` to modify a class
- Applying `property` on a coupon

By the end of this chapter, you should be able to apply built-in functions to reflect on Python objects, apply them to examples, and use them to generate or modify code.

Technical requirements

The code examples shared in this chapter are available on GitHub for this chapter here: `https://github.com/PacktPublishing/Metaprogramming-with-Python/tree/main/Chapter06`.

Introducing built-in functions used in reflection

To understand reflection and the usage of Python's built-in functions to perform reflection, we will continue making use of our core example of *ABC Megamart* throughout this chapter. We will be specifically looking at the concept and examples based on coupons in a retail store throughout this chapter. Coupons are a technique used by retail stores or manufacturers to promote their products among consumers. Coupons are generated and posted through various modes of advertisements, and they are used to attract customers to a specific store or product.

We will make use of the same set of built-in functions as in introspection, to apply reflection on Python objects:

- `id()`
- `eval()`
- `callable()`
- `hasattr()`
- `getattr()`
- `isinstance()`
- `issubclass()`
- `property()`

Reflection on Python objects helps in the metaprogramming of these objects using the built-in functions that can introspect Python objects, and we will look at some examples for these in this chapter.

Using id to delete duplicates

We reviewed the `id` function in the previous chapter, which covered introspection. In Python 3, `id` is used to identify an object using the object's memory address. Identifying `id` of an object can be used to reflect on an object and avoid redundancies or errors that can possibly occur while using an object throughout a program.

To understand this further, we will be creating a class named `Coupon`, which generates a unique random coupon ID and prints a coupon for any product that is provided as input. In the following code, we will start with creating a class named `Coupon` and will be adding the coupon details as attributes. We will also create a method named `generate_coupon` to print five coupons for a product along with its unique random coupon ID:

```
class Coupon:
    def __init__(self, product_name, product_category, \
      brand,source, expiry_date, quantity):
        self.product_name = product_name
        self.product_category = product_category
        self.brand = brand
        self.source = source
        self.expiry_date = expiry_date
        self.quantity = quantity
    def generate_coupon(self):
        import random
        couponId =  random.sample(range(1,9),5)
        for i in couponId:
            pri
nt('***********-----------------***************')
            print('Product:', self.product_name)
            print('Product Category:', \
              self.product_category)
            print('Coupon ID:', i)
            print('Brand:', self.brand)
            print('Source:', self.source)
            print('Expiry Date:', self.expiry_date)
            print('Quantity:', self.quantity)
            pri
nt('***********-----------------***************')
```

Let's now create a `Coupon1` variable and assign the `Coupon` class to it:

```
Coupon1 = Coupon
```

In this case, we are intentionally assigning the `Coupon` class to a variable to demonstrate the usage of the `id` function. Ideally, this function will come in handy to debug and ensure when the class is actually assigned unintentionally and thus leading to issues later on in the code. At this point in time, let's assume that the assignment of the `Coupon` class to a variable is unintentional.

Let's look at how to identify and resolve such unintentional assignments of a class and review the coupon generation results if `Coupon1` was called by some other object when `Coupon` was the only class that should have been available to generate the coupons.

In the preceding `Coupon` class, the expectation was to generate only five coupons for a product with unique random coupon identifiers. Since we have assigned the class to a variable, the class identifier is also assigned to the variable:

```
id(Coupon)
2175775727280
id(Coupon1)
2175775727280
```

Let's now call the `generate_coupon` method of the `Coupon` class along with its attributes and look at the results:

```
Coupon("Potato Chips","Snacks","ABCBrand1","Manhattan
Store","10/1/2021",2).generateCoupon()
```

The output for coupon 1 is as follows:

```
**********-------------------*************
Product: Potato Chips
Product Category: Snacks
Coupon ID: 5
Brand: ABCBrand1
Source: Manhattan Store
Expiry Date: 10/1/2021
Quantity: 2
**********-------------------*************
```

The output for coupon 2 is as follows:

```
**********-------------------*************
Product: Potato Chips
Product Category: Snacks
Coupon ID: 1
Brand: ABCBrand1
Source: Manhattan Store
Expiry Date: 10/1/2021
Quantity: 2
```

```
***********-------------------**************
```

The output for coupon 3 is as follows:

```
***********-------------------**************
Product: Potato Chips
Product Category: Snacks
Coupon ID: 4
Brand: ABCBrand1
Source: Manhattan Store
Expiry Date: 10/1/2021
Quantity: 2
***********-------------------**************
```

The output for coupon 4 is as follows:

```
***********-------------------**************
Product: Potato Chips
Product Category: Snacks
Coupon ID: 8
Brand: ABCBrand1
Source: Manhattan Store
Expiry Date: 10/1/2021
Quantity: 2
***********-------------------**************
```

The output for coupon 5 is as follows:

```
***********-------------------**************
Product: Potato Chips
Product Category: Snacks
Coupon ID: 3
Brand: ABCBrand1
Source: Manhattan Store
Expiry Date: 10/1/2021
Quantity: 2
***********-------------------**************
```

Calling the preceding method resulted in the generation of five unique coupons for the potato chips product. Coupon identifiers are unique and should not be regenerated at any other part of the code in the future; therefore, the preceding method will be called only once in the code. Since we have already assigned the Coupon class to another variable named Coupon1, let's look at what will happen if Coupon1 is called in some other part of the code unintentionally:

```
Coupon1("Potato Chips","Snacks","ABCBrand1","Manhattan
Store","10/1/2021",2).generate_coupon()
```

The output for coupon 1 is as follows:

```
***********------------------*************
Product: Potato Chips
Product Category: Snacks
Coupon ID: 7
Brand: ABCBrand1
Source: Manhattan Store
Expiry Date: 10/1/2021
Quantity: 2
***********------------------*************
```

The output for coupon 2 is as follows:

```
***********------------------*************
Product: Potato Chips
Product Category: Snacks
Coupon ID: 8
Brand: ABCBrand1
Source: Manhattan Store
Expiry Date: 10/1/2021
Quantity: 2
***********------------------*************
```

The output for coupon 3 is as follows:

```
***********------------------*************
Product: Potato Chips
Product Category: Snacks
Coupon ID: 1
Brand: ABCBrand1
```

```
Source: Manhattan Store
Expiry Date: 10/1/2021
Quantity: 2
***********-----------------**************
```

The output for coupon 4 is as follows:

```
***********-----------------**************
Product: Potato Chips
Product Category: Snacks
Coupon ID: 6
Brand: ABCBrand1
Source: Manhattan Store
Expiry Date: 10/1/2021
Quantity: 2
***********-----------------**************
```

The output for coupon 5 is as follows:

```
***********-----------------**************
Product: Potato Chips
Product Category: Snacks
Coupon ID: 2
Brand: ABCBrand1
Source: Manhattan Store
Expiry Date: 10/1/2021
Quantity: 2
***********-----------------**************
```

In this example, Coupon1 should not be called in the code since calling it would generate duplicate coupons, possibly with the same IDs. This might lead to the creation of five more coupons for the same product, which is not required; among these, two of them would be duplicates with coupon identifiers 1 and 8. This leads to making coupons 1 and 8 void when distributed to consumers since each coupon is expected to have one unique identifier to redeem it.

Let's now look at how to resolve this issue by developing a function named delete_duplicates that checks and deletes such duplicate assignments of the Coupon class. This function looks at the list of Python objects in the directory that has duplicates and deletes the duplicates of classes. Refer to the following code:

```python
def delete_duplicates(directory = dir()):
    class_id_count = {}
    duplicates = []
    ids = []
    classes = []
    classnames = []
    for obj in directory:
        if type(eval(obj)) == type:
            ids.append(id(eval(obj)))
            classes.append(eval(obj))
            classnames.append(obj)
    for i in ids:
        if i not in class_id_count:
            class_id_count[i] = 1
        elif (class_id_count[i] == 1):
            duplicates.append(i)
            class_id_count[i] += 1
    dupe_set = {}
    for cls,clsname in zip(classes,classnames):
        for clsid in duplicates:
            if (id(cls)==clsid):
                print(clsname,cls)
                dupe_set[clsname] = \
                    str(cls).split('.')[1].rstrip("'>'")
    for key,value in dupe_set.items():
        if (key!=value):
            del globals()[key]
```

The first three `for` loops in the preceding code were previously discussed in the *Debug unintentional assignments using id* section in the previous chapter, which covered introspection. The last `for` loop checks whether duplicate items are present in the dictionary named `dupe_set`, and deletes the duplicate variables only and not the actual classes.

Calling the preceding function results in the deletion of the duplicate `Coupon1` variable:

```
delete_duplicates(directory = dir())
Coupon <class '__main__.Coupon'>
Coupon1 <class '__main__.Coupon'>
```

```
Coupon
__main__.Coupon
Coupon1
```

Checking whether `Coupon1` still exists results in the following error:

```
-------------------------------------------------------------------------
NameError                                     Traceback (most recent call last)
<ipython-input-11-1b826290f64a> in <module>
----> 1 Coupon1

NameError: name 'Coupon1' is not defined
```

Figure 6.1 – Error on calling Coupon1 after it is deleted

The preceding error confirms that the duplicate variable was deleted by the `delete_duplicates` function. In the following section, we will look at applying reflection using the function named `callable`.

Using callable to dynamically check and generate methods

We will now look into another familiar function named `callable` to check on how it can be used to perform reflection on an object.

> **Note**
> A class, method, or a function is callable in Python, while class objects or variables are not callable.

In this example, we will check whether a class is callable, and if it returns `true`, we will dynamically add a method to the class. To test the usage of the `callable` function, we will first create a coupon class and name it `SimpleCoupon`:

```
class SimpleCoupon:
    pass
```

Let's check whether the preceding class is callable:

```
callable(SimpleCoupon)
True
```

In the following code, we will create a function that generates another function if called. We will create a create_coupon function that, in turn, creates a generate_coupon function or method when called:

```
def create_coupon( product, product_category, brand, source,
expiry_date, quantity:
    def generate_coupon(product, product_category, brand, \
      source, expiry_date, quantity):
        import random
        couponId =  random.
sample(range(100000000000,900000000000),3)
        for i in couponId:
            print(\
            '***********-----------------***************')
            print('Product:',product)
            print('Product Category:', product_category)
            print('Coupon ID:', i)
            print('Brand:', brand)
            print('Source:',  source)
            print('Expiry Date:',  expiry_date)
            print('Quantity:',  quantity)
            print(\
            '***********-----------------***************')
    return generate_coupon
```

Let's now check whether the SimpleCoupon class is callable and if it is callable, we will add a coupon_details variable to provide all the required input parameters to initialize the call:

```
if callable(SimpleCoupon):
    SimpleCoupon.coupon_details = {
                        "product": "Honey Mustard Sauce",
                        "product_category": "Condiments",
                        "brand": "ABCBrand3",
                        "source": "Pasadena Store",
                        "expiry_date": "10/1/2021",
                        "quantity": 2}
```

In the next step, let's check on how to create a method dynamically and add it to the class if the class is callable. To add the `generate_coupon` method to the `SimpleCoupon` class, let's call the `create_coupon` function:

```
if callable(SimpleCoupon):
    SimpleCoupon.generate_coupon = create_
coupon(SimpleCoupon.coupon_details['product'],
SimpleCoupon.coupon_details['product_category'],
SimpleCoupon.coupon_details['brand'],
SimpleCoupon.coupon_details['source'],
SimpleCoupon.coupon_details['expiry_date'],SimpleCoupon.coupon_
details['quantity'])
```

After adding the `generate_coupon` method, we can run the method as follows and check the results:

```
SimpleCoupon.generate_coupon(SimpleCoupon.coupon_
details['product'], SimpleCoupon.coupon_details['product_
category'],                            SimpleCoupon.coupon_
details['brand'], SimpleCoupon.coupon_details['source'],
SimpleCoupon.coupon_details['expiry_date'], SimpleCoupon.
coupon_details['quantity'])
```

The output for coupon 1 is as follows:

```
***********--------------------**************
Product: Honey Mustard Sauce
Product Category: Condiments
Coupon ID: 579494488135
Brand: ABCBrand3
Source: Pasadena Store
Expiry Date: 10/1/2021
Quantity: 2
***********--------------------**************
```

The output for coupon 2 is as follows:

```
***********--------------------**************
Product: Honey Mustard Sauce
Product Category: Condiments
Coupon ID: 657317674875
Brand: ABCBrand3
```

```
**********-----------------**************
Source: Pasadena Store
Expiry Date: 10/1/2021
Quantity: 2
**********-----------------**************
```

The output for coupon 3 is as follows:

```
**********-----------------**************
Product: Honey Mustard Sauce
Product Category: Condiments
Coupon ID: 689256610872
Brand: ABCBrand3
Source: Pasadena Store
Expiry Date: 10/1/2021
Quantity: 2
**********-----------------**************
```

In this section, we have looked at how to make use of `callable` to modify a class and add attributes and methods to a class by externally verifying whether the class is callable. We have successfully verified whether the `SimpleCoupon` class is callable and then we have also added a `coupon_details` list and a `generate_coupon` method to the class. This explains the use of `callable` as a built-in function in handling reflection on Python objects.

With this understanding, we will look at how the `hasattr` function helps in applying reflection on Python objects.

Using hasattr to set values

We will now look into the `hasattr` function, which can be used to check whether a Python object has attributes. Using this function as a condition to test the objects, we can apply reflection on objects externally.

In this example, we will look at creating custom coupons by changing one of its variables using the `hasattr` function. The classes and methods throughout this chapter are used to understand reflection with relevant examples explained under each section. We will now create another class named CustomCoupon. We will add and define class attributes to this class within the class itself and we will be adding a method to generate coupons:

```
class CustomCoupon:
    product_name = "Honey Mustard Sauce"
    product_category = "Condiments"
```

```
    brand = "ABCBrand3"
    source = "Store"
    expiry_date = "10/1/2021"
    quantity = 10
    manufacturer = None
    store = None

    def generate_coupon(self):
        import random
        couponId =  random.sample(
          range(100000000000,900000000000),1)
        for i in couponId:
            pri
nt('***********--------------------***************')
            print('Product:', self.product_name)
            print('Product Category:',
              self.product_category)
            print('Coupon ID:', i)
            print('Brand:', self.brand)
            print('Source:', self.source)
            print('Expiry Date:', self.expiry_date)
            print('Quantity:', self.quantity)
            if(self.manufacturer is not None):
                print('Manufacturer:', self.manufacturer)
            elif(self.store is not None):
                print('Store:', self.store)
            pri
nt('***********--------------------***************')
```

Look at three attributes of the preceding class – source, manufacturer, and store. If we want to change the behavior of these attributes from outside the class, we can do so by first checking whether the class has these attributes, and when the attributes are present, we can then modify the behavior of these attributes. Let's look at how to perform this using the hasattr function. We will first start with creating an object for the class:

```
coupon = CustomCoupon()
```

Let's check whether the object coupon has an attribute named `source`, and if it is present, then we will get the value of the attribute:

```
if hasattr(coupon, 'source'):
    print(getattr(coupon, 'source'))
```

Store

Let's now proceed with calling the method to generate the coupon:

```
coupon.generate_coupon()
```

```
**********-----------------**************
Product: Honey Mustard Sauce
Product Category: Condiments
Coupon ID: 728417424745
Brand: ABCBrand3
Source: Store
Expiry Date: 10/1/2021
Quantity: 10
**********-----------------**************
```

The implementation of reflection on the object coupon will start in the following code. We will create a `check_attribute` function that takes in three parameters. The first parameter is the class object's name followed by the `store` attribute and then the `manufacturer` attribute. This function checks whether the given input object has the attribute named `source` with a `Store` value, and when it returns `true`, it sets a value for the attribute store, and when it returns `false`, it sets `None` as the value for the attribute store. Similarly, when the `source` attribute has a `Manufacturer` value, then the value is set for another attribute manufacturer, as follows:

```
def check_attribute(couponobj, store, manufacturer):
    if hasattr(couponobj, 'source'):
        if(str(getattr(couponobj, 'source')) == 'Store'):
            setattr(couponobj, 'store', store)
        else:
            setattr(couponobj, 'store', None)
        if(str(getattr(couponobj,'source')) ==
           'Manufacturer'):
            setattr(couponobj, 'manufacturer',
                manufacturer)
```

```
        else:
            setattr(couponobj, 'manufacturer', None)
```

Let's now check the value of the `source` attribute:

```
coupon.source
```

'Store'

We can now call `check_attribute` to add a store and let's also add a manufacturer. Since the source has been set to `Store`, the function should set the value for the `store` variable and not for the `manufacturer` variable:

```
check_attribute(coupon,"Brooklyn Store", "XYZ Manufacturer")
coupon.generate_coupon()
```

```
**********-----------------**************
Product: Honey Mustard Sauce
Product Category: Condiments
Coupon ID: 220498341601
Brand: ABCBrand3
Source: Store
Expiry Date: 10/1/2021
Quantity: 10
Store: Brooklyn Store
**********-----------------**************
```

Let's now reset the `source` value to `Manufacturer` and run `check_attribute` again:

```
coupon.source = 'Manufacturer'
check_attribute(coupon,"Brooklyn Store", "XYZ Manufacturer")
coupon.manufacturer
```

'XYZ Manufacturer'

Let's now check what has happened to the `store` variable:

```
coupon.store
```

It returns no value. Resetting the source to `Store` again sets the `store` value and resets `manufacturer` as follows:

```
coupon.source = 'Store'
check_attribute(coupon,"Malibu Store", "XYZ Manufacturer")
coupon.generate_coupon()
***********------------------**************
Product: Honey Mustard Sauce
Product Category: Condiments
Coupon ID: 498746188585
Brand: ABCBrand3
Source: Store
Expiry Date: 10/1/2021
Quantity: 10
Store: Malibu Store
***********------------------**************
```

In this example, we looked at implementing the `hasattr` function on *ABC Megamart* coupon information. This example explains reflection using the `hasattr` function. With this understanding, let's proceed further to look at `isinstance`.

Using isinstance to modify an object

We will now look at another built-in function named `isinstance`. This function is used to identify whether an object is an instance of a class. We will be implementing reflection on class objects by checking whether they are instances of a specific class and then customizing the object of the class accordingly. This example uses the same attributes (`source`, `store`, and `manufacturer`) as in the preceding example of the `hasattr` function.

To begin with, let's create two objects for two different classes and apply the `isinstance` function to the objects of the classes to understand how this function can help in changing the behavior of Python objects. We will be reusing the `CustomCoupon` class from the preceding section and we will also be creating another `SimpleCoupon` class. We will then add two objects, `coupon1` and `coupon2`, as follows:

```
coupon1 = CustomCoupon()
class SimpleCoupon:
    product_name = "Strawberry Ice Cream"
    product_category = "Desserts"
    brand = "ABCBrand3"
```

```
    store = "Los Angeles Store"
    expiry_date = "10/1/2021"
    quantity = 10
coupon2 = SimpleCoupon()
```

In the following figure, let's look at the attributes of each object:

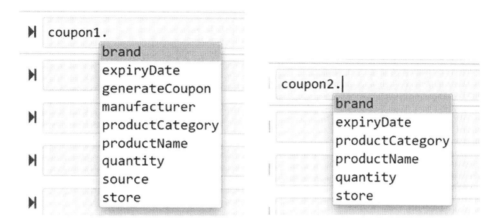

Figure 6.2 – Attributes of the coupon 1 and coupon 2 objects

Let's now check whether the objects are instances of a specific class using the isinstance function:

```
isinstance(coupon1, CustomCoupon)
```

True

```
isinstance(coupon2, SimpleCoupon)
```

True

We will now define a function named check_instance, which makes use of isinstance to implement reflection that customizes the object externally. This function takes an object, a class name, a store value, and a manufacturer value as input parameters and checks whether the object is an instance of a specific coupon class, and also checks whether it has the attribute named source and updates the store or manufacturer values accordingly. If none of these conditions are met, it returns a message that the object cannot be customized:

```
def check_instance(couponobject, couponclass, store,
manufacturer):
    if isinstance(couponobject, couponclass):
```

```
        if hasattr(couponobject, 'source'):
            if(str(getattr(couponobject, 'source')) ==
              'Store'):
                setattr(couponobject, 'store', store)
            else:
                setattr(couponobject, 'store', None)
            if(str(getattr(couponobject,'source')) ==
              'Manufacturer'):
                setattr(couponobject,'manufacturer',
                  manufacturer)
            else:
                setattr(couponobject,'manufacturer', None)
    else:
        print(couponobject,'cannot be customized')
```

Let's now call check_instance on the coupon1 object and see whether the store value is updated in the object:

```
check_instance(coupon1, CustomCoupon, 'Malibu Beach Store',
'XYZ Manufacturer')
coupon1.store
'Malibu Beach Store'
coupon1.generate_coupon()
**********------------------**************
Product: Honey Mustard Sauce
Product Category: Condiments
Coupon ID: 535933905876
Brand: ABCBrand3
Source: Store
Expiry Date: 10/1/2021
Quantity: 10
Store: Malibu Beach Store
**********------------------**************
```

Let's further call `check_instance` on the `coupon2` object and check whether the object is customized:

```
check_instance(coupon2, CustomCoupon, 'Malibu Beach Store',
'XYZ Manufacturer')
<__main__.SimpleCoupon object at 0x0000023B51AD2B88> cannot be
customized
```

In the preceding object, the conditions specified in `check_instance` were not met and so the object could not be customized.

This example explains reflection using the `isinstance` function. With this understanding, let's proceed further to look at `issubclass`.

Using issubclass to modify a class

In this section, we will look at the `issubclass` built-in function. This function can be used to apply reflection on classes that are inherited by one or more parent classes or superclasses. This function is used to verify whether a class is a subclass of a specific parent and then modify the class accordingly.

Let's begin by creating two classes with a simple set of variables. The classes will be named `StoreCoupon` and `ManufacturerCoupon`:

```
class StoreCoupon:
    product_name = "Strawberry Ice Cream"
    product_category = "Desserts"
    brand = "ABCBrand3"
    store = "Los Angeles Store"
    expiry_date = "10/1/2021"
    quantity = 10

class ManufacturerCoupon:
    product_name = "Strawberry Ice Cream"
    product_category = "Desserts"
    brand = "ABCBrand3"
    manufacturer = "ABC Manufacturer"
    expiry_date = "10/1/2021"
    quantity = 10
```

We will also create two functions that in turn create new functions to generate `store coupon` and `manufacturer coupon`, respectively:

```
def create_store_coupon(product_name, product_category, brand,
store, expiry_date, quantity):
    def generate_store_coupon(product_name,
      product_category, brand, store, expiry_date,
      quantity):
        import random
        couponId =  random.sample(
          range(100000000000,900000000000),1)
        for i in couponId:
            pri
nt('***********------------------**************')
            print('Product:', product_name)
            print('Product Category:', product_category)
            print('Coupon ID:', i)
            print('Brand:', brand)
            print('Store:', store)
            print('Expiry Date:', expiry_date)
            print('Quantity:', quantity)
            pri
nt('***********------------------**************')
    return generate_store_coupon
def create_manufacturer_coupon(product_name, product_category,
brand, manufacturer, expiry_date, quantity):
    def generate_manufacturer_coupon(product_name, product_
category, brand, manufacturer, expiry_date, quantity):
        import random
        couponId =  random.sample(
          range(100000000000,900000000000),1)
        for i in couponId:
            pri
nt('***********------------------**************')
            print('Product:', product_name)
            print('Product Category:', product_category)
            print('Coupon ID:', i)
            print('Brand:', brand)
```

```
            print('Manufacturer:', manufacturer)
            print('Expiry Date:', expiry_date)
            print('Quantity:', quantity)
            pri
nt('***********-----------------***************')
        return generate_manufacturer_coupon
```

We will further create a new class named `IceCreamCoupon`, which inherits `StoreCoupon` as the parent:

```
class IceCreamCoupon(StoreCoupon):
    pass
```

Let's now define a function to check whether a specific class is the parent class of `IceCreamCoupon`. If the subclass has `StoreCoupon` as a parent class, a function to generate `StoreCoupon` should be created, and if it has `ManufacturerCoupon` as a parent class, then a function to generate `ManufacturerCoupon` should be created:

```
def check_parent():
    if issubclass(IceCreamCoupon, StoreCoupon):
        IceCreamCoupon.generate_store_coupon =
create_store_coupon(IceCreamCoupon.product_name,
IceCreamCoupon.product_category,
IceCreamCoupon.brand, IceCreamCoupon.store,
IceCreamCoupon.expiry_date, IceCreamCoupon.quantity)
    elif issubclass(IceCreamCoupon, ManufacturerCoupon):
        IceCreamCoupon.generate_manufacturer_coupon =
create_manufacturer_coupon(IceCreamCoupon.product_name,
IceCreamCoupon.product_category,
IceCreamCoupon.brand,
IceCreamCoupon.manufacturer,
IceCreamCoupon.expiry_date,
IceCreamCoupon.quantity)
```

Running `check_parent` will now add `generate_store_coupon` to the `IceCreamCoupon` class, as follows:

```
check_parent()
IceCreamCoupon.generate_store_coupon(IceCreamCoupon.
product_name, IceCreamCoupon.product_category,
IceCreamCoupon.brand,IceCreamCoupon.store,
IceCreamCoupon.expiry_date,IceCreamCoupon.quantity)
```

```
**********------------------**************
Product: Strawberry Ice Cream
Product Category: Desserts
Coupon ID: 548296039957
Brand: ABCBrand3
Store: Los Angeles Store
Expiry Date: 10/1/2021
Quantity: 10
**********------------------**************
class IceCreamCoupon(ManufacturerCoupon):
    pass
check_parent()
IceCreamCoupon.generate_manufacturer_coupon(IceCreamCoupon.
product_name,IceCreamCoupon.product_category,
IceCreamCoupon.brand,IceCreamCoupon.manufacturer,
IceCreamCoupon.expiry_date,IceCreamCoupon.quantity)
**********------------------**************
Product: Strawberry Ice Cream
Product Category: Desserts
Coupon ID: 193600674937
Brand: ABCBrand3
Manufacturer: ABC Manufacturer
Expiry Date: 10/1/2021
Quantity: 10
**********------------------**************
```

In this example, we looked at how to make use of the `issubclass` function to implement reflection on Python classes and, in turn, modify the classes from a metaprogram rather than directly changing the function definition. With this understanding, we will look at the last section of this chapter on implementing property on a class.

Applying property on a class

In this section, we will look at the usage of `property`, which is another built-in function that can be added as a decorator in a class and can update the properties of the methods of the class by implementing the `getter`, `setter`, and `delete` methods on a class method. In *Chapter 5*, we looked at the usage of `property` as a function. In this section, we will implement `property` in an example to check how it works on reflection. We will be looking at the same coupon example to understand this.

Let's now create a new class and name it `CouponwithProperty`, initialize the class with a `_coupon_details` variable, and set it to none. We will then add `property` as a decorator and define a `coupon_details` method and add `getter`, `setter`, and `delete` to get, set, and delete values for the coupon details. In this example, we will define `getter` to get coupon details and `setter` to set coupon details, but we will define `deleter` in such a way that `coupon_details` can never be deleted. This is possible through reflection:

```python
class CouponwithProperty:
    def __init__(self):
        self._coupon_details = None
    @property
    def coupon_details(self):
        return self.coupon_details
    @coupon_details.getter
    def coupon_details(self):
        print("get coupon_details")
        return self._coupon_details
    @coupon_details.setter
    def coupon_details(self, coupon):
        print("set coupon_details")
        self._coupon_details = coupon
    @coupon_details.deleter
    def coupon_details(self):
        print("Sorry this attribute cannot be
            deleted")
```

Let's now create an object for the preceding class:

```python
fmcgCoupon = CouponwithProperty()
```

We can test whether `getter` is working by calling the `coupon_details` attribute:

```python
fmcgCoupon.coupon_details
get coupon_details
```

Similarly, we can check whether `setter` is working by setting a value for the `coupon_details` attribute:

```
fmcgCoupon.coupon_details = {
        'Product': 'Strawberry Ice Cream',
        'Product Category': 'Desserts',
        'Coupon ID': 190537749828,
        'Brand': 'ABCBrand3',
        'Manufacturer': 'ABCBrand3',
        'Expiry Date': 'ABC Manufacturer',
        'Quantity': '10/1/2021'
        }
set coupon_details
```

Calling `getter` again after setting the values will result in the following:

```
fmcgCoupon.coupon_details
get coupon_details
{'Product': 'Strawberry Ice Cream',
 'Product Category': 'Desserts',
 'Coupon ID': 190537749828,
 'Brand': 'ABCBrand3',
 'Manufacturer': 'ABCBrand3',
 'Expiry Date': 'ABC Manufacturer',
 'Quantity': '10/1/2021'}
```

The most important change we made on the attribute was disabling the `delete` operation from happening by setting `deleter`. Let's check whether it is working as expected:

```
del fmcgCoupon.coupon_details
Sorry this attribute cannot be deleted
fmcgCoupon.coupon_details
get coupon_details
{'Product': 'Strawberry Ice Cream',
 'Product Category': 'Desserts',
 'Coupon ID': 190537749828,
 'Brand': 'ABCBrand3',
 'Manufacturer': 'ABCBrand3',
```

```
'Expiry Date': 'ABC Manufacturer',
'Quantity': '10/1/2021'}
```

When we call `del` on an attribute, it deletes the attribute but, in this case, `del` is unable to delete the attribute because we have programmed `deleter` to disable deletion.

These are some of the examples of how reflection can be applied to Python objects using Python's built-in functions.

Summary

In this chapter, we have learned how to examine function objects in Python using the concept of reflection and the corresponding applications of reflection, in which we saw how to implement reflection using built-in functions such as `id`, `callable`, `hasattr`, `isinstance`, `issubclass`, and `property` on various Python objects, and we also learned how to apply them to our core example. From all of these concepts, we learned how to examine Python objects such as classes, methods, and functions. From the examples covered under each topic, we also learned how to apply reflection in practical use cases.

Similar to other chapters covered in this book, this chapter, which covered the concept of reflection, also covered changing the behavior of Python objects externally using metaprogramming.

In the next chapter, we will be looking at the concept of *generics* with some interesting examples.

7
Understanding Generics and Typing

In this chapter, we will look at what generics are and how to perform type checking in Python 3 and understand how it is useful in metaprogramming.

Python is a programming language where variables are declared as generics and they don't get a data type assigned to them on the declaration. Python resolves the data types dynamically during runtime depending on the values assigned to variables. In other programming languages such as C++, generics need to be programmatically designed to make the variables generic, whereas in Python, generics are how the variables are defined. In such cases, how we would declare a variable with typing and restrict the behavior of the variables is what we will be focusing on in detail in this chapter.

Throughout this chapter, we will look at understanding how generics work in Python and how to define type checks so that we can apply metaprogramming on variables to statically type them so that we don't have to wait for the complete program to run to determine that we have unintentionally used incorrect typing in our code.

In this chapter, we will be covering the following main topics:

- What are generics?
- What happens when data types are specified?
- Typing with explicit type checks – approach 1
- Typing with explicit type checks – approach 2
- Adding data types with constraints
- Creating a simple custom data type
- Creating a domain-specific data type

By the end of this chapter, you should be able to apply generics and type checking on Python variables. You should also be able to create your own domain-specific data types.

Technical requirements

The code examples shared in this chapter are available on GitHub under the code for this chapter here: `https://github.com/PacktPublishing/Metaprogramming-with-Python/tree/main/Chapter07`.

What are generics?

Generics are a programming paradigm where any attribute or variable is a function in a language that is not assigned to any specific type. When we speak of type, it is either the variable data type or the function return type.

How are generics connected to metaprogramming?

Metaprogramming deals with the concepts of Python 3 and above, where we can develop scripts or programs that manipulate the objects of Python externally without actually impacting the definition of classes, methods, or functions in a program. Generics are the way in which Python has built the handling of data types for its objects. If we need to change the data type handling in Python from generics to specific types, we can perform it through metaprogramming. To understand how to make specifics work, we need to understand generics with examples. Let's look at generics in the following section.

How are generics handled in Python?

Here, we can investigate generics with an example. Throughout this chapter, we will look into another interesting section of our core example, *ABC Megamart*. In this chapter, we will be covering our examples using the clothing and fashion department of *ABC Megamart*.

Let's consider the fashion department of *ABC Megamart* in this example. This department covers various clothing products. To examine generics, we will first define a class named `Fashion` with attributes such as `clothing_category`, `gender`, `model`, `design`, `dress_type`, `size`, and `color`. We will also add a method named `get_item` to return the preceding attributes. The code is defined as follows:

```
class Fashion:
    def __init__(self,clothing_
category,gender,model,design,dress_type,size, color):
        self.clothing_category = clothing_category
        self.gender = gender
        self.model = model
```

```
        self.design = design
        self.dress_type = dress_type
        self.size = size
        self.color = color
    def get_item(self):
        return self.clothing_category,self.gender,self.
model,self.design,self.dress_type, self.size,self.color
```

This code handles generics. Let's explain this statement by assigning values of any data types to the attributes of `Fashion`:

```
fashion =
Fashion("Clothing","Women","Western","Dotted","Jumpsuits",38,
"blue")
```

We have added string values to `clothing_category`, `gender`, `model`, `design`, `dress_type`, and `color`, while we added an integer value to the `size` attribute. Since the language handles generics by default, we did not have to declare the data types and the values are accepted without throwing any errors. We can call the `get_item` method to display these generic values:

```
fashion.get_item()
('Clothing', 'Women', 'Western', 'Dotted', 'Jumpsuits', 38,
'blue')
```

Examining the data types of `clothing_category` and `size` results as follows:

```
type(fashion.clothing_category)
str
type(fashion.size)
int
```

Let's double-check our statement on generics now. What happens when we change the data types of input variables? Will they be accepted by Python? To test this, let's change the data types of `clothing_category` and `size`:

```
fashion = Fashion(102,"Women","Western","Floral","T-
Shirt","XS","green")
fashion.get_item()
(102, 'Women', 'Western', 'Floral', 'T-Shirt', 'XS', 'green')
```

The change in data types is accepted and processed by Python and can be viewed as follows:

```
type(fashion.clothing_category)
int
type(fashion.size)
str
```

In the preceding example, no matter which data type the input value belongs to, they are processed successfully. In the following section, let's explicitly assign data types and check further.

What happens when data types are specified?

Annotations in Python are added to code to provide additional information or help to end users with a piece of code while creating libraries. Annotations can be used to add data types to a specific code so that the information on data types can later be retrieved using the annotations by developers.

Type hints as annotations

In the context of typing, which is the topic of this chapter, let's look at type hints in this section. Data types of a function or method can be defined in Python using a functionality of annotations called **type hinting**. Type hinting is a concept laid out in **PEP 483** (**Python Enhancement Proposals**) for **Python 3.5** by *Guido van Rossum* and *Ivan Levkivskyi*. Type hinting can be read in detail in the Python documentation available at *PEP 483 – The Theory of Type Hints* at peps.python.org. Type hinting is used to provide information to the developers on the data types and return types of Python objects and is not a strict requirement in Python coding. With or without type hinting, Python code executes the same way since it is a dynamically typed language. Let's look at another example of the Fashion class by declaring type hints on the methods of the class. To implement this, we can explicitly assign a data type and its return type to a variable while declaring a variable and adding it to a method in Python. We will also add a type hint for the return type of a method.

Let's declare the Fashion class initialized with its attributes or variables along with the data types, which we would expect the variables to be on:

```
class Fashion:
    def __init__(self,clothing_category:
str,gender:str,model:str,design:str,dress_type:str,size:int,
color:str):
        self.clothing_category = clothing_category
        self.gender = gender
        self.model = model
        self.design = design
```

```
        self.dress_type = dress_type
        self.size = size
        self.color = color
    def get_item(self) -> list:
        return self.clothing_category,self.gender,self.model,
  self.design,self.dress_type, self.size,self.color
```

In the preceding code, we have specifically tagged a data type to each variable. In this class, we will also add a `get_item` method and add annotation with a type hint specifying that this method returns a `list` item.

Let's now check what happens when these data types are not followed while creating an object and assigning values to these variables:

```
fashion = Fashion(104,"Women","Western","Cotton","Shirt","S",
"white")
fashion.get_item()
[104, 'Women', 'Western', 'Cotton', 'Shirt', 'S', 'white']
```

We have declared `clothingCategory_c` as a string and `size` as an integer in the preceding class definition but we have assigned an integer to `clothing_category` and a string to the `size` variables. The program still ran successfully without throwing any type error, while there should, ideally, have been a type error in this case. This example again proves that types are handled as generics in Python when we assign a data type during variable declaration.

Let's also look at the annotation for the `get_item` method in the following code:

```
 print(Fashion.get_item.__annotations__)
```

Calling `__annotations__` on the method provides the list data type annotated as the return type for the method:

```
 {'return': <class 'list'>}
```

Let's look further into the concept of typing, in which we can look at how to deal with specific types instead of generics.

Typing with explicit type checks – approach 1

In the preceding section, we looked at Python's ability to handle data types as generics. While building an application, there can be scenarios where a variable will need a specific data type, and we might expect metaprogramming to have the ability to handle such specific data types. In this section, let's look at creating a class to perform type checking.

Creating a class to implement type checking

In this example, we will be creating a class named `typecheck` and adding methods to check each data type specifically. If a data type, for instance, an integer type, is provided as input to the method, it returns the input and, if the condition fails, it returns a message to provide the input value as an integer. Similarly, we will add various methods to check string, float, list, tuple, and dictionary objects:

```
class typecheck:
```

Let's now define a method named `intcheck`. The purpose of this method is to perform an integer type check of any input explicitly. In this method, a value will be provided as input and the method will verify whether the input value is an integer. If the input value is an integer, we will return the input value. If the value is not an integer, we will return a message that says `"value should be an integer"`:

```
def intcheck(self,inputvalue):
    if type(inputvalue) != int:
        print("value should be an integer")
    else:
        return inputvalue
```

In the following method, let's check that the input variable is not a string (for example, `Orangesexample`) and return an error message when the condition is `true` and return the input value when the condition is `false`:

```
def stringcheck(self,inputvalue):
    if type(inputvalue) != str:
        print("value should be a string")
    else:
        return inputvalue
```

In the following method, let's check that the input variable is not a floating-point value (for example, `example, 2335.2434`) and return an error message when the condition is `true` and return the input value when the condition is `false`:

```
def floatcheck(self,inputvalue):
    if type(inputvalue) != float:
        print("value should be a float")
    else:
        return inputvalue
```

In the following method, let's check that the input variable is not a list of variables (for example, `['fruits','flowers',1990]`) and return an error message when the condition is `true` and return the input value when the condition is `false`:

```
def listcheck(self,inputvalue):
    if type(inputvalue) != list:
        print("value should be a list")
    else:
        return inputvalue
```

In the following method, let's check that the input variable is not a tuple of variables (for example, example, `('fruits','flowers',1990))` and return an error message when the condition is `true` and return the input value when the condition is `false`:

```
def tuplecheck(self,inputvalue):
    if type(inputvalue) != tuple:
        print("value should be a tuple")
    else:
        return inputvalue
```

In the following method, let's check that the input variable is not a dictionary with key/value pairs (for example, `example: {'one': 1, 'two': 2}`) and return an error message when the condition is `true` and return the input value when the condition is `false`:

```
def dictcheck(self,inputvalue):
    if type(inputvalue) != dict:
        print("value should be a dict")
    else:
        return inputvalue
```

Now let's , we will proceed further to create the `Fashion` class to perform type checks using the `typecheck` class.

Creating a class to test type checking

Let's now create the `Fashion` class with the same set of variables, that is, `clothing_category`, `gender`, `model`, `design`, `dress_type`, `size`, and `color`. In this example too, we will assign a specific data type to each variable. In the following class definition, let's create an object for the `typecheck` class and call type-specific methods to store the variables of each type. For instance, a `price` variable will be declared as `float`, and the `floatcheck` method from `typecheck` will be used to store the variable instead of using generics:

```
class Fashion:
```

In the following method, let's initialize the variables for the `Fashion` class along with their specific data types defined using the type checking methods of the `typecheck` class:

```
    def __init__(self,clothing_category:
str,gender:str,price:float,design:str,dress_type:str,size:int,
color:list):
        tc = typecheck()
        self.clothing_category = tc.stringcheck(clothing_
category)
        self.gender = tc.stringcheck(gender)
        self.price = tc.floatcheck(price)
        self.design = tc.stringcheck(design)
        self.dress_type = tc.stringcheck(dress_type)
        self.size = tc.intcheck(size)
        self.color = tc.listcheck(color)
```

In the following method, let's return all the variables initialized in the `Fashion` class:

```
    def get_item(self):
        return self.clothing_category,self.gender,self.
price,self.design,self.dress_type, self.size,self.color
```

Calling the `floatcheck` method on the `price` variable acts as a typing mechanism for the variable declaration, and if the input provided is not a float, then an error will be displayed in the variable declaration phase itself:

```
fashion =
Fashion(112,"Men","Western","Designer","Shirt",38.4,"black")
value should be a string
value should be a float
```

```
value should be an integer
value should be a list
```

In the preceding example, we have declared four variables with incorrect data types; clothing_category should be a string, price should be a float, size should be an integer, and color should be a list. All these incorrect variables were not accepted by the code and hence we have received corresponding variable type errors:

```
fashion.get_item()
(None, 'Men', None, 'Designer', 'Shirt', None, None)
```

While we get the items from the fashion object, all incorrect type variables have no values assigned to them. Let's now look at the correct values and how they are accepted by the fashion object:

```
:fashion =
Fashion("112","Men",20.0,"Designer","Shirt",38,["blue","white"])
fashion.get_item()
('112', 'Men', 20.0, 'Designer', 'Shirt', 38, ['blue', 'white'])
```

In the preceding code, we have corrected the input values by assigning values of specific data types and the error is now resolved. By developing such explicit typing libraries, we can convert Python's generics into specifics.

Typing with explicit type checks – approach 2

In this section, we will look at another approach for applying specific data types to variables. In the first approach, we developed a typecheck class and used the type checking methods themselves to create new data types. In this example, we will be creating the typecheck class with each type checking method to check that the input value belongs to the expected type and returns a Boolean value based on the condition's result. This method of type checking gives us the flexibility of modifying the Fashion class to provide variable-specific error messages when the condition is not met.

Creating a class to implement type checking

In this example, let's begin by creating the typecheck class.

The typecheck class is created here to make all the methods in this class reusable just in case all the methods in the type check code need to be exported into a different file for later use.

All the methods in this example can be created with or without a class and used throughout this chapter:

```
class typecheck
```

- In the following method, let's check that the input variable is not an integer (for example, 23348) and return False when the condition is true and return True when the condition is false:

```
def intcheck(self,inputvalue):
    if type(inputvalue) != int:
        return False
    else:
        return True
```

- In the following method, let's check that the input variable is not a string (for example, Orangesexample) and return False when the condition is true and return True when the condition is false:

```
def stringcheck(self,inputvalue):
    if type(inputvalue) != str:
        return False
    else:
        return True
```

- In the following method, let's check that the input variable is not a floating point value (for example, 2335.2434) and return False when the condition is true and return True when the condition is false:

```
def floatcheck(self,inputvalue):
    if type(inputvalue) != float:
        return False
    else:
        return True
```

- In the following method, let's check that the input variable is not a list of variables (for example, ['fruits','flowers',1990]) and return False when the condition is true and return True when the condition is false:

```
def listcheck(self,inputvalue):
    if type(inputvalue) != list:
        return False
    else:
        return True
```

- In the following method, let's check that the input variable is not a tuple of variables (for example, `('fruits','flowers',1990)`) and return `False` when the condition is true and return `True` when the condition is false:

```
def tuplecheck(self,inputvalue):
    if type(inputvalue) != tuple:
        return False
    else:
        return True
```

- In the following method, let's check that the input variable is not a dictionary with key/value pairs (for example, `{'one': 1, 'two': 2}`) and return `False` when the condition is true and return `True` when the condition is false:

```
def dictcheck(self,inputvalue):
    if type(inputvalue) != dict:
        return False
    else:
        return True
```

Now, we can proceed further to create the `Fashion` class to perform type checks using the `typecheck` class.

Creating a class to test type checking

In this section, let's look at creating a `Fashion` class with a different variable type definition as follows:

```
class Fashion:
```

- Let's initialize the variables along with the specific data types for each:

```
def __init__(self,clothing_category:
str,gender:str,model:tuple,design:int,price:float,
size:dict, color:list):
    tc = typecheck()
```

- In the following code, let's check whether the `clothing_category` input is a string and return the value if it is true, and return an error specific to `clothing_category` if it is false:

```
if tc.stringcheck(clothing_category):
    self.clothing_category = clothing_category
else:
    print("clothing category should be a string")
```

- In the following code, let's check whether the `gender` input is a string and return the value if it is true and return an error specific to the `gender` variable if it is false:

```
if tc.stringcheck(gender):
    self.gender = gender
else:
    print("gender should be a string")
```

- In the following code, let's check whether the `model` input is a tuple and return the value if it is true and return an error specific to the `model` variable if it is false:

```
if tc.tuplecheck(model):
    self.model = model
else:
    print("model should be a tuple")
```

- In the following code, let's check whether the `design` input is an integer and return the value if it is true and return an error specific to the `design` variable if it is false:

```
if tc.intcheck(design):
    self.design = design
else:
    print("design should be an integer")
```

- In the following code, let's check whether the `price` input is a floating point value and return the value if it is true and return an error specific to the `price` variable if it is false:

```
if tc.floatcheck(price):
    self.price = price
else:
    print("price should be a floating point
value")
```

- In the following code, let's check whether the `size` input is a dictionary object and return the value if it is true and return an error specific to the `size` variable if it is false:

```
if tc.dictcheck(size):
    self.size = size
else:
    print("size should be a dictionary object")
```

- In the following code, let's check whether the `color` input is a list object and return the value if it is true and return an error specific to the `color` variable if it is false:

```
if tc.listcheck(color):
        self.color = color
    else:
        print("color should be a list of values")
```

- In the following code, let's create a method to return all the variables listed in the preceding code:

```
    def get_item(self):
        return self.clothing_category,self.gender,self.
model,self.design,self.price, self.size,self.color
```

To test this approach of type checking, let's pass some incorrect values as input for some of these variables and check:

```
fashion = Fashion(12,"Women","Western","Floral","Maxi
Dress",34,"yellow")
```

Executing the preceding code results in the following list of errors:

```
clothing category should be a string
model should be a tuple
price should be a floating point value
size should be a dictionary object
color should be a list of values
```

Further, calling the `get_item` method on the preceding `fashion` object results in the following error:

```
fashion.get_item()
```

The graphical representation of the error message is as follows:

```
-------------------------------------------------------------------
AttributeError                        Traceback (most recent call last)
<ipython-input-6-fa1ce8e899e3> in <module>
----> 1 fashion.getitem()

<ipython-input-4-796edca1116a> in getitem(self)
     32
     33     def getitem(self):
---> 34         return self.clothingCategory,self.gender,self.model,self.design,self.price, self.size,self.color

AttributeError: 'Fashion' object has no attribute 'clothingCategory'
```

Figure 7.1 – Error on calling the get_item method

In the preceding error, the first variable, `clothing-category`, was not accepted by the method since type expectations were not met by this variable.

We can check further by providing the right input types as follows:

```
fashion =
Fashion("Rayon","Women",("Western","Floral"),12012,100.50,
{'XS': 36, 'S': 38, 'M': 40},["yellow","red"])
```

There were no errors from the preceding value assignments. Calling the `get_item` method on the `fashion` object now results in the following output:

```
fashion.get_item()
('Rayon',
 'Women',
 ('Western', 'Floral'),
 12012,
 100.5,
 {'XS': 36, 'S': 38, 'M': 40},
 ['yellow', 'red'])
```

The preceding output meets all the type requirements and the end goal of type checking is achieved successfully through this approach. Now that you understand this, let's look further into the concept of data types with constraints.

Adding data types with constraints

In this section, we will look at an example of adding constraints to data types and checking constraints along with type checking. There might be scenarios where we would like to create an integer variable and restrict its length to two digits or to create a string and restrict its length to 10 characters and more. With this example, let's explore how to add such constraints or restricts during the static type checking.

In this example, let's create a `typecheck` class with only two methods to check an integer and a string. While checking these data types, let's also add a few more constraints within the method definition:

```
class typecheck:
```

- In the following method, let's check that the input variable is not an integer or its length is greater than two, and return `False` when the condition is true, and return `True` when the condition is false:

```
def intcheck(self,inputvalue):
    if (type(inputvalue) != int) and
```

```
        (len(str(inputvalue))>2):
                return False
        else:
                return True
```

- In the following method, let's check that the input variable is not a string or its length is greater than 10, and return `False` when the condition is true, and return `True` when the condition is false:

```
    def stringcheck(self,inputvalue):
        if (type(inputvalue) != str) and
    (len(str(inputvalue))>10):
                return False
        else:
                return True
```

With just two methods with type checks and constraints, we can look into creating a `Fashion` class with two variables and one method:

```
class Fashion:
```

- Let's initialize the class with `clothing_category` as a string and `size` as an integer:

```
    def __init__(self,clothing_category: str,size:int):
        tc = typecheck()
```

- In the following code, let's declare `clothing_category` using the `stringcheck` method:

```
        if tc.stringcheck(clothing_category):
            self.clothing_category = clothing_category
        else:
            print("value should be a string of length
    less than or equal to 10")
```

- In the following code, let's declare `size` using the `intcheck` method:

```
        if tc.intcheck(size):
            self.size = size
        else:
            print("value should be an integer of 2 digits
    or less")
```

- In the following code, let's add the method to get the items and return them:

```
def get_item(self):
    return self.clothing_category,self.size
```

Let's further create an object for the `fashion` class and assign two variables that do not match the type-checking conditions:

```
fashion = Fashion("Clothing & Accessories",384)
value should be a string of length less than or equal to 10
value should be an integer of 2 digits or less
```

The preceding error messages indicate that both the type checks and constraints are not met for the string as well as integer data types. Let's now provide the right type of input values and perform static type checking:

```
fashion = Fashion("Cotton",34)
fashion.get_item()
('Cotton', 34)
```

The value assignments are now working as expected in the preceding code. With this understanding, let's proceed further to create simple custom data types.

Creating a simple custom data type

Until the preceding section, we looked at adding explicit type checks and converting generic type variables into specific types to handle specific data needs we might get while programming an application, and we also added errors to help debug incorrect data types assigned to variables.

In this section, let's look at creating our own simple data types and what will be required to do so. First of all, let's answer the question of why we need our own data types. Any custom data type is a derivation of basic data types in Python along with certain variations to fulfill the purpose of our data needs in an application. Any data type will have its own set of operations that can be performed on top of the data of that specific type. For instance, an integer data type will support arithmetic operations such as addition, subtraction, multiplication, and division. Similarly, a string supports concatenation in the place of addition, and so on. So, when we create our own data type, we can override these basic operations to fulfill the need of our custom data type.

To demonstrate this, let's first create our own data type and override the basic operators to perform the operations that we expect. Please note that custom data types may be required only in situations where we would like to make it domain-specific or application-specific. We can always use default data types and avoid creating custom data types where there is no requirement:

1. We will create a class named `DressSize` and initialize it with the `size` variable of the integer type. If the input value for `size` is not an integer and the input values do not follow a specific list of dress sizes, type checking returns an error message in red (as shown in *Figure 7.2*):

```
class DressSize:
    def __init__(self,size:int):
        self.limit = [28, 30, 32, 34, 36, 38, 40, 42, 44,
46, 48]
        if type(size)==int and size in self.limit:
            self.size = size
        else:
            print("\x1B[31mSize should be a valid dress
size")
```

2. Next, let's override the default `str` method of a class to return the string version of the `size` variable:

```
    def __str__(self):
        return str(self.size)
```

3. Then, let's add a new method named `value` to return the value of the `size` attribute:

```
    def value(self):
        return self.size
```

4. Now, let's override the addition (+) operator of the integer method to increase `size` values from one dress size object created for the `DressSize` class:

```
    def __add__(self, up):
        result = self.size + up
        if result in self.limit:
            return result
        else:
            return "Input valid size increments"
```

5. Then, let's override the subtraction (`-`) operator of the integer method to decrease `size` values from one size object created for the `DressSize` class:

```
    def __sub__(self, down):
        result = self.size - down
        if result in self.limit:
            return result
        else:
            return "Input valid size decrements"
```

6. We will then create an object for the class, in this case, our new custom data type, `DressSize`, and initialize it with a string instead of an integer, as follows:

```
s = DressSize("30")
```

Incorrect input type results in an error with a red font similar to how error messages are usually displayed while debugging:

```
Size should be an integer    Size should be a valid dress size
```

Figure 7.2 – Error message for DressSize

7. Calling the `value` method would also result in an error since the type checking failed for the `DressSize` data type:

```
s.value()
```

The value error is displayed as follows:

```
---------------------------------------------------------------------------
AttributeError                            Traceback (most recent call last)
<ipython-input-53-3d2db1bf7adf> in <module>
----> 1 s.value()

<ipython-input-51-5269406ba653> in value(self)
     10 
     11     def value(self):
---> 12         return self.size
     13 
     14     def __add__(self,second):

AttributeError: 'DressSize' object has no attribute 'size'
```

Figure 7.3 – Value error due to incorrect DressSize input type

8. Let's correct this error by providing the correct input type while creating a `DressSize` object:

```
s = DressSize(30)
s
<__main__.DressSize at 0x22c4bfc4a60>
```

9. In the following code, we can look at how the addition operation (+) works on the objects of `DressSize`:

```
DressSize(30) + 6
36
DressSize(30) + 3
'Input valid size increments'
```

10. The addition of two objects works like a regular addition since we have overloaded the addition operator (+) to add the initialized variables of two objects. Similarly, we can check the results of subtraction, as follows:

```
DressSize(32) - 4
26
DressSize(30) - 3
'Input valid size decrements'
```

11. The subtraction of two objects works like a regular subtraction since we have overloaded the subtraction operator (-) to subtract the initialized variables of two objects. Similarly, printing the object results in printing the string format of the `size` variable since we have overloaded the `str` method to do this:

```
print(s)
30
```

12. We have also added a `value` method to display the value of the `size` variable, and it works as follows:

```
s.value()
30
```

13. Calling the `type` method on the variable or the `s` object displays the class name, `DressSize`, which is the data type of `s` in this case:

```
type(s)
__main__.DressSize
```

Now, we can consider creating a more detailed data type of our own in the next section.

Creating a domain-specific data type

In this section, let's create an even more customized data type to deal with the dress size of the fashion department of *ABC Megamart*. The `DressSize` data type we defined in the preceding section handles any integer as input and performs the operations we overloaded. When we look at the domain of the fashion industry and consider the dress size as a domain-specific variable, the `DressSize` data type should ideally be considering only specific values for `size` and not accept all integers. The dress size will be based on the size of dresses held in the inventory of *ABC Megamart*.

The accepted input for dress size in this example should be the list of integers, `[36,38,40,42,44,46,48]`, or the list of strings that indicates the equivalent text values for dress size such as `[XS,S,M,L,XL,XXL,XXXL]`:

1. Let's begin by creating the `DressSize` class along with its methods to work as a domain-specific data type, and initialize `size` as its only input value:

    ```
    class DressSize:
        def __init__(self, size):
    ```

2. Let's further define two domain-specific lists that holds the valid set of values for dress size in text and integer formats, respectively:

    ```
    self.romanchart = ['XS','S','M','L','XL','XXL','XXXL']
    self.sizenum = [36,38,40,42,44,46,48]
    ```

3. In the following code, we will be creating a dictionary object that holds the integer and text format of `size` as key/value pairs. The reason behind adding this dictionary object is to use it further in the data type-specific methods created for this data type:

    ```
    self.chart = {}dict(zip(self.romanchart,self.sizenum))
    ```

4. Let's now add the condition that accepts the input value as `size` if it meets the data type criteria and then rejects the input value with an error if it does not meet the criteria:

    ```
            if (size in self.romanchart) or (size in self.
    sizenum ):
                self.size = size
            else:
                print("\x1B[31mEnter valid size")
    ```

In the preceding code, the input value will be accepted if it is present in the romanchart list variable or if it is present in the sizenum list variable. If both the criteria are not met, the value will be rejected by the DressSize data type and an error message will be displayed in a red-colored font. Why do we need to set these strict constraints in this particular domain-specific data type? If we look at the size values of a dress, the size usually is an even number and there are no odd-numbered dress sizes in a shopping cart or in a clothing store. Also, the size of the clothing in most of the generic clothing stores falls between 36 and 48 in general. If the store holds clothes of lesser or greater sizes, we can adjust the lists accordingly and redefine the data type. In this specific scenario, let's consider the dress sizes between 36 and 48 and their corresponding text codes between XS and XXXL as acceptable values. Now, we have added the acceptance criteria for the data type:

1. Let's add specific methods that can be processed on the data type. In the following method, let's override the default str method of a class to return the string version of the size variable:

    ```
    def __str__(self):
        return str(self.size)
    ```

2. In the following code, let's add a new method named value to return the value of the size attribute:

    ```
    def value(self):
        return self.size
    ```

3. In the following code, let's add a method to increment the size value. The size value should increment by 2 since dress size is always measured in even numbers:

    ```
    def increase(self):
        if (self.size in self.romanchart) :
            result = self.chart[self.size] + 2
            for key, value in self.chart.items():
                if value == result:
                    return resultkey
        elif (self.size in self.sizenum ):
            return self.size + 2
    ```

In the preceding code, we have added a logic to look up the value of a dress size such as XL if DressSize is a text input to the data type, and then increment the value by 2. We have also added a logic to check the integer value of the dress size and increment by 2 if the dress size input is an integer.

4. Let's add one more method to decrement the `DressSize` attribute:

```
def decrease(self):
    if self.size in self.romanchart :
        result = self.chart[self.size] - 2
        for key, value in self.chart.items():
            if value == result:
                return key
    elif (self.size in self.sizenum ):
        return self.size - 2
```

In the preceding code, we have added a logic to look up the value of a dress size such as XL if `DressSize` is a text input to the data type, and then decrement the value by 2. We have also added a logic to check the integer value of `DressSize` and decrement by 2 if the dress size input is an integer. This defines the overall creation of a domain-specific data type named `DressSize`.

5. The next step is to test this data type by creating an object:

```
s = DressSize("XXL")
```

In the preceding code, we have created an object named `s`, so let's look at how various methods and attributes work on this object:

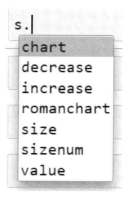

Figure 7.4 – Attributes of DressSize

6. In the following code, let's call `chart` from the `s` object:

```
s.chart
{'XS': 36, 'S': 38, 'M': 40, 'L': 42, 'XL': 44, 'XXL':
46, 'XXXL': 48}
```

7. Printing the object results in the string format representation of the value of the s object:

```
print(s)
XS
XL
```

8. Calling the value method results as follows:

```
s.value()
'XXL'
```

9. Calling the increment method results as follows:

```
s.increase()
XXXL
```

10. Calling the decrement method results as follows:

```
s.decrease()
XL
```

11. Let's now create the Fashion class and initialize variables out of which the size variable will be initialized as the DressSize type:

```
class Fashion:
    def __init__(self,clothing_category:
str,gender:str,model:str,design:str,dress_
type:str,color:str,size:DressSize):
        self.clothing_category = clothing_category
        self.gender = gender
        self.model = model
        self.design = design
        self.dress_type = dress_type
        self.color = color
```

12. In the following code, let's define the type checking condition for DressSize. If size is an instance of DressSize, then it returns the instance, and if it is not an instance, an appropriate error message will be displayed:

```
if isinstance(size,DressSize):
        self.size = size
    else:
        print("value should be of type DressSize")
```

13. Let's further add the `get_item` method to return the attributes of the `Fashion` class:

```
def get_item(self):
    return self.clothing_category,self.gender,self.
model,self.design,self.dress_type,self.color,self.size
```

14. Creating the object further results as follows:

```
fashion =
Fashion("Clothing","Women","Western","Dotted","Jumpsuits",
'blue',"XL")
value should be of type DressSize
```

In the preceding code, we did not assign the correct data type for the size variable.

15. To correct it, let's create an instance of `DressSize` and provide it as input to the `Fashion` class:

```
M = DressSize("M")
fashion = Fashion("Clothing","Women","Western","Dotted",
"Jumpsuits",'blue',M)
```

The preceding code did not result in any error and is accepted as input by the `Fashion` class. Calling the `get_item` method would result in the following output:

```
fashion.get_item()
('Clothing',
 'Women',
 'Western',
 'Dotted',
 'Jumpsuits',
 'blue',
 <__main__.DressSize at 0x22c4cf4ba60>)
```

If we want to look at the specific value of the M object, we can call the `value` method as follows:

```
fashion.size.value()
'M'
```

In this section, we looked at how to create a domain-specific custom data type and how to use it on another class as a type variable.

These are some of the examples of how generics work in Python and how specifics can be applied to Python objects using user-defined functions.

Summary

In this chapter, we have learned the concepts of generics and type checking. We also looked at creating user-defined data types with specific constraints and we've also seen how to apply them to our core example. We created our own domain-specific data type and overloaded operators and methods to work according to the data type. Similar to other chapters covered in this book, this chapter is also used to change the behavior of Python objects externally using the concept of metaprogramming.

In the next chapter, we will be looking at the concept of templates with some interesting examples.

8

Defining Templates for Algorithms

In this chapter, we will look at what templates are and how to implement template programming in Python.

What are templates and where are they useful? The main usage of applying the concepts of metaprogramming during the process of developing an application is to design a reusable framework that can be manipulated externally through the programming of metadata of Python objects rather than modifying the object itself. Templates, as the name suggests, can act as a template, a format, or a model on how a sequence of operations can be performed on a Python object. These templates can be used to define the common functionalities of methods within a class and to reuse them through the application of the object-oriented programming concept of **inheritance**.

Throughout this chapter, we will look at understanding how templates can be defined and used in Python and how a sequence of common operations can be designed into a template that fits into a framework. Speaking of designs, template programming is one of the main concepts within the design patterns of Python. Design patterns will be covered in detail in *Chapter 12* on design patterns.

In this chapter, we will be taking a look at the following main topics:

- Explaining a sequence of operations
- Defining the sequence of methods
- Identifying the common functionalities
- Designing templates

By the end of this chapter, you should be able to apply generics and type checking on Python variables. You should also be able to create your own domain-specific data types.

Technical requirements

The code examples shared in this chapter are available on GitHub under the code for this chapter here: `https://github.com/PacktPublishing/Metaprogramming-with-Python/tree/main/Chapter08`.

Explaining a sequence of operations

Developing algorithms is always interesting, especially in a language like Python where less code needs to be written to complete an action compared to any other programming language. An **algorithm** is a simple sequence of steps that need to be performed to accomplish a task. While developing any algorithm, the most important aspect is to ensure that we are following the steps to perform the action in the right sequence. This section covers examples of a sequence of operations and how they can be defined in a Python program.

Back to our core example

In this chapter, we will continue using our core example of *ABC Megamart*, and we will specifically look at the billing counter where we can perform a sequence of operations. The reason we are focusing on a sequence of operations here is to especially understand how **templates** can be utilized to perform a set of tasks, and also how they can be reused to perform similar kinds of other tasks too. So, let's begin.

At *ABC Megamart*, we have four different checkout counters to check out the shopping items from the cart. The details of the counters are as follows:

- The first one is to check out items that contain vegetables and dairy.

- The second one is to check out items that contain less than 10 assorted items, excluding electronics, vegetables, and dairy.

- The third one is to check out items that contain more than 10 assorted items, excluding electronics, vegetables, and dairy.

- The fourth one is to check out electronic goods.

Each of these counters is performing a sequence of operations and at this point in time, they might look like they are an independent set of operations. The goal of this chapter is to create templates and look at a common way of connecting these independent operations. To connect them and create a template, we need to understand the sequence of operations in each of these counters.

Let's now look at what each of the counters will work on.

The vegetables and dairy counter

The journey of a customer to the billing counter starts from the vegetable section, where vegetables are added to the shopping cart, the customer then stands in a queue at the respective billing counter, vegetables and fruit are weighed and packed, a price tag with a bar code is added on the packet, the bar code is scanned and the bill is added to the invoice for each item, a tax component is added for each item, and the bill is totaled, printed, and handed over to the customer, who then pays the bill.

The graphical representation of the steps is as follows:

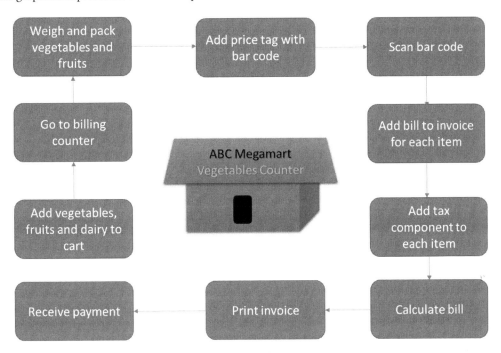

Figure 8.1 – Vegetables counter

The following functions will be defined to perform each of these operations:

```
return_cart()
goto_vege_counter()
weigh_items()
add_price_tag()
scan_bar_code()
add_billing()
add_tax()
calc_bill()
```

```
print_invoice()
receive_payment()
```

Let's further look at the next counter, which handles less than 10 items.

Less than 10 items counter

When a customer adds less than 10 items to the cart and the items do not contain vegetables, fruit, dairy, or electronics, then the customer goes to the less than 10 items counter where the bar code on each item is scanned and the bill is added to the invoice for each item, a tax component is added for each item, and the bill is totaled, printed, and handed over to the customer, who then pays the bill.

The graphical representation of the steps is as follows:

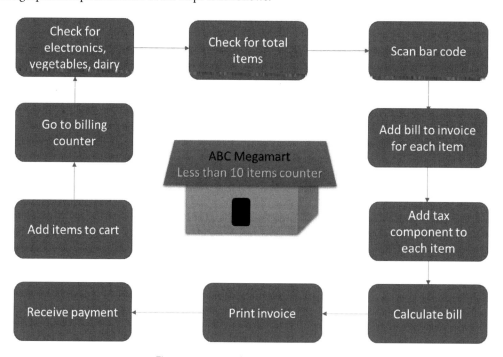

Figure 8.2 – Less than 10 items counter

The following functions will be defined to perform each of these operations:

```
return_cart()
goto_less_t10_counter()
review_items()
count_items()
```

```
scan_bar_code()
add_billing()
add_tax()
calc_bill()
print_invoice()
receive_payment()
```

Let's further look at the next counter, which handles more than 10 items.

The greater than 10 items counter

When a customer adds more than 10 items to the cart and the items do not contain vegetables, fruit, dairy, or electronics, then the customer goes to the greater than 10 items counter where the bar code on each item is scanned and the bill is added to the invoice for each item, coupons are applied, a tax component is added for each item, and the bill is totaled, printed, and handed over to the customer, who then pays the bill.

The graphical representation of the steps is as follows:

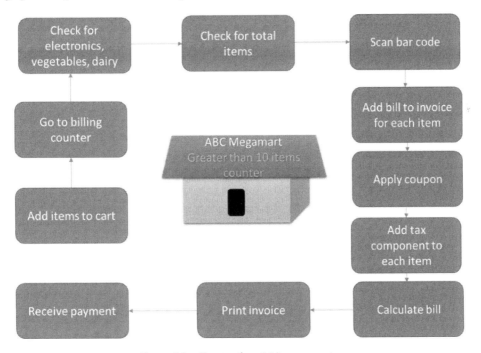

Figure 8.3 – Greater than 10 items counter

The following functions will be defined to perform each of these operations:

```
return_cart()
gotoGreatT10Counter()
review_items()
count_items()
scan_bar_code()
add_billing()
apply_coupon()
add_tax()
calc_bill()
print_invoice()
receive_payment()
```

Let's further look at the next counter, which handles electronic items.

Electronics counter

The last counter is the electronics counter, where a customer goes to the counter, gets the electronic items tested, the item is scanned, and the bill is added to the invoice for each item. A tax component is added for each item and the bill is totaled, printed, and handed over to the customer, who then pays the bill.

The graphical representation of the steps is as follows:

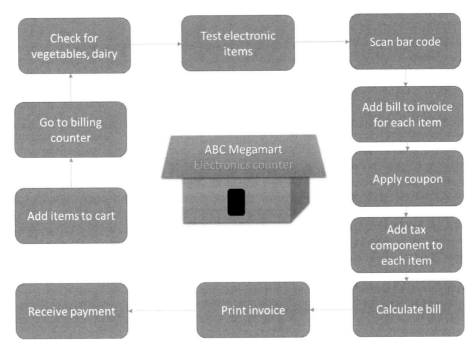

Figure 8.4 – Electronics counter

The following functions will be defined to perform each of these operations:

```
return_cart()
goto_electronics_counter()
review_items()
test_electronics()
scan_bar_code()
add_billing()
apply_coupon()
add_tax()
calc_bill()
print_invoice()
receive_payment()
```

In each of the preceding billing counters, we looked at the sequence of operations that happens for a sale to complete.

With this understanding, let's look at defining each of the operations into methods in the following section.

Defining the sequence of methods

Defining the methods helps us in understanding each of the operations performed at each counter in detail. Let's define the classes and methods required to fulfill the actions to be performed in each operation. We will be covering the following counters in this section:

- The vegetable counter
- Less than 10 items counter
- Greater than 10 items counter
- The electronics counter

Let's begin with the vegetable counter.

The vegetable counter

The following are the steps for the operation of this counter:

1. We will first create the `VegCounter` class as follows:

```
class VegCounter():
```

2. In the following code, we will be defining the `return_cart` method that returns the list of items added to the shopping cart:

```
def return_cart(self,*items):
    cart_items = list(items)
    return cart_items
```

3. Let's now return the name of the counter to be included in the bill. For this example, the counter name is `Vegetables & Dairy`:

```
def goto_vege_counter(self):
    return 'Vegetables & Dairy'
```

4. In the following code, let's define the method to weigh the items in the cart and return a dictionary of items and their corresponding weights:

```
def weigh_items(self,*weights,cart_items = None):
    weight = list(weights)
    item_weight = dict(zip(cart_items, weight))
    return item_weight
```

5. Next, let's define a method to take the unit price and weights as input and calculate the price of each item by multiplying the weights and unit price:

```
def add_price_tag(self,*units,weights = None):
    pricetag = []
    for item,price in zip(weights.
items(),list(units)):
        pricetag.append(item[1]*price)
    return pricetag
```

6. In the following method, let's input bar codes to each of the items in the cart and return the bar codes as a list:

```
def scan_bar_code(self,*scan):
    codes = list(scan)
    return codes
```

7. Next, let's add a method to add price tags to the bar codes by creating a dictionary object and adding the codes and their corresponding price tags as key-value pairs:

```
def add_billing(self,codes=None,pricetag=None):
    self.codes = codes
    self.pricetag = pricetag
    bill = dict(zip(self.codes, self.pricetag))
    return bill
```

8. Then, let's add tax percentages for each of the items and return the tax values as a list:

```
def add_tax(self,*tax):
    taxed = list(tax)
    return taxed
```

9. Let's further use the price tags and the tax values and calculate the bill for each of the items in the cart, and create a dictionary to add the items and their corresponding billing amount:

```
def calc_bill(self,bill,taxes,cart_items):
    items = []
    calc_bill = []
    for item,tax in zip(bill.items(),taxes):
        items.append(item[1])
        calc_bill.append(item[1] + item[1]*tax)
```

```
        finalbill = dict(zip(cart_items, calc_bill))
        return finalbill
```

10. In the following method, let's print the invoice with the counter name, items in the cart, price, and the total bill amount:

```
    def print_invoice(self,finalbill):
        final_total = sum(finalbill.values())
        print('**************ABC
Megamart*****************')
        print('***********------------------
**************')
        print('Counter Name: ', self.goto_vege_counter())
        for item,price in finalbill.items():
            print(item,": ", price)
        print('Total:',final_total)
        print('***********------------------
**************')
```

11. Then, let's print the invoice with a statement stating that the invoice is paid:

```
    def receive_payment(self,finalbill):
        final_total = sum(finalbill.values())
        print('**************ABC
Megamart*****************')
        print('***********------------------
**************')
        print('Counter Name: ', self.goto_vege_counter())
        for item,price in finalbill.items():
            print(item,": ", price)
        print('Total:',final_total)
        print('***********------------------
**************')
        print('**************P
AID***********************')
```

12. Executing the preceding code results in the following. The methods are called in a sequence so that the results from one method are provided as input to the next step:

```
veg = VegCounter()
cart = veg.return_
```

```
cart('onions','tomatoes','carrots','lettuce')
item_weight = veg.weigh_items(1,2,1.5,2.5,cart_items =
cart)
pricetag = veg.add_price_tag(7,2,3,5,weights = item_
weight)
codes = veg.scan_bar_code(113323,3434332,2131243,2332783)
bill = veg.add_billing(codes,pricetag)
taxes = veg.add_tax(0.04,0.03,0.035,0.025)
finalbill = veg.calc_bill(bill,taxes,cart)
veg.print_invoice(finalbill)
```

The output of the printed invoice looks as follows:

```
**************ABC Megamart*****************
**********-------------------**************
Counter Name:  Vegetables & Dairy
onions :  7.28
tomatoes :  4.12
carrots :  4.6575
lettuce :  12.8125
Total: 28.87
**********-------------------**************
```

13. Next, let's print the invoice that has been paid by the customer, `veg.receive_payment(finalbill)`.

    The output of the paid invoice looks as follows:

```
**************ABC Megamart*****************
**********-------------------**************
Counter Name:  Vegetables & Dairy
onions :  7.28
tomatoes :  4.12
carrots :  4.6575
lettuce :  12.8125
Total: 28.87
**********-------------------**************
**************PAID*********************
```

Less than 10 items counter

Similar to the class defined for the vegetable counter, we can also define the methods for the remaining three counters. The detailed code for the remaining counters is available at `https://github.com/PacktPublishing/Metaprogramming-with-Python/tree/main/Chapter08`.

For the code for this counter, let's create the `LessThan10Counter` class and add all of its methods, which includes `return_cart`, `goto_less_t10_counter`, `review_items`, `count_items`, `scan_bar_code`, `add_billing`, `add_tax`, `calc_bill`, `print_invoice`, and `receive_payment`. For simplicity, let's look at the additional methods that we have in each counter instead of repeating all of the methods:

1. Let's start by creating the `LessThan10Counter` class:

    ```
    class LessThan10Counter():
        ...
    ```

2. In this class, we have a `goto_less_t10_counter` method, which returns the name of the counter:

    ```
    def goto_less_t10_counter(self):
        return 'Less than 10 counter'
    ```

3. We also have the following method to review the items in the cart to make sure that they are not electronic, vegetable, fruit, or dairy products:

    ```
    def review_items(self,item_type = None):
        veg_cart = ['Vegetables', 'Dairy', 'Fruits']
        if (item_type == 'Electronics'):
            print("Move to Electronics Counter")
        elif (item_type in veg_cart):
            print("Move to Vege Counter")
    ```

4. In the following method, let's count the items to make sure that the total number of items in the cart is less than `10`:

    ```
    def count_items(self,cart_items = None):
        if len(cart_items)<=10:
            print("Move to Less than 10 items counter")
        else:
    ```

```
                 print("Move to Greater than 10 items
    counter")
        ...
```

5. Executing all of the methods for this class in a sequence results in the following:

```
less10 = LessThan10Counter()
cart = less10.return_cart('paperclips','blue
pens','stapler','pencils')
less10.review_items(item_type = ['stationary'])
less10.count_items(cart)
codes = less10.scan_bar_code(113323,3434332,2131243,23327
83)
bill = less10.add_billing(10,15,12,14,codes = codes)
taxes = less10.add_tax(0.04,0.03,0.035,0.025)
finalbill = less10.calc_bill(bill,taxes,cart)
less10.print_invoice(finalbill)
less10.receive_payment(finalbill)
```

The output for the paid invoice looks as follows:

```
**************ABC Megamart*****************
**********-----------------***************
Counter Name:  Less than 10 counter
paperclips :  10.4
blue pens :  15.45
stapler :  12.42
pencils :  14.35
Total: 52.620000000000005
**********-----------------***************
**************PAID***********************
```

Greater than 10 items counter

In this section, let's define the class and methods for the counter for greater than 10 items.

For the code here, let's create the GreaterThan10Counter class and add all of its methods, which includes return_cart, goto_greater_t10_counter, review_items, count_items, scan_bar_code, add_billing, add_tax, apply_coupon, calc_bill, print_invoice, and receive_payment. For simplicity, let's look at the additional methods that we have in each counter instead of repeating all of the methods:

1. We will first create the `GreaterThan10Counter` class:

    ```
    class GreaterThan10Counter():
    …
    ```

2. In this class, we have a `goto_greater_t10_counter` method counter that returns the name of the counter:

    ```
    def goto_greater_t10_counter(self):
        return 'Greater than 10 counter'
    …
    ```

3. Next, let's add a method to apply a discount coupon to the items purchased:

    ```
    def apply_coupon(self):
        coupon_discount = 0.1
        return coupon_discount
    …
    ```

4. Executing all of the methods for this class in a sequence results in the following:

    ```
    greater = GreaterThan10Counter()
    cart = greater.return_cart('paper clips','blue
    pens','stapler','pencils','a4paper','a3paper','chart',
                            'sketch pens','canvas','water
    color','acrylic colors')
    greater.review_items(item_type = ['stationary'])
    greater.count_items(cart)
    codes = greater.scan_bar_code(113323,3434332,2131243,2332
    783)
    bill = greater.add_billing(10,15,12,14,codes = codes)
    taxes = greater.add_tax(0.04,0.03,0.035,0.025)
    greater.apply_coupon()
    finalbill = greater.calc_bill(bill,taxes,cart)
    greater.print_invoice(finalbill)
    greater.receive_payment(finalbill)
    ```

    The output for the paid invoice looks as follows:

    ```
    **************ABC Megamart****************
    **********--------------------**********
    Counter Name:  Greater than 10 counter
    ```

```
paper clips :  10.4
blue pens :  15.45
stapler :  12.42
pencils :  14.35
Total: 47.358000000000004
***********------------------*************
***************PAID***********************
```

In this class, we had a different method definition for `goto_greater_t10_counter` and a new `apply_coupon` method.

The electronics counter

In this section, let's define the class and methods for the electronic items counter. In the following code, let's create the `ElectronicsCounter` class and add all of its methods, which includes `return_cart`, `goto_electronics_counter`, `review_items`, `test_electronics`, `scan_bar_code`, `add_billing`, `add_tax`, `apply_coupon`, `calc_bill`, `print_invoice`, and `receive_payment`. For simplicity, let's look at the additional methods that we have in each counter instead of repeating all of the methods:

1. We will first create the class for the electronics counter:

    ```
    class ElectronicsCounter():
        ...
    ```

2. In this class, we have a method to go to the electronics counter that returns the name of the counter:

    ```
    def goto_electronics_counter(self):
        return 'Electronics counter'
    ```

3. Next, let's define a method that provides the status of the electronic goods and checks whether they are working:

    ```
    def test_electronics(self,*status):
        teststatus = list(status)
        return teststatus
    ```

4. Executing all of the methods for this class in a sequence results in the following:

    ```
    electronics = ElectronicsCounter()
    cart = electronics.return_
    cart('television','keyboard','mouse')
    ```

```
electronics.review_items(item_type = ['Electronics'])
electronics.test_electronics('pass','pass','pass')
codes = electronics.scan_bar_code(113323,3434332,2131243)
bill = electronics.add_billing(100,16,14,codes = codes)
taxes = electronics.add_tax(0.04,0.03,0.035)
electronics.apply_coupon()
finalbill = electronics.calc_bill(bill,taxes,cart)
electronics.print_invoice(finalbill)
electronics.receive_payment(finalbill)
```

The output for the paid invoice looks as follows:

```
***************ABC Megamart******************
***********------------------***************
Counter Name:  Greater than 10 counter
television :  104.0
keyboard :  16.48
mouse :  14.49
Total: 134.97
***********------------------***************
***************PAID***************************
```

In this class, we had different method definitions for `goto_electronics_counter` and a new `test_electronics` method.

Having defined the sequences, let's proceed further to look at the common functionalities of each of these counters.

Identifying the common functionalities

In this section, let's look at a graphical representation that shows the list of functions to be performed at each counter and the common functionalities between all four of them as follows. The common functionalities are highlighted in bold font in the following figure:

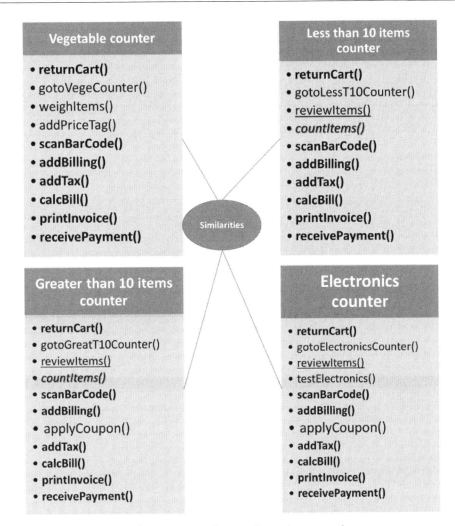

Figure 8.5 – Common operations performed across each counter

From *Figure 8.5*, all the functions highlighted in the bold font are common across all four counters. The review_items function is common across the less than 10 items counter, greater than 10 items counter, and electronics counter. The count_items function is common across the less than 10 items counter and greater than 10 items counter. The apply_coupon function is common across the greater than 10 items counter and the electronics counter. Since there are common functions or operations performed across all of the counters, we can look at creating a common way of designing them, too. This is where we can introduce the concept of templates.

Designing templates

As the name suggests, **templates** define a common template or format in which we can design an algorithmic flow of operations and reuse them when similar kinds of activities are performed. A template is one of the methods of design patterns in Python and can be used effectively while developing frameworks or libraries. Templates emphasize the concept of reusability in programming.

In this section, we will look at creating a class that handles all the common functions of all four counters discussed throughout this chapter, and create a method that handles the template that sequences or pipelines the steps to be executed in all the counters:

1. To begin with, let's create an abstract class named `CommonCounter`, and initialize the class with all the variables that will be used across all four counters. Refer to the following code:

```
from abc import ABC, abstractmethod
class CommonCounter(ABC):
    def __init__(self,items,name,scan,units,tax,item_type
= None, weights = None, status = None):
        self.items = items
        self.name = name
        self.scan = scan
        self.units = units
        self.tax = tax
        self.item_type = item_type
        self.weights = weights
        self.status = status
```

2. Next, we will be defining the `return_cart`, `goto_counter`, and `scan_bar_code` methods to take the input variables that are initialized in the class:

```
    def return_cart(self):
        cart_items = []
        for i in self.items:
            cart_items.append(i)
        return cart_items
    def goto_counter(self):
        countername = self.name
        return countername
    def scan_bar_code(self):
        codes = []
        for i in self.scan:
```

```
        codes.append(i)
    return codes
```

3. Then, we will be defining the add_billing, add_tax, and calc_bill methods to take the input variables that are initialized in the class:

```
def add_billing(self):
    self.codes = self.scan_bar_code()
    pricetag = []
    for i in self.units:
        pricetag.append(i)
    bill = dict(zip(self.codes, pricetag))
    return bill
def add_tax(self):
    taxed = []
    for i in self.tax:
        taxed.append(i)
    return taxed
def calc_bill(self):
    bill = self.add_billing()
    items = []
    cart_items = self.return_cart()
    calc_bill = []
    taxes = self.add_tax()
    for item,tax in zip(bill.items(),taxes):
        items.append(item[1])
        calc_bill.append(item[1] + item[1]*tax)
    finalbill = dict(zip(cart_items, calc_bill))
    return finalbill
```

4. For simplicity, we will not be defining the print invoice method, and instead, will define the receive_payment method, which contains the definition of the print invoice method as well within the following code:

```
def receive_payment(self):
    finalbill = self.calc_bill()
    final_total = sum(finalbill.values())
    print('*************ABC
Megamart****************')
```

```
        print('**********-------------------
**************')
        print('Counter Name: ', self.goto_counter())
        for item,price in finalbill.items():
            print(item,": ", price)
        print('Total:',final_total)
        print('**********-------------------
**************')
        print('***************p
AID***********************')
```

5. Next, we will be defining the `apply_coupon` method, which returns a 0 value. This method can be redefined in the child classes if required:

```
def apply_coupon(self):
        return 0
```

6. In the preceding code snippets, we defined all the methods that are common across all four counters, whereas in the following code, we will be defining methods without statements so that they can be redefined within the child classes as and when required:

```
def weigh_items(self):
        pass
def add_price_tag(self):
        pass
def count_items(self):
        pass
def test_electronics(self):
        pass
```

7. Then, let's create review items as an abstract method that needs to have a definition within the child classes:

```
@abstractmethod
    def review_items(self):
        pass
```

Now, the most important concept of templates is defined in the next code.

1. Let's define a method that handles the sequence of operations of a billing counter, and let's use this method as a template for all the child classes that will be created for each billing counter:

```
def pipeline_template(self):
        self.return_cart()
        self.goto_counter()
        self.review_items()
        self.count_items()
        self.test_electronics()
        self.weigh_items()
        self.add_price_tag()
        self.scan_bar_code()
        self.add_billing()
        self.add_tax()
        self.apply_coupon()
        self.calc_bill()
        self.receive_payment()
```

2. We have defined the common class for all counters along with its template method, which can be reused for each individual billing counter.

3. In the following code, we will create a child class for VegeCounter, with CommonCounter as a parent class:

```
class VegeCounter(CommonCounter):
    def review_items(self):
        if ('Vegetables' in self.item_type):
            print("Move to Vege Counter")
        if ('Dairy' in self.item_type):
            print("Move to Vege Counter")
        if ('Fruits' in self.item_type):
            print("Move to Vege Counter")
    def weigh_items(self):
        item_weight = dict(zip(self.items, self.weights))
        return item_weight
    def add_price_tag(self):
        pricetag = []
        item_weight = self.weigh_items()
```

```
            for item,price in zip(item_weight.items(),self.
    units):
                pricetag.append(item[1]*price)
            return pricetag
```

4. In the preceding code, we have defined the `review_items` abstract method and we have also added statements in the definition of the `weight_items` and `add_price_tag` methods.

5. Similarly, in the following code, let's create a child class for `ElectronicsCounter` and define `review_items` (which is an abstract method), followed by redefining `test_electronics` (which did not have a definition in the `CommonCounter` base class):

```
class ElectronicsCounter(CommonCounter):
    def review_items(self):
        if ('Electronics' in self.item_type):
            print("Move to Electronics Counter")
    def test_electronics(self):
        teststatus = []
        for i in self.status:
            teststatus.append(i)
        return teststatus
```

6. Let's now create a function to run the `pipeline_template` method for each of its child classes:

```
def run_pipeline(counter = CommonCounter):
    counter.pipeline_template()
```

7. Executing the `run_pipeline` method for each of the child classes results in the sequence of steps executed according to each billing counter. Let's execute the `pipeline` method for the vegetable counter:

```
run_pipeline(VegeCounter(items = ['onions', 'lettuce',
'apples', 'oranges'],
                        name = ['Vegetable Counter'],
                        scan = [113323,3434332,2131243,2
332783],
                        units = [10,15,12,14],
                        tax = [0.04,0.03,0.035,0.025],
                        item_type = ['Vegetables'],
                        weights = [1,2,1.5,2.5]))
```

The output after running the pipeline for `VegeCounter` is as follows:

```
Move to Vege Counter
**************ABC Megamart*****************
**********-------------------**************
Counter Name:  ['Vegetable Counter']
paperclips :  10.4
blue pens :  15.45
stapler :  12.42
pencils :  14.35
Total: 52.620000000000005
**********-------------------**************
***************PAID**********************
```

8. Let's now execute the `pipeline` method for `ElectronicsCounter`:

```
run_pipeline(ElectronicsCounter(items =
['television','keyboard','mouse'],
                                name = ['Electronics
Counter'],
                                scan =
[113323,3434332,2131243],
                                units = [100,16,14],
                                tax = [0.04,0.03,0.035],
                                item_type =
['Electronics'],
                                status =
['pass','pass','pass']))
```

The output after running the pipeline for `ElectronicsCounter` is as follows:

```
Move to Electronics Counter
**************ABC Megamart*****************
**********-------------------**************
Counter Name:  ['Electronics Counter']
television :  104.0
keyboard :  16.48
mouse :  14.49
Total: 134.97
**********-------------------**************
***************PAID**********************
```

In this section, we have created a template, but we have not repeated the same methods in multiple class definitions. The same CommonCounter abstract class can be reused for the definitions of the less than 10 items counter and the greater than 10 items counter as well. We learned how to create a template and implement template programming that emphasizes reusability in Python application development. We created a template that covers all the common functionalities across multiple sets of operations and reused the template multiple times.

Summary

In this chapter, we have learned the concepts of defining methods for a sequence of operations that follows an algorithm. We also defined classes that follow a sequence of operations from our core example. We created an abstract class that defines all the common functionalities of our core example, and we applied the templates design pattern to understand the concept of templates using the sequences from our core example.

Similar to other chapters covered in this book, this chapter also covered templates, which is a design pattern applied in metaprogramming to change the behavior of Python objects externally.

In the next chapter, we will be looking at the concept of abstract syntax trees with some interesting examples.

Part 3: Deep Dive – Building Blocks of Metaprogramming II

This section is a continuation of *Part 2*. The objective of this section is to give you a deeper understanding of the concepts of metaprogramming by looking at much more advanced building blocks, such as abstract syntax trees and MRO, among others, in detail, along with examples of how they can be applied in a practical scenario. This section will have chapters that provide an explanation of the concepts with an implementation-based approach to give hands-on experience along with guided coding knowledge to users while reading this book. The chapters in this section can be read sequentially or independently.

This part contains the following chapters:

- *Chapter 9, Understanding Code through Abstract Syntax Trees*
- *Chapter 10, Understanding Method Resolution Order of Inheritance*
- *Chapter 11, Creating Dynamic Objects*
- *Chapter 12, Applying GOF Design Patterns – Part 1*
- *Chapter 13, Applying GOF Design Patterns – Part 2*
- *Chapter 14, Code Generation*
- *Chapter 15, Development of an End-to-End Case Study-Based Application*
- *Chapter 16, Following Best Practices*

9

Understanding Code through Abstract Syntax Tree

In this chapter, we will look at what abstract syntax trees are and how to understand the syntax tree of each unit of the Python code we write.

Any programming language is designed with its own syntax, which is used by developers while coding in the language following specific syntax. The interpreter or compiler of a programming language interprets the syntax of the language and compiles or interprets the code and executes it to achieve the desired result.

In Python, an **abstract syntax tree** (**AST**) provides an abstract representation of the syntax of the code in the form of a tree. Python has a library named `ast` that can be used to understand the abstract syntax of the code that we develop.

Throughout this chapter, we will look at understanding the syntax tree of some of the important code snippets that we developed in previous chapters, and we will also look at modifying or adding more information to the code through a few examples. We will be making use of abstract syntax trees throughout this chapter to perform an analysis of the code.

In this chapter, we will be taking a look at the following main topics:

- Exploring the `ast` library
- Inspecting Python code with abstract syntax trees
- Understanding abstract syntax trees with applications

By the end of this chapter, you should be able to understand the abstract syntax tree of Python code. You should also be able to inspect, parse, and modify the abstract syntax tree of source code through metaprogramming.

Technical requirements

The code examples shared in this chapter are available on GitHub under the code for this chapter here: `https://github.com/PacktPublishing/Metaprogramming-with-Python/tree/main/Chapter9`.

Exploring the ast library

In this section, we will explore the `ast` Python library, which can be imported from Python 3 to analyze the Python code written by developers. We can also use it to modify the code through its abstract syntax tree at a metaprogramming level rather than modifying the syntax of the code itself. This helps in understanding how the code is syntactically represented and how the syntax tree of the code can be used to modify its behavior without modifying the original source code. We will look at some of the important functions of the `ast` library, as those functions will be used throughout this chapter to understand the code from our core example.

Let's start by importing the `ast` library:

```
import ast
```

Once we import the library, we can look at analyzing a piece of code using this library. We will now create a variable named `assignment` and assign a string format of the code to it:

```
assignment = "product_name = 'Iphone X'"
```

The output of the `assignment` variable appears as follows:

```
assignment
```

```
"product_name = 'Iphone X'"
```

The preceding code can be parsed into its corresponding nodes using the `parse` method of the `ast` library. We will now create a variable named `assign_tree` and store the parsed node of the lines of code stored under `assignment`:

```
assign_tree = ast.parse(assignment)
assign_tree
```

The output of the parsed node looks as follows:

```
<ast.Module at 0x1b92b3f6520>
```

Now, we can make use of another method called dump to print the tree structure of the node with each of its values and fields. This helps in debugging the code:

```
print(ast.dump(assign_tree,indent = 4))
```

The output of the code is as follows:

```
Module(
    body=[
        Assign(
            targets=[
                Name(id='productName', ctx=Store())],
            value=Constant(value='Iphone X'))],
    type_ignores=[])
```

Figure 9.1 – Example of an abstract syntax tree

The "product_name = 'Iphone X'" code is broken down into multiple parts. The syntax of any code in Python is grammatically embedded into Module followed by body. We have assigned the Iphone X value to the product_name variable and so the code that performs a value assignment is identified by the Assign branch, which has attributes mapped with the corresponding ID, context, and value. This is an example of what a simple representation of a node would look like. For multiple lines of code with various other operations, the node will have multiple other branches in the tree.

Let's start inspecting the Python code for a few examples of using abstract syntax trees in the following section.

Inspecting Python code with abstract syntax trees

In this section, we will review and understand the code for a simple arithmetic addition example, and we will also further look into parsing the code and modifying it using abstract syntax trees.

Reviewing simple code using ast

In this section, let's review simple code that adds two numbers, and let's look at all the elements of the node, and also how the elements are organized in the tree. Let's begin by writing code to assign two variables, a and b, with numerical values, and c as the sum of a and b. Finally, let's print the c value. This is shown in the following code:

```
addfunc = """
a = 1098
b = 2032
c = a + b
print(c)
```

```
"""
```

We will now parse the preceding addfunc and store the node in another variable called add_tree:

```
add_tree = ast.parse(addfunc)
add_tree
```

The output of the parsed node is as follows:

```
<ast.Module at 0x19c9b2bf2e0>
```

The base element of the node is Module, and all the other lines of code are split into semantics that are stored within the module of the node.

Let's look at the detailed tree representation in the following code by calling the dump method on the tree:

```
print(ast.dump(add_tree, indent=4))
```

The tree begins with Module as its base element, or the trunk followed by multiple branches. Module is followed by body as a list item that lists down all other elements of the code.

Within body, there will be four list items that describe the operations of addfunc. The first one, which is also the first line of addfunc, is to assign the Constant value 1098 to a variable with a name whose id is a and the context of the value is Store since we are storing the value in the variable. Here is how it appears:

```
Module(
    body=[
        Assign(
            targets=[
                Name(id='a', ctx=Store())],
            value=Constant(value=1098)),
```

Figure 9.2 – Code snippet output

Similarly, the second line of addfunc is to store the 2032 value in the b variable, which is represented grammatically in the following list item:

```
Assign(
    targets=[
        Name(id='b', ctx=Store())],
    value=Constant(value=2032)),
```

Figure 9.3 – Code snippet output

The third line of code in addfunc has the arithmetic operation of adding the two values stored in a and b:

```
Assign(
    targets=[
        Name(id='c', ctx=Store())],
    value=BinOp(
        left=Name(id='a', ctx=Load()),
        op=Add(),
        right=Name(id='b', ctx=Load()))),
```

Figure 9.4 – Code snippet output

The preceding code has an additional element, BinOp, followed by left, op, and right variables to indicate the left numerical value, addition operation, and right numerical value, respectively.

The last line of the code in addfunc is the Expr expression element, which represents the printing of the c variable with a context value of Load:

```
Expr(
    value=Call(
        func=Name(id='print', ctx=Load()),
        args=[
            Name(id='c', ctx=Load())],
        keywords=[]))],
type_ignores=[])
```

Figure 9.5 – Code snippet output

To execute `addfunc`, we need to first compile the parsed tree as follows:

```
add_code = compile(add_tree, 'add_tree', 'exec')
```

Post-compilation, we should be able to execute the compiled tree, which results in the addition of `a` and `b`:

```
exec(add_code)
```

The following is the output of the code:

```
3130
```

In this section, we reviewed the abstract syntax tree of the simple arithmetic `add` function. In the following section, let's look at modifying the code of the `add` function using metaprogramming.

Modifying simple code using ast

In this section, let's consider the example of `addfunc` from the preceding section and look at how to modify the code in the example through metaprogramming, without modifying the actual code. The operation performed by the code in `addfunc` is arithmetic addition. What if we want to perform arithmetic multiplication instead of addition and we don't want the actual code to be modified? What if there are multiple locations where we want arithmetic addition to be replaced by arithmetic multiplication, and browsing through thousands of lines of code and modifying them is not a feasible option as it might impact or break something else in the code? In such scenarios, we can modify the node of the code using its syntax tree instead of modifying the actual code itself. To achieve this, let's make use of the abstract syntax tree of the code.

Let's reuse the `add_tree` parsed tree variable from the code in the preceding section:

```
add_tree
<ast.Module at 0x19c9b2bf2e0>
```

To understand which fields to modify, let's look at the following representation of the node and look at each section of the node marked by an identifier. The elements of interest for this example are represented inside a box in the following figure:

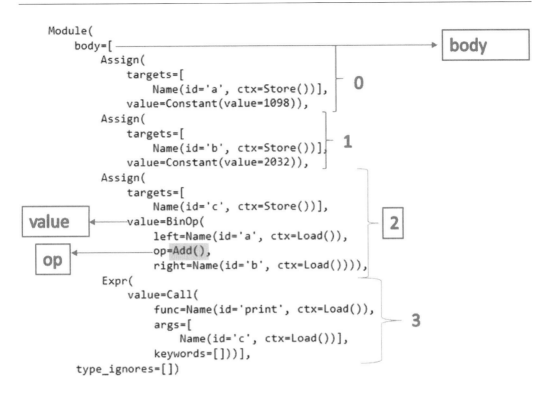

Figure 9.6 – Parsed node of addfunc

To modify the add operation into a multiplication operation, the tree for this node traverses through `body` followed by its list item 2, followed by the `value` field of the item, followed by the `op` field. The `Add()` operation of the `op` field will have to be modified into a multiplication operation to achieve our goal for this section. Here's how:

```
add_tree.body[2].value.op=ast.Mult()
```

Executing the preceding code results in a change of the tree:

```
print(ast.dump(add_tree, indent=4))
```

The figure of the updated tree structure is represented as follows, with the Add() operation replaced by the Mult() operation:

```
Module(
    body=[
        Assign(
            targets=[
                Name(id='a', ctx=Store())],
            value=Constant(value=1098)),
        Assign(
            targets=[
                Name(id='b', ctx=Store())],
            value=Constant(value=2032)),
        Assign(
            targets=[
                Name(id='c', ctx=Store())],
            value=BinOp(
                left=Name(id='a', ctx=Load()),
                op=Mult(),
                right=Name(id='b', ctx=Load())))),
        Expr(
            value=Call(
                func=Name(id='print', ctx=Load()),
                args=[
                    Name(id='c', ctx=Load())],
                keywords=[]))],
    type_ignores=[])
```

Modified using metaprogramming

Figure 9.7 – Tree modified to perform multiplication

To verify whether the preceding modification on the tree node works, let's compile the tree and execute it to check the results:

```
add_code = compile(add_tree, 'add_tree', 'exec')
exec(add_code)
```

Executing the preceding code should have ideally provided an output of 3130, which is the addition of two numbers, 1098 and 2032. But we have modified ast to perform multiplication instead and so it would result in the value, which is a product of the two numbers:

```
2231136
```

Thus the tree is now modified and can be compiled to achieve the desired result without modifying the actual code.

With this understanding, let's proceed further to look at how to parse and understand the classes in Python.

Understanding abstract syntax trees with applications

In this section, we will look into applying the concept of abstract syntax trees to our core example of *ABC Megamart* and explore how `ast` is defined in the classes, such as the `Branch` class and the `VegCounter` class of *ABC Megamart*. We will also look at modifying the behavior of these classes using `ast` at a metaprogramming level instead of modifying the actual source code of the class.

Understanding the ast of a class

In this section, we will look at understanding the abstract syntax tree of a class, which will help us in exploring how to modify the elements of a class through metaprogramming. We can try it as follows:

1. Let's begin by creating a class with empty definitions and look at its abstract syntax tree:

```
branch_code = """
class Branch:
    '''attributes...'''
    '''methods...'''
"""
```

2. Next, let's parse the code:

```
branch_tree = ast.parse(branch_code)
branch_tree
<ast.Module at 0x216ed8b5850>
```

3. Let's further look at the elements of the node and understand how the class is grammatically defined:

```
print(ast.dump(branch_tree, indent=4))
```

The structure of the node is as follows:

```
Module(
    body=[
        ClassDef(
            name='Branch',
            bases=[],
            keywords=[],
            body=[
                Expr(
                    value=Constant(value='attributes...')),
                Expr(
                    value=Constant(value='methods...'))],
            decorator_list=[])],
    type_ignores=[])
```

Figure 9.8 – Code snippet output

In the preceding output, we have `Module` followed by `body`, with `ClassDef` within the body element. This `ClassDef` has a `name` element followed by two expressions.

4. Let's redefine this empty class definition with an attribute and a method along with a decorator and recheck the structure of the node:

```
branch_code = """class Branch:
    branch_id = 1001
    @staticmethod
    def get_product(self):
        return 'product'
    """
```

5. We will now parse `branch_code` in the following step:

```
branch_tree = ast.parse(branch_code)
print(ast.dump(branch_tree, indent=4))
```

The structure of the `Branch` class in the form of an abstract syntax tree is as follows. We can see that the node starts with the `Module` element followed by `body`.

Within `body`, we have a `ClassDef` element that contains the class name followed by its attributes, which include `branch_id` stored as a constant value followed by the `get_product` method with its arguments. Refer to the following output:

```
Module(
    body=[
        ClassDef(
            name='Branch',
            bases=[],
            keywords=[],
            body=[
                Assign(
                    targets=[
                        Name(id='branchID', ctx=Store())],
                    value=Constant(value=1001)),
                FunctionDef(
                    name='getProduct',
                    args=arguments(
                        posonlyargs=[],
                        args=[
                            arg(arg='self')],
                        kwonlyargs=[],
                        kw_defaults=[],
                        defaults=[]),
                    body=[
                        Return(
                            value=Constant(value='product'))],
```

Figure 9.9 – Code snippet output

6. We also have a `decorator` method loaded under `decorator_list` as follows:

```
decorator_list=[
        Name(id='staticmethod', ctx=Load())])],
    decorator_list=[])],
type_ignores=[])
```

Figure 9.10 – Code snippet output

7. If we create an object for the class, the code for the object can also be parsed similarly to the preceding class example:

```
branch_code = """
branch_albany = Branch()
"""
branch_tree = ast.parse(branch_code)
print(ast.dump(branch_tree, indent=4))
```

8. The node of the object will have the following structure:

```
Module(
    body=[
        Assign(
            targets=[
                Name(id='branchAlbany', ctx=Store())],
            value=Call(
                func=Name(id='Branch', ctx=Load()),
                args=[],
                keywords=[]))],
    type_ignores=[])
```

Figure 9.11 Code snippet output

In this section, we reviewed the abstract syntax tree of a class to understand the various elements of its syntax. With this understanding, let's look further into modifying the abstract syntax tree of a class from our core example, *ABC Megamart*.

Modifying the ast of a code block by parsing

In this section, let's look at how to modify the attributes in the code of a class by using its abstract syntax tree instead of modifying the actual class itself.

Let's consider having developed a robust library with multiple classes and methods. A robust library definition may be too big to be disturbed or modified. Instead of modifying the source code, we can make changes to some specific attributes in the library without impacting the actual code, through metaprogramming. In such a scenario, modifying `ast` of the library would be a better way of making changes rather than impacting the source code of the library.

In this example, we will be following these steps:

9. We will be creating a `vegCounter` class and adding a `return_cart` method to return the items within the cart. We will also be creating an object for the class and calling the `return_cart` method on the object. Refer to the following code:

```
vegctr = """
class VegCounter():
    def return_cart(self,*items):
        cart_items = list(items)
        return cart_items
veg = VegCounter()
print(veg.return_
cart('onions','tomatoes','carrots','lettuce'))
"""
```

10. Next, let's parse the code for `vegCounter` and look at the structure of the node:

```
vegctr_tree = ast.parse(vegctr)
print(ast.dump(vegctr_tree, indent=4))
```

The output of the node is as follows. There is a class definition followed by a function definition in `ast`:

```
Module(
  body=[
    ClassDef(
      name='VegCounter',
      bases=[],
      keywords=[],
      body=[
        FunctionDef(
          name='returnCart',
          args=arguments(
            posonlyargs=[],
            args=[
              arg(arg='self')],
            vararg=arg(arg='items'),
            kwonlyargs=[],
            kw_defaults=[],
            defaults=[]),
```

Figure 9.12 – Code snippet output

11. The following output has the elements for the list item and the logic that reads items to the list:

```
body=[
  Assign(
    targets=[
      Name(id='cartItems', ctx=Store())],
    value=List(elts=[], ctx=Load())),
  For(
    target=Name(id='i', ctx=Store()),
    iter=Name(id='items', ctx=Load()),
    body=[
      Expr(
        value=Call(
          func=Attribute(
            value=Name(id='cartItems', ctx=Load()),
            attr='append',
            ctx=Load()),
          args=[
            Name(id='i', ctx=Load())],
          keywords=[]))],
    orelse=[]),
  Return(
    value=Name(id='cartItems', ctx=Load()))],
    decorator_list=[])],
  decorator_list=[]),
```

Figure 9.13 – Code snippet output

12. The following output has the syntax for creating the object for the VegCounter class:

```
Assign(
  targets=[
    Name(id='veg', ctx=Store())],
  value=Call(
    func=Name(id='VegCounter', ctx=Load()),
    args=[],
    keywords=[])),
```

Figure 9.14 – Code snippet output

13. The following output displays the elements that print the cart items by calling the `return_cart` method on a list of cart items:

```
Expr(
  value=Call(
    func=Name(id='print', ctx=Load()),
    args=[
      Call(
        func=Attribute(
          value=Name(id='veg', ctx=Load()),
          attr='returnCart',
          ctx=Load()),
        args=[
          Constant(value='onions'),
          Constant(value='potatoes'),
          Constant(value='carrots'),
          Constant(value='lettuce')],
        keywords=[])],
    keywords=[]))],
  type_ignores=[])
```

Figure 9.15 – Code snippet output

14. Let's now compile the abstract syntax tree and execute it to display the list of items added to the cart:

```
vegctr_code = compile(vegctr_tree, 'vegctr_tree', 'exec')
exec(vegctr_code)
['onions', 'tomatoes', 'carrots', 'lettuce']
```

15. Next, let's navigate through the values in the cart items and look at the path of the second value in the `return_cart` method output:

```
vegctr_tree.body[2].value.args[0].args[1].n
'tomatoes'
```

16. Let's now change the second value of the cart item from tomatoes to potatoes by parsing through the node elements hierarchically:

```
vegctr_tree.body[2].value.args[0].args[1].n = 'potatoes'
print(ast.dump(vegctr_tree, indent=4))
```

17. In the following output, let's look at the updated value for the second item in the cart, which is modified without changing the source code:

```
Expr(
    value=Call(
        func=Name(id='print', ctx=Load()),
        args=[
            Call(
                func=Attribute(
                    value=Name(id='veg', ctx=Load()),
                    attr='returnCart',
                    ctx=Load()),
                args=[
                    Constant(value='onions'),
                    Constant(value='potatoes'),
                    Constant(value='carrots'),
                    Constant(value='lettuce')],
                keywords=[])],
            keywords=[]))],
    type_ignores=[])
```

Figure 9.16 – Modifying value within ast

18. We can now unparse the node using the unparse method in the ast library as follows:

```
print(ast.unparse(vegctr_tree))
```

19. The modified source code now looks as follows:

```
class VegCounter:
    def return_cart(self, *items):
        cart_items = list(items)
        return cart_items
veg = VegCounter()
print(veg.return_cart('onions', 'potatoes', 'carrots',
'lettuce'))
```

This is one approach to modifying the Python source code using an abstract syntax tree.

With this understanding, let's proceed with the next approach, where we will be transforming the nodes of the abstract syntax tree.

Modifying the ast of a code block by transforming nodes

In this section, we will look at another approach to modifying the source code of a class by modifying the abstract syntax tree instead of changing the actual code:

1. Let's now create the `VegCounter` class as follows:

```
class VegCounter():
    def return_cart(self,*items):
        cart_items = []
        for i in items:
            cart_items.append(i)
        return cart_items
veg = VegCounter()
```

2. Next, let's create a variable named `cart` and add the function call on the object as a string:

```
cart = """veg.return_
cart('onions','tomatoes','carrots','lettuce')"""
cart_tree = ast.parse(cart)
print(ast.dump(cart_tree, indent = 4))
```

3. Parsing the preceding code provides the following output:

```
Module(
    body=[
        Expr(
            value=Call(
                func=Attribute(
                    value=Name(id='veg', ctx=Load()),
                    attr='returnCart',
                    ctx=Load()),
                args=[
                    Constant(value='onions'),
                    Constant(value='tomatoes'),
                    Constant(value='carrots'),
                    Constant(value='lettuce')],
                keywords=[]))],
    type_ignores=[])
```

Figure 9.17 – AST of the object variable

In this section, instead of traversing through the structure of the node, we will be using `NodeTransformer` from the `ast` library to perform code transformation:

```
from ast import NodeTransformer
```

4.   The attributes of `NodeTransformer` are as follows:

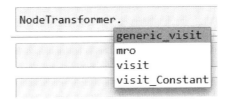

Figure 9.18 – Attributes of NodeTransformer

5.   Next, let's create a class named `ModifyVegCounter` inherited from the `NodeTransfomer` class. We will be redefining the `visit_Constant` method to modify the constant values of the cart items by adding a string prefix whenever the constant value occurs in the code:

```
class ModifyVegCounter(NodeTransformer):
    def visit_Constant(self, node):
        modifiedValue = ast.Constant('item:' + str(node.
value))
        return modifiedValue
```

6.   We can make use of the `visit` method to visit the node and use the `dump` method to print the tree:

```
ModifyVegCounter().visit(cart_tree)
print(ast.dump(cart_tree, indent = 4))
```

The transformed node looks as follows:

```
Module(
    body=[
        Expr(
            value=Call(
                func=Attribute(
                    value=Name(id='veg', ctx=Load()),
                    attr='returnCart',
                    ctx=Load()),
                args=[
                    Constant(value='item:onions'),
                    Constant(value='item:tomatoes'),
                    Constant(value='item:carrots'),
                    Constant(value='item:lettuce')],
                keywords=[]))],
    type_ignores=[])
```

Figure 9.19 – Source code transformed with NodeTransformer

7. We can further unparse the code using the `ast` library's `unparse` method:

```
print(ast.unparse(cart_tree))
```

The output of the code is represented as follows:

```
veg.return_cart('item:onions', 'item:tomatoes',
'item:carrots', 'item:lettuce')
```

This is another example of how an abstract syntax tree can be used in metaprogramming.

In this section, we covered the approach of transforming the nodes of an abstract syntax tree using the `NodeTransformer` method of the `ast` library.

Summary

In this chapter, we have learned about the concept of the abstract syntax tree by exploring the `ast` library in Python 3. We also inspected Python code using abstract syntax trees. We understood the applications of abstract syntax trees by modifying the code at the node level using source code from our core example.

Similar to other chapters in this book, this chapter covered the concept of abstract syntax trees in metaprogramming. This also helps in understanding how to modify the behavior of Python objects externally without modifying the source code. Modifying the abstract syntax tree instead of the actual methods and attributes in the code helps migrate source code from different versions of Python or the application development platform conveniently without impacting the actual logic of the code.

In the next chapter, we will be looking at the concept of **method resolution order** with some other interesting examples.

10
Understanding Method Resolution Order of Inheritance

In this chapter, we will look at the concept of **method resolution order** (**MRO**) in Python 3 and how it works on inheritance.

As the name suggests, MRO is the order in which methods of a class get resolved while calling them in a program.

Throughout this chapter, we will look at understanding the MRO through a few examples, how method resolution can go wrong, and how the current Python 3 implementation handles methods defined in a class. We will be making use of MRO throughout this chapter to understand the behavior of code while inheritance is implemented in Python 3.

Why should we understand MRO? In scenarios where we are using multiple classes in Python code, we need to inherit methods from multiple parent classes or superclasses. Understanding the order in which the methods would get resolved from the existing class to its parent class helps in avoiding incorrect method calls. This in turn helps in avoiding incorrect results in the algorithm of Python code.

In this chapter, we will be taking a look at the following main topics:

- Understanding the MRO of a class
- Understanding the impact of modifying the order of inheritance
- Impact of unintended change of order in inheritance

By the end of this chapter, you should be able to get an understanding of how methods are resolved in Python class hierarchy, understand how methods are processed in multiple inheritances, and write the methods on your own with the knowledge of how they would get resolved.

Technical requirements

The code examples shared in this chapter are available on GitHub under the code for this chapter here: `https://github.com/PacktPublishing/Metaprogramming-with-Python/tree/main/Chapter10`.

Understanding the MRO of a class

In this section, let's explore how methods are resolved in a class that has no inheritance specified within its code. A class by default in Python 3 is inherited by `object`. To understand how MRO works on a class that has no parent class, looking at it in its simplest form is the easiest approach. We will then see how MRO works on a class with single, multiple, and multilevel inheritance.

In this example, let's create a class for a branch of *ABC Megamart* as follows:

1. In the `Branch` class, let's create attributes for branch ID, street, city, state and ZIP code, product, sales, and invoice. Let's also create methods such as `get_product` (which returns the product), `get_sales` (which returns sales), and `get_invoice` (which returns the invoice). The following code represents the `Branch` class:

    ```
    class Branch:
        def __init__(self, branch_id, branch_street,
                        branch_city, branch_state,
                        branch_zip, product, sales, invoice):
            self.branch_id = branch_id
            self.branch_street = branch_street
            self.branch_city = branch_city
            self.branch_state = branch_state
            self.branch_zip = branch_zip
            self.product = product
            self.sales = sales
            self.invoice = invoice
        def get_product(self):
            return self.product
        def get_sales(self):
            return self.sales
        def get_invoice(self):
            return self.invoice
    ```

There are five attributes and three methods in the preceding class. The MRO for the preceding class can be reviewed by calling a built-in method on the class, known as mro.

2. Next, let's call the mro method of the Branch class:

```
Branch.mro()
```

The mro of the Branch class is represented as follows:

[__main__.Branch, object]

In the preceding output, we can see that the Branch class did not have any explicit definition of a superclass or parent class, and so it is, by default, inherited from the object.

In this section, we understood the concept of MRO along with an example of how to look at the MRO of a class. Now, let's look further to see how MRO works on a class that has a single parent class or superclass.

Understanding MRO in single inheritance

When a class inherits one parent class or superclass, it is single inheritance. Let's look at how methods are resolved in the case of the Branch class example when it becomes a parent class:

1. Before proceeding with the creation of the child class, let's redefine the Branch class with suitable methods that can be used for testing this concept:

```
class Branch:
    def __init__(self, branch, sales, product):
        self.branch = branch
        self.sales = sales
        self.product = product

    def set_branch(self, value):
        self.branch = value

    def set_sales(self, value):
        self.sales = value

    def set_product(self, value):
        self.product = value

    def calc_tax(self):
        branch = self.branch
```

```
        product = self.product
        sales = self.sales
        pricebeforetax = sales['purchase_price'] +
                         sales['purchase_price'] *
                         sales['profit_margin']
        finalselling_price = pricebeforetax +
            (pricebeforetax * sales['tax_rate'])
        sales['selling_price'] = finalselling_price
        return branch, product, sales
```

2. For this example, let's create another class, named NYC, which inherits from the Branch class:

```
class NYC(Branch):
    def __init__(self, intercitybranch):
        self.intercitybranch = intercitybranch

    def set_management(self, value):
        self.intercitybranch = value

    def calc_tax_nyc(self):
        branch = self.branch
        intercitybranch = self.intercitybranch
        product = self.product
        sales = self.sales
        pricebeforetax = sales['purchase_price'] +
                         sales['purchase_price'] *
                         sales['profit_margin']
        finalselling_price = pricebeforetax +
            (pricebeforetax * (sales['tax_rate'] +
                sales['local_rate']))
        sales['selling_price'] = finalselling_price
        return branch, intercitybranch, product,
                sales

NYC.mro()
```

In the preceding code, we have the NYC class inherited from the `Branch` class, and the NYC class has two methods defined. The `set_management` method returns the value stored in `intercitybranch`, and the `calc_tax_nyc` method calculates tax for NYC.

The MRO of the NYC class is represented in the following output:

```
[__main__.NYC, __main__.Branch, object]
```

The methods present in NYC will be resolved first, followed by the methods of `Branch` and then the methods of `object`.

3. Let's look at what happens when a method required by NYC is not present in NYC but instead defined in its parent class. In the NYC class, `calc_tax_nyc` is the method that calculates tax for the NYC branch, and this method needs values for attributes such as `branch`, `intercitybranch`, `product`, and `sales`. The value for the `intercitybranch` attribute alone can be set within the NYC class using the `set_management` method, whereas the remaining attributes, such as `branch`, `product`, and `sales`, do not have a set method in NYC.

4. Let's start by creating a variable named `intercitybranch` and defining an instance for NYC:

```
intercitybranch = {
    }
branch_manhattan = NYC(intercitybranch)
```

5. Let's set the value for `intercitybranch` first, and then look at how to deal with the set methods for the remaining attributes:

```
branch_manhattan.set_management({'regionalManager' :
'John M',
    'branchManager' : 'Tom H',
    'subbranch_id' : '2021-01' })
```

6. The set methods required to set `branch`, `product`, and `sales` are available in the parent class of `Branch`. Since the MRO of the NYC class is to resolve from NYC followed by `Branch` followed by `object`, the set methods of `Branch` can now be called by NYC to set the values for `branch`, `product`, and `sales` as follows:

```
branch = {'branch_id' : 2021,
    'branch_street' : '40097 5th Main Street',
    'branchBorough' : 'Manhattan',
    'branch_city' : 'New York City',
    'branch_state' : 'New York',
    'branch_zip' : 11007}
```

```
product = {'productId' : 100002,
    'productName' : 'WashingMachine',
    'productBrand' : 'Whirlpool'
}

sales = {
    'purchase_price' : 450,
    'profit_margin' : 0.19,
    'tax_rate' : 0.4,
    'local_rate' : 0.055
}
branch_manhattan.set_branch(branch)
branch_manhattan.set_product(product)
branch_manhattan.set_sales(sales)
```

7. Now that the required values are set, we are good to call the `calc_tax_nyc` method from the NYC class that inherited the `Branch` class:

```
branch_manhattan.calc_tax_nyc()
```

8. The selling price calculated using the tax rate and the other supporting values of `branch`, `product`, and `sales` set using the parent class is represented in the following output:

```
({'branch_id': 2021,
  'branch_street': '40097 5th Main Street',
  'branchBorough': 'Manhattan',
  'branch_city': 'New York City',
  'branch_state': 'New York',
  'branch_zip': 11007},
 {'regionalManager': 'John M',
  'branchManager': 'Tom H',
  'subbranch_id': '2021-01'},
 {'productId': 100002,
  'productName': 'WashingMachine',
  'productBrand': 'Whirlpool'},
 {'purchase_price': 450,
  'profit_margin': 0.19,
  'tax_rate': 0.4,
```

```
    'local_rate': 0.055,
    'selling_price': 779.1525})
```

In this section, we looked at how MRO works in classes that have a single inheritance. Now, let's look at what happens when a class inherits from two classes.

Understanding MRO in multiple inheritances

In this section, we will look at inheriting from more than one superclass or parent class and its corresponding MRO.

For this example, let's create two parent classes, Product and Branch, as follows:

1. The Product class will have a set of attributes followed by a method named get_product:

```
class Product:
    _product_id = 100902
    _product_name = 'Iphone X'
    _product_category = 'Electronics'
    _unit_price = 700


    def get_product(self):
        return self._product_id, self._productName,
    self._product_category, self._unit_price
```

2. The Branch class will have a set of attributes followed by a method named get_branch:

```
class Branch:
    _branch_id = 2021
    _branch_street = '40097 5th Main Street'
    _branch_borough = 'Manhattan'
    _branch_city = 'New York City'
    _branch_state = 'New York'
    _branch_zip = 11007


    def get_branch(self):
        return self._branch_id, self._branch_street,
            self._branch_borough, self._branch_city,
            self._branch_state, self._branch_zip
```

3. Let's next create a child class or subclass named `Sales` and inherit from the `Product` and `Branch` classes. `Sales` will have one attribute date and a `get_sales` method:

```
class Sales(Product, Branch):
    date = '08/02/2021'
    def get_sales(self):
        return self.date, Product.get_product(self),
            Branch.get_branch(self)
```

4. The `Sales` class inherits `Product` followed by `Branch`:

```
Sales.mro()
```

5. Let's look at the order of its method resolution:

```
[__main__.Sales, __main__.Product, __main__.Branch,
object]
```

In the preceding output, the methods are resolved in the order of `Sales` followed by `Product` followed by `Branch` followed by `object`. If a method called by an object of the `Sales` class is not present in `Sales`, the MRO algorithm searches for it within the `Product` class followed by the `Branch` class.

6. Let's create another class (named `Invoice`) and inherit both `Branch` and `Product` in an order that's different from the inheritance of the `Sales` class:

```
class Invoice(Branch, Product):
    date = '08/02/2021'
    def get_invoice(self):
        return self.date, Branch.get_branch(self),
            Product.get_product(self)
```

7. Let's examine mro for the `Invoice` class:

```
Invoice.mro()
```

8. The mro for the `Invoice` class is represented in the following output:

```
[__main__.Invoice, __main__.Branch, __main__.Product,
object]
```

In the preceding output, the methods are resolved in the order of `Invoice` followed by `Branch` followed by `Product` followed by `object`. If a method called by an object of the `Invoice` class is not present in `Invoice`, the MRO algorithm searches for it within the `Branch` class followed by the `Product` class.

In the case of multiple inheritances, we reviewed how the order of method resolution changes when the order of inheriting superclasses or parent classes changes in Python 3.

Now, let's look at what happens to MRO in the case of multilevel inheritance.

Reviewing MRO in multilevel inheritance

Classes in Python can also inherit from superclasses at multiple levels, and the MRO gets more complicated as the number of superclasses or parent classes increases. In this section, let's look at the order of method resolution for such multiple inheritances with a few more examples.

In this example, we will perform the following steps:

1. Let's first create a class named `StoreCoupon`, where we will be defining attributes for a store such as product name, product category, the brand of the product, store name where the product is sold, expiry date of the product, and quantity to be purchased to get a coupon.

2. We will then define a method named `generate_coupon`, where we will be generating two coupons for the product with random coupon ID values and all the details of the product and its store:

```python
class StoreCoupon:
    productName = "Strawberry Ice Cream"
    product_category = "Desserts"
    brand = "ABCBrand3"
    store = "Los Angeles Store"
    expiry_date = "10/1/2021"
    quantity = 10

    def generate_coupon(self):
        import random
        coupon_id =  random.sample(range(
                100000000000,900000000000),2)
        for i in coupon_id:
            print('***********-------------------
***************')
            print('Product:', self.productName)
            print('Product Category:',
                    self.product_category)
            print('Coupon ID:', i)
            print('Brand:', self.brand)
```

```
                    print('Store:', self.store)
                    print('Expiry Date:', self.expiry_date)
                    print('Quantity:', self.quantity)
                    print('***********------------------
                        **************')
```

3. Let's now define a class, SendStoreCoupon, that inherits StoreCoupon and does not add any methods or attributes to it:

```
class SendStoreCoupon(StoreCoupon):
    pass
SendStoreCoupon.mro()
```

4. The MRO of this class is represented in the following output:

```
[__main__.SendStoreCoupon, __main__.StoreCoupon, object]
```

5. The methods in SendStoreCoupon are resolved first, followed by the methods in the StoreCoupon class, followed by object.

6. Let's add one more level of inheritance by defining another class, named SendCoupon, and inheriting it from the SendStoreCoupon classes:

```
class SendCoupon(SendStoreCoupon):
    pass
SendCoupon.mro()
```

7. The MRO of this class is represented in the following output:

```
[__main__.SendCoupon,
    __main__.SendStoreCoupon,
    __main__.StoreCoupon,
    object]
```

8. In the preceding output, the methods are resolved from SendCoupon followed by SendStoreCoupon followed by StoreCoupon followed by object.

9. Let's create an object for the SendCoupon class and call the generate_coupon method:

```
coupon = SendCoupon()
coupon.generate_coupon()
```

10. The `SendCoupon` class does not have a definition for the `generate_coupon` method and so, as per the MRO, the parent class or superclass' `SendStoreCoupon` method will be called, as in the following output:

```
**********-----------------**************
Product: Strawberry Ice Cream
Product Category: Desserts
Coupon ID: 532129664296
Brand: ABCBrand3
Store: Los Angeles Store
Expiry Date: 10/1/2021
Quantity: 10
**********-----------------**************
**********-----------------**************
Product: Strawberry Ice Cream
Product Category: Desserts
Coupon ID: 183336814176
Brand: ABCBrand3
Store: Los Angeles Store
Expiry Date: 10/1/2021
Quantity: 10
**********-----------------**************
```

In this example, we looked at how the methods are resolved from one level of inheritance to the other.

Now, let's look further into the impact of modifying the order of inheritance.

Understanding the importance of modifying the order of inheritance

In this section, we will look at inheriting from more than one parent class. We will see what happens to the method resolution when the order of the parent class changes in addition to the `SendStoreCoupon` class that was created in the preceding section:

1. First, we will be creating another class, named `ManufacturerCoupon`, where we will be defining attributes for a manufacturer such as the product name, product category, brand of the product, manufacturer name where the product is sold, expiry date of the product, and quantity to be purchased to get a coupon.

2. We will then define a method named `generate_coupon`, where we will be generating two coupons for the product with random coupon ID values and all the details of the product and its manufacturer:

```
class ManufacturerCoupon:
    productName = "Strawberry Ice Cream"
    product_category = "Desserts"
    brand = "ABCBrand3"
    manufacturer = "ABC Manufacturer"
    expiry_date = "10/1/2021"
    quantity = 10

    def generate_coupon(self):
        import random
        coupon_id =  random.sample(range(
                     100000000000,900000000000),2)
        for i in coupon_id:
            print('***********------------------
***************')
            print('Product:', self.productName)
            print('Product Category:',
                    self.product_category)
            print('Coupon ID:', i)
            print('Brand:', self.brand)
            print('Manufacturer:', self.manufacturer)
            print('Expiry Date:', self.expiry_date)
            print('Quantity:', self.quantity)
            print('***********------------------
                    **************')
```

3. Let's also define the `SendCoupon` class with two parent classes—`ManufacturerCoupon` and `SendStoreCoupon`:

```
class SendCoupon(ManufacturerCoupon,SendStoreCoupon):
    pass
SendCoupon.mro()
```

4. The MRO of the class is represented in the following output:

```
[__main__.SendCoupon,
 __main__.ManufacturerCoupon,
 __main__.SendStoreCoupon,
 __main__.StoreCoupon,
 object]
```

5. Let's further create an object for the class and call the `generate_coupon` method:

```
coupon = SendCoupon()
coupon.generate_coupon()
```

6. The `generate_coupon` method generated coupons for the manufacturer in this example since the first parent that has the `generate_coupon` method definition is `ManufacturerCoupon`. The following coupons are generated from the `generate_coupon` method:

```
***********------------------**************
Product: Strawberry Ice Cream
Product Category: Desserts
Coupon ID: 262335232934
Brand: ABCBrand3
Manufacturer: ABC Manufacturer
Expiry Date: 10/1/2021
Quantity: 10
***********------------------**************
***********------------------**************
Product: Strawberry Ice Cream
Product Category: Desserts
Coupon ID: 752333180295
Brand: ABCBrand3
Manufacturer: ABC Manufacturer
Expiry Date: 10/1/2021
Quantity: 10
***********------------------**************
```

7. Let's further change the order of inheritance in the SendCoupon class and look at how the methods are resolved:

```
class SendCoupon(SendStoreCoupon,ManufacturerCoupon):
    pass
SendCoupon.mro()
```

8. The MRO of the class is represented in the following output:

```
[__main__.SendCoupon,
 __main__.SendStoreCoupon,
 __main__.StoreCoupon,
 __main__.ManufacturerCoupon,
 object]
```

9. Let's further create an object for the class and call the generate_coupon method:

```
coupon = SendCoupon()
coupon.generate_coupon()
```

10. The generate_coupon method generated coupons for the store in this example since the first parent that has the generate_coupon method definition is SendStoreCoupon, which in turn inherits the method from its StoreCoupon parent class, as represented in the following output:

```
***********------------------**************
Product: Strawberry Ice Cream
Product Category: Desserts
Coupon ID: 167466225705
Brand: ABCBrand3
Store: Los Angeles Store
Expiry Date: 10/1/2021
Quantity: 10
***********------------------**************
***********------------------**************
Product: Strawberry Ice Cream
Product Category: Desserts
Coupon ID: 450583881080
Brand: ABCBrand3
Store: Los Angeles Store
```

```
Expiry Date: 10/1/2021
Quantity: 10
***********-----------------***************
```

In this section, we understood the impact of the order in which a child class resolved the parent classes or the superclasses.

With this understanding, let's look at what happens when the inheritance becomes even more complex and where it can lead to errors.

Impact of unintended change of order in inheritance

In this section, we will be looking at examples that demonstrate how important the order of inheritance is to resolve the methods in the case of multilevel inheritance, and what happens when the order changes in one of the parent or superclasses unintentionally.

This is how it works:

1. Let's start by creating a class named CommonCounter that initializes with two attributes, items and name. Let's also add two methods to this class, return_cart (which returns the items in the cart) and goto_counter (which returns the name of the counter). This is how the code looks:

    ```
    class CommonCounter():
        def __init__(self,items,name):
            self.items = items
            self.name = name
        def return_cart(self):
            cartItems = []
            for i in self.items:
                cartItems.append(i)
            return cartItems
        def goto_counter(self):
            countername = self.name
            return countername
    CommonCounter.mro()
    ```

2. The MRO of the class is represented in the following output:

    ```
    [__main__.CommonCounter, object]
    ```

3. Let's now create another class, named `CheckItems`, which is also going to be a parent class in multilevel inheritance applied in this section. This class will have one attribute named `item_type` and one method named `review_items` that returns the name of the counter based on the type of items in the cart:

```
class CheckItems():
    def __init__(self, item_type = None):
        self.item_type = item_type


    def review_items(self, item_type = None):
        veg_cart = ['Vegetables', 'Dairy', 'Fruits']
        if (item_type == 'Electronics'):
            print("Move to Electronics Counter")
        elif (item_type in veg_cart):
            print("Move to Vege Counter")
CheckItems.mro()
```

4. The MRO of the class is represented in the following output:

```
[__main__.CheckItems, object]
```

5. On the second level of inheritance, let's create a class named `ElectronicsCounter`, which inherits from the `CommonCounter` and `CheckItems` classes, in that order:

```
class ElectronicsCounter(CommonCounter,CheckItems):
    def __init__(status = None):
        self.status = status
    def test_electronics(self):
        teststatus = []
        for i in self.status:
            teststatus.append(i)
        return teststatus
ElectronicsCounter.mro()
```

6. The MRO of the class is represented in the following output:

```
[__main__.ElectronicsCounter,
 __main__.CommonCounter,
 __main__.CheckItems,
 object]
```

7. On the second level of inheritance, let's also create a class named VegeCounter, which inherits from the CheckItems and CommonCounter classes, in that order:

```
class VegeCounter(CheckItems,CommonCounter):
    def __init__(weights = None):
        self.weights = weights
    def weigh_items(self):
        item_weight = dict(zip(self.items,
                                  self.weights))
        return item_weight
VegeCounter.mro()
```

8. The MRO of the class is represented in the following output:

```
[__main__.VegeCounter,
 __main__.CheckItems,
 __main__.CommonCounter,
 object]
```

9. Let's now create another class, named ScanCode, which inherits the ElectronicsCounter and VegCounter classes:

```
class ScanCode(ElectronicsCounter,VegeCounter):
    pass
```

The preceding code results in the following error message:

```
---------------------------------------------------------------------------
TypeError                                 Traceback (most recent call last)
~\AppData\Local\Temp/ipykernel_2164/409991840.py in <module>
----> 1 class ScanCode(ElectronicsCounter,VegeCounter):
      2     pass

TypeError: Cannot create a consistent method resolution
order (MRO) for bases CommonCounter, CheckItems
```

Figure 10.1 – MRO error

10. Even though the MRO of the class is ScanCode followed by ElectronicsCounter followed by VegeCounter followed by CommonCounter followed by CheckItems followed by object, the MROs of the CommonCounter and CheckItems base classes are reversed. Therefore, the overall class definition throws an error in this scenario.

This example demonstrates the impact of unintended change in the order of inheritance. It is important to ensure that the order of classes is correct while defining classes with multilevel inheritance in Python so that the MRO is consistent for base classes.

Summary

In this chapter, we have learned about the concept of method resolution by exploring the MRO method in Python 3. We also inspected the MRO of Python code by implementing different types of inheritance. We understood the impact of MRO by modifying the order of inheritance at various levels for multiple classes from our core example.

Similar to other chapters covered in this book, this chapter explains that the MRO also focuses on metaprogramming and its impact on Python code.

In the next chapter, we will be looking at the concept of dynamic objects, with some other interesting examples.

11
Creating Dynamic Objects

In this chapter, we will look at the concept of dynamic objects in Python 3 and the process that can be followed to create any dynamic Python objects including classes, instances of classes, methods, and attributes.

As the name suggests, dynamic objects are objects that can be created at runtime or execution time rather than while coding, provided certain conditions are met.

Throughout this chapter, we will look at how to create classes, class instances, functions, methods, and attributes dynamically using our core example of *ABC Megamart*.

Why should we understand the creation of dynamic objects? In scenarios where we want to build applications that can generate code at runtime, the basic building blocks for Python code are the objects that are created at runtime. Dynamic creation of objects gives the flexibility and choice of creating an object only when it is required. Any object defined will occupy a certain amount of memory. When an object created during the coding time is not required by the rest of the code or application, it occupies memory that can otherwise be used more efficiently.

In this chapter, we will be taking a look at the following main topics:

- Exploring type for dynamic objects
- Creating multiple instances of a class dynamically
- Creating dynamic classes
- Creating dynamic attributes and methods

By the end of this chapter, you should have an understanding of how Python objects can be created at runtime and how they can be implemented in various applications.

Technical requirements

The code examples shared in this chapter are available on GitHub under the code for this chapter at `https://github.com/PacktPublishing/Metaprogramming-with-Python/tree/main/Chapter11`.

Exploring type for dynamic objects

In this section, let's explore the function named `type` from the perspective of dynamic object creation. Why do we need to create an object dynamically? Let's consider the scenarios where we want to change the attributes of the class only for specific instances/objects of the class and not for the original class itself. In such scenarios, we can create dynamic objects for the class and define the attributes of the class dynamically within the specific dynamic object and not for the whole class itself.

In multiple chapters throughout this book, we have looked at the various uses of the `type` function. In this chapter, we will look at how to use `type` to dynamically create Python objects.

Let's look at the graphical representation of the signature of the `type` function in Python in the following screenshot:

```
type()

Init signature: type(self, /, *args, **kwargs)
Docstring:
type(object_or_name, bases, dict)
type(object) -> the object's type
type(name, bases, dict) -> a new type
Type:           type
Subclasses:     ABCMeta, EnumMeta, NamedTupleMeta, _TypedDictMeta, _ABC, MetaHasDescripto
rs, PyCStructType, UnionType, PyCPointerType, PyCArrayType, ...
```

Figure 11.1 – Signature of type

The type function accepts a self-object followed by a tuple and a dictionary of arguments as input. When we provide an object as input to the `type` function, it returns the type of the object as in the following example:

```
type(object)
```

The output for the type of object is `type` itself:

```
type
```

From *Figure 11.1*, we can also see that the other variation of `type` accepts an object followed by `bases` and `dict`. The argument value for `bases` denotes the base classes and the argument value for `dict` denotes various attributes of the class.

To examine the `type` function for creating dynamic objects, let's define a class named `Branch`:

```
class Branch:
    '''attributes...'''

    '''methods...'''
    pass
```

Let's further create an object dynamically using the `type` function in the following code:

```
branchAlbany = type('Branch', (object,), {'branchID' : 123,
                    'branchStreet' : '123 Main Street',
                    'branchCity' : 'Albany',
                    'branchState' : 'New York',
                    '  'branch'ip' : 12084})
```

In the preceding code, the `branchAlbany` variable is the object to be defined dynamically, the first argument is the class name for which an object needs to be created, the second argument is the tuple of base classes for the class argument, and the third argument is the list of attributes or methods to be added to the object.

We can look at the definition of the `branchAlbany` object in the following code and output:

```
branchAlbany

__main__.Branch
```

The following screenshot is a representation of the attributes added to `branchAlbany` once the preceding code is executed:

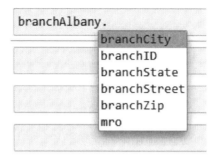

Figure 11.2 – Attributes of branchAlbany

The method resolution order of the dynamic class instance is the same as the `Branch` class:

```
branchAlbany.mro
```

```
<function Branch.mro()>
```

All the dynamic attributes added to the class instance are now part of the `branchAlbany` class instance:

```
branchAlbany.branchID
123
branchAlbany.branchStreet
'123 Main Street'
branchAlbany.branchCity
'Albany'
branchAlbany.branchState
'New York'
branchAlbany.branchZip
12084
```

To understand this further, let's look at the attributes of `branchAlbany` and compare them to the attributes of the `Branch` class for which the `branchAlbany` instance is created. A graphical representation of the comparison is shown in *Figure 11.3*:

Branch

```
['__class__',
 '__delattr__',
 '__dict__',
 '__dir__',
 '__doc__',
 '__eq__',
 '__format__',
 '__ge__',
 '__getattribute__',
 '__gt__',
 '__hash__',
 '__init__',
 '__init_subclass__',
 '__le__',
 '__lt__',
 '__module__',
 '__ne__',
 '__new__',
 '__reduce__',
 '__reduce_ex__',
 '__repr__',
 '__setattr__',
 '__sizeof__',
 '__str__',
 '__subclasshook__',
 '__weakref__']
```

branchAlbany

```
['__class__',
 '__delattr__',
 '__dict__',
 '__dir__',
 '__doc__',
 '__eq__',
 '__format__',
 '__ge__',
 '__getattribute__',
 '__gt__',
 '__hash__',
 '__init__',
 '__init_subclass__',
 '__le__',
 '__lt__',
 '__module__',
 '__ne__',
 '__new__',
 '__reduce__',
 '__reduce_ex__',
 '__repr__',
 '__setattr__',
 '__sizeof__',
 '__str__',
 '__subclasshook__',
 '__weakref__',
 'branchCity',
 'branchID',
 'branchState',
 'branchStreet',
 'branchZip']
```

Figure 11.3 – Attributes of Branch versus branchAlbany

The preceding figure clarifies that the attributes defined as part of the dynamic object creation for the Branch class did not get included in the Branch class itself. The definition of the Branch class remains intact and only the definition of the dynamic object changed in this scenario.

To explore further, we can create another dynamic instance of the Branch class with a different set of attributes:

```
branchNYC = type('Branch', (object,), {'branchID' : 202,
                        'productId': 100001,
                        'productName': 'Refrigerator',
                        'productBrand': 'Whirlpool'})
```

The branchNYC instance now has its own set of dynamic attributes that are not part of either the Branch class or the branchAlbany instance. A comparison of the three is in *Figure 11.4*:

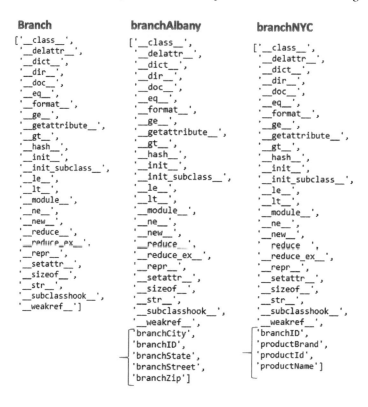

Figure 11.4 – Attributes of Branch, branchAlbany, and branchNYC

With this understanding, let's look further at creating multiple instances or objects of a class dynamically.

Creating multiple instances of a class dynamically

In this section, let's look at creating more than one instance of a class dynamically. For this example, we will be making use of a built-in Python function named globals to create dynamic object names, along with the type function that we use to create dynamic objects. Refer to the following steps:

1. Let's create a new class named Product without any attributes or methods. Instead of defining the attributes within the class and creating an instance of the class, let's create multiple instances with their own attributes:

```python
class Product():
    '''attributes...'''
```

```
        '''methods...'''
        pass
```

2. Next, we will be creating three dictionary items in a list named `details`:

```
details = [{'branchID' : 202,
        'ProductID' : 100002,
        'ProductName' : 'Washing Machine',
        'ProductBrand' : 'Whirlpool',
        'PurchasePrice' : 450,
        'ProfitMargin' : 0.19},
    {
        'productID' : 100902,
        'productName' : 'Iphone X',
        'productCategory' : 'Electronics',
        'unitPrice' : 700
    },
    {
        'branchID' : 2021,
        'branchStreet' : '40097 5th Main Street',
        'branchBorough' : 'Manhattan',
        'branchCity' : 'New York City',
        'Product ID': 100003,
        'Product Name': 'Washing Machine',
        'Product Brand': 'Samsung',
        'Purchase Price': 430,
        'Profit Margin': 0.18
    },
    ]
```

3. These dictionary items are going to be provided as attributes for multiple instances of objects that we are going to create using `globals` and `type`:

```
for obj,var in
zip(['product1','product2','product3'],details):
    globals()[obj] = type('Product', (object,), var)
```

4. In the preceding code, we have created three objects `product1`, `product2`, and `product3` with variables defined in the `details` list. Each object is created dynamically and will have its own set of attributes.

    The `Product` class has its default set of attributes since we did not define any custom attributes in the class. These are presented in *Figure 11.5*:

Product

```
['__class__',
 '__delattr__',
 '__dict__',
 '__dir__',
 '__doc__',
 '__eq__',
 '__format__',
 '__ge__',
 '__getattribute__',
 '__gt__',
 '__hash__',
 '__init__',
 '__init_subclass__',
 '__le__',
 '__lt__',
 '__module__',
 '__ne__',
 '__new__',
 '__reduce__',
 '__reduce_ex__',
 '__repr__',
 '__setattr__',
 '__sizeof__',
 '__str__',
 '__subclasshook__',
 '__weakref__']
```

Figure 11.5 – Attributes of Product

5. The attributes of the three objects we created in this example have their own set of attributes defined dynamically. The dynamic attributes of the dynamic objects are in the following figure:

Figure 11.6 – Attributes of product1, product2, and product3

In this section, we learned how to create multiple instances of a class dynamically with each instance having its own dynamic set of attributes. With this understanding, let's further look at creating multiple classes dynamically.

Creating dynamic classes

In this section, let's look at how to create classes dynamically with different names and different attributes by making use of the built-in functions of type and globals. To explore this concept further, we will first create one dynamic class using the type function:

```
Product = type('Product', (object,), {'branchID' : 202,
                        'productId': 100001,
```

```
                                    'productName': 'Refrigerator',
                                    'productBrand': 'Whirlpool'})
```

In the preceding code, we created a class named `Product` and provided the class name, followed by the base classes and their corresponding attributes.

Let's test the created class with the following code:

```
Product
__main__.Product
type(Product)
type
Product.branchID
202
```

With this understanding, let's now take it further and create multiple dynamic classes.

Creating multiple dynamic classes

In this section, we will be creating multiple dynamic classes using `type` and `globals`:

1. Let's define three functions to be added as dynamic methods while creating multiple dynamic classes as follows:

   ```
   def setBranch(branch):
           return branch

   def setSales(sales):
           return sales

   def setProduct(product):
           return product
   ```

2. Next, let's create a dictionary of attributes:

   ```
   details = [{'branch': 202,
               'setBranch' : setBranch
     },
     {'purchasePrice': 430,
      'setSales' : setSales
      },
   ```

```
{'product': 100902,
 'setProduct' : setProduct
 }]
```

3. In the next step, we will be creating multiple classes dynamically using `type` and `globals` in a loop:

```
for cls,var in
zip(['productcls1','productcls2','productcls3'],details):
    globals()[cls] = type(cls, (object,), var)
```

4. The preceding code creates three classes named `productcls1`, `productcls2`, and `productcls3`, and also creates dynamic variables and methods that can be further reviewed for their usage in the following code and their corresponding output:

```
productcls1.setBranch(productcls1.branch)
202
productcls2.setSales(productcls2.purchasePrice)
430
productcls3.setProduct(productcls3.product)
100902
```

In the preceding code, we have successfully executed the methods created within the dynamic classes.

In this section, we have learned how to create multiple classes dynamically. With this understanding, let's proceed further by creating dynamic methods in classes.

Creating dynamic attributes and methods

In this section, let's explore how to create dynamic methods within classes. A dynamic method is a method created for a class during runtime, unlike the regular class methods that we create while coding within the class definition itself.

Dynamic methods are created to avoid modifying the structure or the original class definition once it is defined. Instead of modifying the class definition, we can define and call a runtime template method that will in turn create a dynamic method for the class.

Let's start by creating a simple class definition for managing the coupons of *ABC Megamart* named SimpleCoupon:

```
class SimpleCoupon:
    '''attributes'''''

  ''''''methods''''''
    pass
```

We did not define any attributes or methods for this class, but we will define them more clearly in the following sections.

Defining attributes dynamically

Let's now define a set of coupon attributes for the SimpleCoupon class during runtime using Python's built-in setattr function. This function accepts a Python object, the name of the attribute, and its corresponding value:

```
setattr(SimpleCoupon,'couponDetails',
[["Honey Mustard Sauce","Condiments","ABCBrand3","Pasadena
Store","10/1/2021",2],
["Potato Chips","Snacks","ABCBrand1","Manhattan
Store","10/1/2021",2],
["Strawberry Ice Cream","Desserts","ABCBrand3","ABC
Manufacturer","10/1/2021",2]])
```

In the preceding code, we have provided the class name SimpleCoupon as the input object, followed by the attribute name as couponDetails, and its corresponding values as three lists of product details, one for each type of coupon: Condiments, Snacks, and Desserts.

Now that we have dynamically created the attribute, let's check whether it has been added to the SimpleCoupon class and is available for use by looking at the list of attributes and methods available in the class as represented in *Figure 11.7*:

SimpleCoupon

```
['__class__',
 '__delattr__',
 '__dict__',
 '__dir__',
 '__doc__',
 '__eq__',
 '__format__',
 '__ge__',
 '__getattribute__',
 '__gt__',
 '__hash__',
 '__init__',
 '__init_subclass__',
 '__le__',
 '__lt__',
 '__module__',
 '__ne__',
 '__new__',
 '__reduce__',
 '__reduce_ex__',
 '__repr__',
 '__setattr__',
 '__sizeof__',
 '__str__',
 '__subclasshook__',
 '__weakref__',
 'couponDetails']
```

Figure 11.7 – couponDetails added to SimpleCoupon

With this understanding, let's further dynamically create methods in the `SimpleCoupon` class.

Defining methods dynamically

In this section, let's create a new function that acts as a template function to dynamically generate methods within the `SimpleCoupon` class. We will now create a function named `createCoupon` that accepts a class object, method name, and the coupon details as input.

Within the function definition, let's also define a `generateCoupon` function that will be generated as a dynamic method in the class:

```
def createCoupon(classname,methodname,couponDetails):

    def generateCoupon(couponDetails):
        import random
        couponId =  random.sample(range(
```

```
      100000000000,900000000000),1)
    for i in couponId:
        print('***********------------------
    **************')
        print('Product:', couponDetails[0])
        print('Product Category:', couponDetails[1])
        print('Coupon ID:', i)
        print('Brand:', couponDetails[2])
        print('Source:', couponDetails[3])
        print('Expiry Date:', couponDetails[4])
        print('Quantity:', couponDetails[5])
        print('***********------------------
    **************')


    setattr(classname,methodname,generateCoupon)
```

In the preceding code, we call the `setattr` function to define the method dynamically in the class object provided as input to `setattr`.

In the next step, let's generate three `generateCoupon` methods dynamically using the same method definition but with three different names and test them with three different sets of attributes.

```
for method,var in
zip(['generateCondimentsCoupon','generateSnacksCoupon',
'generateDessertsCoupon'],SimpleCoupon.couponDetails):
    createCoupon(SimpleCoupon, method,var)
```

Now, the `SimpleCoupon` class has three different methods added to it with the names `generateCondimentsCoupon`, `generateSnacksCoupon`, and `generateDessertsCoupon` respectively. The dynamics methods added to the `SimpleCoupon` class are shown in the following figure:

SimpleCoupon

```
['__class__',
 '__delattr__',
 '__dict__',
 '__dir__',
 '__doc__',
 '__eq__',
 '__format__',
 '__ge__',
 '__getattribute__',
 '__gt__',
 '__hash__',
 '__init__',
 '__init_subclass__',
 '__le__',
 '__lt__',
 '__module__',
 '__ne__',
 '__new__',
 '__reduce__',
 '__reduce_ex__',
 '__repr__',
 '__setattr__',
 '__sizeof__',
 '__str__',
 '__subclasshook__',
 '__weakref__',
 'couponDetails',
 'generateCondimentsCoupon',
 'generateDessertsCoupon',
 'generateSnacksCoupon']
```

Figure 11.8 – Dynamic methods added to SimpleCoupon

Let's run each method by calling them from the SimpleCoupon class. The generateCondimentsCoupon method is called in the following code:

```
SimpleCoupon.generateCondimentsCoupon(SimpleCoupon.
couponDetails[0])
```

The output is generated as follows:

```
***********-------------------**************
Product: Honey Mustard Sauce
Product Category: Condiments
Coupon ID: 666849488635
Brand: ABCBrand3
Source: Pasadena Store
```

```
Expiry Date: 10/1/2021
Quantity: 2
**********-----------------**************
generateSnacksCoupon is called in the following code:
SimpleCoupon.generateSnacksCoupon(SimpleCoupon.
couponDetails[1])
```

The output for this is as follows:

```
**********-----------------**************
Product: Potato Chips
Product Category: Snacks
Coupon ID: 394693383743
Brand: ABCBrand1
Source: Manhattan Store
Expiry Date: 10/1/2021
Quantity: 2
**********-----------------**************
```

The generateDessertsCoupon method is called in the following code:

```
SimpleCoupon.generateDessertsCoupon(SimpleCoupon.
couponDetails[2])
```

The output is generated as follows:

```
**********-----------------**************
Product: Strawberry Ice Cream
Product Category: Desserts
Coupon ID: 813638596228
Brand: ABCBrand3
Source: ABC Manufacturer
Expiry Date: 10/1/2021
Quantity: 2
**********-----------------**************
```

In this section, we have understood the concept of generating methods dynamically in a Python class along with examples. This concept will help while designing applications with automated code generation capabilities.

Summary

In this chapter, we have learned the concept of dynamic objects by exploring methods of creating various dynamic objects in Python 3. We also covered the concepts of creating multiple instances of a class dynamically. We looked at the concept of creating dynamic classes. We also looked at the concepts of creating attributes and methods dynamically within classes.

Similar to other chapters covered in this book, while this chapter explained dynamic objects, it also provided some focus on metaprogramming and its impact on Python code.

In the next chapter, we will be looking at the concept of design patterns with some other interesting examples.

12
Applying GOF Design Patterns – Part 1

In this chapter, we will look at the concept of design patterns in Python 3 and its various categories, along with examples of how they can be applied while developing software using Python.

The concept of design patterns originated from the book Design Patterns Elements of Reusable Object-Oriented Software by Erich Gamma, Richard Helm, Ralph Johnson, and John Vlissides, Addison-Wesley, which was written in C++. This concept was later extended to other **object-oriented programming** (**OOP**) languages.

In this chapter, we are going to look at how these design patterns can be applied in Python using our core example of *ABC Megamart*.

We will cover the following main topics:

- An overview of design patterns
- Exploring behavioral design patterns

By the end of this chapter, you should understand some important behavioral design patterns and how they can be implemented in various applications.

Technical requirements

The code examples in this chapter are available in this book's GitHub repository at `https://github.com/PacktPublishing/Metaprogramming-with-Python/tree/main/Chapter12`.

An overview of design patterns

Every programming language has its elements uniquely designed and communicated to others. Design patterns give a structured and well-designed approach to developing software or applications in Python. In Python, every element is an object. Design patterns express how we are going to sequence or structure these objects to perform various operations. This allows them to become reusable.

The design patterns are divided into three categories – behavioral, structural, and creational. In this chapter, we will cover behavioral design patterns and look at three in particular, as follows:

- The chain of responsibility
- Command
- Strategy

More than 20 different design patterns are available in Python and covering all of them would require a book of its own. Therefore, we will only focus on some of the most interesting design patterns in this chapter and the next. With that, let's explore some behavioral design patterns.

Exploring behavioral design patterns

As the name suggests, behavioral design patterns deal with the behavior of objects and how they talk to each other. In this section, we will learn about the elements of the chain of responsibility, command, and strategy design patterns, which belong to the behavioral design pattern category, and understand them by applying them to *ABC Megamart*.

Understanding the chain of responsibility

The chain of responsibility is a design pattern where the responsibility of the actions that can be performed by objects are transferred from one object to another, similar to a chain of events or actions. To explain this further and to implement this design pattern, we need the following elements to be developed in our code:

- **Parent handler**: A base class that defines a base function that specifies how a sequence of actions should be handled.

- **Child handlers**: One or more subclasses that overwrite the base function from the base class to perform the respective action.

- **Exception handler**: A default handler that performs a specific action in case of exceptions. It also overwrites the base function from the base class.

- **Requestor**: A function or method that calls the child handlers to initiate a chain of responsibility.

Let's look at the chain of responsibility with an example.

In this example, we will be calculating tax by state and generating an invoice for the New York and California branches of *ABC Megamart*. Follow these steps:

1. To illustrate the design pattern further, let's create a parent handler class named `InvoiceHandler`. In this class, we will initiate a `next_action` variable to handle the next action in the chain and define a `handle` method to handle the requested action:

    ```python
    class InvoiceHandler(object):
        def __init__(self):
            self.next_action = None
        def handle(self,calctax):
            self.next_action.handle(calctax)
    ```

2. Next, we will create a supporting class to support the actions that we are going to perform in this example. Here, we want to calculate tax for a state based on the request and generate an invoice:

    ```python
    class InputState(object):
        state_ny = ['NYC','NY','New York','new york']
        state_ca = ['CA', 'California', 'california']
    ```

    The `InputState` class has two attributes for the list of acceptable values for the states of New York and California.

3. Now, let's create another class that adds a header to the invoice, as follows:

    ```python
    class Print_invoice(object):
        def __init__(self,state):
            self.state = state
            self.header = 'State specific Sales tax is
    applicable
                            for the state of ' + self.state
    ```

4. Next, we will create a class for the child handler that has a method for generating an invoice, calculating New York's state-specific tax for a product, and overwriting the `handle` method from the `InvoiceHandler` class:

    ```python
    class NYCHandler(InvoiceHandler):
        def generate_invoice(self, header, state):
            product = 'WashingMachine'
            pricebeforetax = 450 + (450 * 0.19)
            tax_rate = 0.4
    ```

```
            local_rate = 0.055
            tax = pricebeforetax * (tax_rate + local_rate)
            finalsellingprice = pricebeforetax + tax
            print('**************ABC
Megamart****************')
            print('***********------------------
**************')
            print(header)
            print('Product: ', product)
            print('Tax: ', tax)
            print('Total Price: ', finalsellingprice)
            print('***********------------------
**************')


    def handle(self,print_invoice):
            if print_invoice.state in InputState.state_ny:
                self.generate_invoice(print_invoice.header,
                                    print_invoice.state)
            else:
                super(NYCHandler, self).handle(print_invoice)
```

5. Then, we will create a class for the child handler that has a method for generating an invoice, calculating California's state-specific tax for a product, and overwriting the `handle` method from the `InvoiceHandler` class:

```
class CAHandler(InvoiceHandler):
    def generate_invoice(self, header, state):
        product = 'WashingMachine'
        pricebeforetax = 480 + (480 * 0.14)
        tax_rate = 0.35
        local_rate = 0.077
        tax = pricebeforetax * (tax_rate + local_rate)
        finalsellingprice = pricebeforetax + tax
        print('**************ABC
Megamart****************')
        print('***********------------------
**************')
        print(header)
```

```
            print('Product: ', product)
            print('Tax: ', tax)
            print('Total Price: ', finalsellingprice)
            print('***********------------------
***************')


    def handle(self,print_invoice):
        if print_invoice.state in InputState.state_ca:
            self.generate_invoice(print_invoice.header,
                                    print_invoice.state)
        else:
            super(CAHandler, self).handle(print_invoice)
```

6. Now, let's define a class that will handle exceptions such as scenarios where the request does not invoke one of the child handler's methods:

```
class ExceptionHandler(InvoiceHandler):
    def handle(self,print_invoice):
        print("No branches in the state")
```

7. Now, let's create a requestor function that instantiates one of the child handler subclasses and initiates a chain of responsibility that transfers from one action to another:

```
def invoice_requestor(state):
    invoice = Print_invoice(state)
    nychandler = NYCHandler()
    cahandler = CAHandler()
    nychandler.next_action = cahandler
    cahandler.next_action = ExceptionHandler()
    nychandler.handle(invoice)
```

In the preceding code, we defined the requestor to set the next action for NYCHandler to CAHandler and the next action for CAHandler to be the exception handler. Let's test this design pattern by calling the invoice_requestor function with the input state's name; that is, CA:

```
invoice_requestor('CA')
```

The preceding code returns the invoice for the state of California since we provided the input as CC instead of NY. If NY was provided as input, the design pattern would have invoked NYHandler. However, since CA was provided, the next-in-the-chain and relevant CAHandler is invoked as follows:

```
**************ABC Megamart*****************
**********------------------**************
State specific Sales tax is applicable for the state of CA
Product:  WashingMachine
Tax:  233.6544
Total Price:  780.8544
**********------------------**************
```

If `invoice_requestor` is provided with NY as the input state name instead, it should call NYHandler, not CAHandler:

```
invoice requestor('NYC')
```

The preceding code returns the NYHandler class's invoice and not the CAHandler class's invoice, as expected:

```
**************ABC Megamart*****************
**********------------------**************
State specific Sales tax is applicable for the state of NYC
Product:  WashingMachine
Tax:  243.6525
Total Price:  779.1525
**********------------------**************
```

As the final part of the request, let's call ExceptionHandler by providing an input state that is neither NY nor CA:

```
invoice_requestor('TEXAS')
```

The preceding code returns the following output by invoking the action from ExceptionHandler:

```
No branches in the state
```

Let's connect the elements of this design pattern with its corresponding objects:

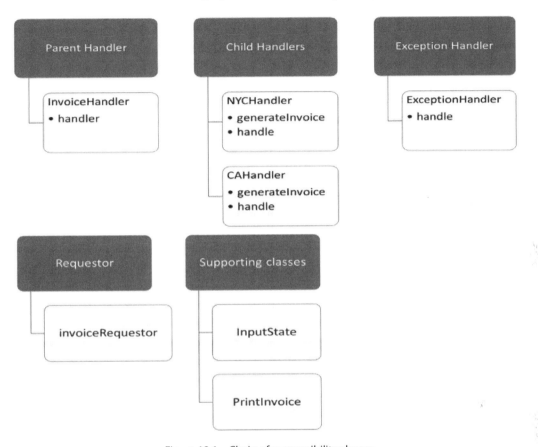

Figure 12.1 – Chain of responsibility classes

In this section, we looked at the chain of responsibility design pattern. Now, let's look at the command design pattern.

Learning about the command design pattern

In this section, we will look at the next design pattern of interest: the command design pattern. The command design pattern can be used to create a sequence for executing commands and reverting to a previous state if a command is executed by mistake. Similar to the chain of responsibility pattern, the command design pattern is also created by defining multiple elements that can execute an action and revert the action that's performed by an object.

To explain this further and to implement this design pattern, we need to develop the following elements in our code:

- **Parent command**: This is a base class that defines the base functions for one or more commands that need to be executed.

- **Child commands**: Child commands specify one or more actions that are inherited from the parent command class and overwritten at the individual child command level.

- **Executor**: This is a base class for executing the child commands. It provides a method to execute the action and a method to revoke the action.

- **Sub-executors**: These inherit executors and overwrite the methods to execute while also revoking the actions that are performed by the child commands.

- **Requestor**: The requestor is a class that requests the executors to execute commands and revert to a previous state.

- **Tester**: This class tests if the design pattern is working as expected.

Now, let's look at this design pattern in action. To understand this design pattern, we'll go back to *ABC Megamart* and calculate the selling price for a product, as well as apply a discount to the selling price. The command pattern can help us design billing in such a way that we can either sell at the actual selling price or apply a discount. Whenever a discount is applied by mistake, we can revert it. Similarly, whenever a discount is not applied, we can reapply it. Follow these steps:

1. Let's start by creating the `Billing` class. This is going to be the parent command and it will have an attribute named `sales`. This is a dictionary object. There will be two abstract methods – one to apply a discount and another to remove the discount:

```python
from abc import ABC, abstractmethod
class Billing:
    sales = {'purchase_price': 450,
             'profit_margin': 0.19,
             'tax_rate': 0.4,
             'discount_rate': 0.10
             }
    @abstractmethod
    def apply_discount(self):
        pass
    @abstractmethod
    def remove_discount(self):
        pass
```

2. Now, let's create the first child command class, `DiscountedBilling`, which will overwrite the `apply_discount` method from its parent class, `Billing`. Applying the `Discount` method will take in the sales dictionary object from the `Billing` class and calculate the discounted price, as shown here:

```
class DiscountedBilling(Billing):
    def apply_discount(self):
        sales = self.sales
        pricebeforetax = sales['purchase_price'] +
            sales['purchase_price'] * sales['profit_
margin']
        finalsellingprice = pricebeforetax +
(pricebeforetax *
        sales['tax_rate'])
        sales['sellingPrice'] = finalsellingprice
        discountedPrice = sales['sellingPrice'] * (1 -
            sales['discount_rate'])
        return discountedPrice
```

3. Next, we will create the next child command class, `ActualBilling`, which will remove the discount. – That is, it will calculate the selling price without a discount:

```
class ActualBilling(Billing):
    def remove_discount(self):
        sales = self.sales
        pricebeforetax = sales['purchase_price'] +
            sales['purchase_price'] * sales['profit_
margin']
        actualprice = pricebeforetax + (pricebeforetax *
            sales['tax_rate'])
        return actualprice
```

4. Now, let's create the base class for the executor. This will have two methods: `exec_discount` and `revoke_discount`. The first is an abstract method for executing the command that applies the discount. And the second is an abstract method for executing the command that revokes the discount:

```
class ExecuteBilling:
    @abstractmethod
    def exec_discount(self):
```

```
        pass
    @abstractmethod
    def revoke_discount(self):
        pass
```

5. Now, let's define a child class named `ExecuteDiscountedBilling` that inherits from the `ExecuteBilling` class. This will overwrite the `exec_discount` and `revoke_discount` methods from its superclass. We will call the `apply_discount` method from the `DiscountedBilling` class within the `exec_discount` method of this child class. We will also set the `ActualBilling` command class from the `ExecuteActualBilling` class within the `revoke_discount` method:

```python
class ExecuteDiscountedBilling(ExecuteBilling):
    def __init__(self, instance):
        self.instance = instance
    def exec_discount(self):
        print('Discount applied...')
        return self.instance.apply_discount()
    def revoke_discount(self, revokeInstance):
        revokeInstance.reset(ExecuteActualBilling(
                            ActualBilling()))
        return revokeInstance.runcalc()
```

6. Now, let's define a child class named `ExecuteActualBilling` that inherits from the `ExecuteBilling` class. This will overwrite the `exec_discount` and `revoke_discount` methods from its superclass. We will call the `remove_discount` method from the `ActualBilling` class within the `exec_discount` method of this child class. We will also set the `DiscountedBilling` command class from the `ExecuteDiscountedBilling` class within the `revoke_discount` method:

```python
class ExecuteActualBilling(ExecuteBilling):
    def __init__(self, instance):
        self.instance = instance

    def exec_discount(self):
        print('Discount removed...')
        return self.instance.remove_discount()

    def revoke_discount(self, revokeInstance):
```

```
            revokeInstance.reset(ExecuteDiscountedBilling(
                        DiscountedBilling()))
        return revokeInstance.runcalc()
```

7. Next, we will define the requestor class, `RequestAction`, which will request the commands to be executed and reverted as required. We will also define three methods:

- The `reset` method, which will set or reset the command

- The `runcalc` method, which will execute the discount calculation

- The `revert` method, which will revert to the previous action by revoking the discount calculation:

In the code block:

```
class RequestAction:
    def __init__(self, action):
        self.action = action
    def reset(self, action):
        print("Resetting command...")
        self.action = action
    def runcalc(self):
        return self.action.exec_discount()
    def revert(self):
        print("Reverting the previous action...")
        return self.action.revoke_discount(self)
```

8. Finally, we must create the final class in this design pattern to test that the command design pattern works as expected:

```
class Tester:
    def __init__(self):
        billing = Billing()
        discount =
                ExecuteDiscountedBilling
    (DiscountedBilling())
        actual = ExecuteActualBilling(ActualBilling())
        requestor = RequestAction(discount)
        print(requestor.runcalc())
        requestor.reset(actual)
        print(requestor.runcalc())
```

```
print(requestor.revert())
print(requestor.revert())
```

In the preceding code, we defined an object instance of the `Billing` class, followed by the instances that can be discounted and the actual `ExecuteBilling` subclasses. We also created an instance of the `RequestAction` requestor class. After that, we sequenced a set of operations to run the discount calculation, then the `reset` command, followed by rerunning the calculation to remove the discount. This will revert the previous command and thus reapply the discount before reverting the previous command, which will, in turn, remove the discount.

Let's call the `Tester` class, as follows:

```
Tester()
```

The output of the preceding code is as follows:

```
Discount applied...
674.73
Resetting command...
Discount removed...
749.7
Reverting the previous action...
Resetting command...
Discount applied...
674.73
Reverting the previous action...
Resetting command...
Discount removed...
749.7
<__main__.Tester at 0x261f09e3b20>
```

Now, let's connect the elements of this design pattern with its corresponding objects:

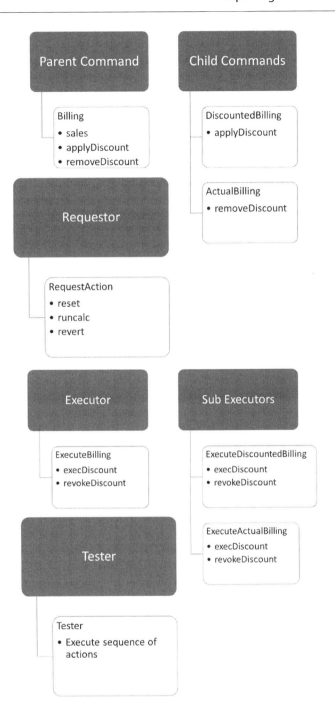

Figure 12.2 – Command design pattern classes

In this section, we looked at the concept of the command design pattern. Now, let's look at the strategy design pattern.

The strategy design pattern

In this section, we'll look at the final design pattern under the category of behavioral design patterns that we will be covering in this chapter. Let's look at the elements of the strategy pattern, as follows:

- **Domain**: A domain or base class defines all the base methods and attributes required for Python objects to perform a sequence of operations. This class also makes decisions concerning the operation that's performed within the class according to the strategy method defined in the strategy classes.

- **Strategies**: These are one or more independent classes that define one specific strategy within its strategy method. The same strategy method name will be used in each of the strategy classes.

- **Tester**: A tester function calls the domain class and executes the strategy.

To understand how the strategy design pattern is implemented, we'll look at various billing counters that we covered in *Chapter 8*. There are various billing counters in *ABC Megamart*, including a vegetable counter, a less than 10 item counter, an electronics counter, and so on.

In this example, we will define a vegetable counter and an electronics counter as strategy classes. Follow these steps:

1. To begin with, we will define a domain class named `SuperMarket` with methods that do the following:

   I.   Initialize attributes

   II.   Display details about the items in the cart

   III. Go to a specific counter

   Here is what the code for this looks like:

   ```python
   class SuperMarket():


       def __init__(self,STRATEGY, items, name, scan, units,
   tax,
                       itemtype = None):
           self.STRATEGY = STRATEGY
           self.items = items
           self.name = name
           self.scan = scan
           self.units = units
   ```

```
            self.tax = tax
            self.itemtype = itemtype

    def return_cart(self):
        cartItems = []
        for i in self.items:
            cartItems.append(i)
        return cartItems

    def goto_counter(self):
        countername = self.name
        return countername
```

2. Next, we will define methods that do the following:

- Scan the bar codes

- Add the bill details

- Add the tax details

Here is the code for this:

```
    def scan_bar_code(self):
        codes = []
        for i in self.scan:
            codes.append(i)
        return codes

    def add_billing(self):
        self.codes = self.scan_bar_code()
        pricetag = []
        for i in self.units:
            pricetag.append(i)
        bill = dict(zip(self.codes, pricetag))
        return bill

    def add_tax(self):
        taxed = []
        for i in self.tax:
```

```
            taxed.append(i)
        return taxed
```

3. The operations for calculating the bill and printing the invoice are also defined in the `SuperMarket` class. Refer to the following code:

```python
    def calc_bill(self):
        bill = self.add_billing()
        items = []
        cartItems = self.return_cart()
        calc_bill = []
        taxes = self.add_tax()
        for item,tax in zip(bill.items(),taxes):
            items.append(item[1])
            calc_bill.append(item[1] + item[1]*tax)
        finalbill = dict(zip(cartItems, calc_bill))
        return finalbill


    def print_invoice(self):
        finalbill = self.calc_bill()
        final_total = sum(finalbill.values())
        print('**************ABC
Megamart****************')
        print('***********------------------
**************')
        print('Counter Name: ', self.goto_counter())
        for item,price in finalbill.items():
            print(item,": ", price)
        print('Total:',final_total)
        print('***********------------------
**************')
        print('***************P
AID**********************')
```

4. The final method within the `SuperMarket` class is the `pipeline_template` method, which creates a pipeline for running the sequence of methods:

```python
    def pipeline_template(self):
        self.return_cart()
```

```
                self.goto_counter()
                self.STRATEGY.redirect_counter()
                self.scan_bar_code()
                self.add_billing()
                self.add_tax()
                self.calc_bill()
                self.print_invoice()
```

In this method, we have called the strategy method to change the strategy that's performed by the `SuperMarket` class.

5. Now, let's define a simple strategy class for the vegetable counter, as follows:

```
class VegeCounter():
    def redirect_counter():
        print("**************Move to Vege
Counter**************")
```

6. Let's also create a simple strategy class for the electronic counter, as follows:

```
class ElectronicsCounter():
    def redirect_counter():
        print("**************Move to Electronics
            Counter**************")
```

7. Now, we must define a tester function to test the strategy:

```
def run_pipeline(domain = SuperMarket):
    domain.pipeline_template()
```

8. Let's test the strategy for the vegetable counter by running the pipeline and providing `VegeCounter` as the strategy value:

```
run_pipeline(SuperMarket(STRATEGY = VegeCounter,
        items =
['Onions','Tomatoes','Cabbage','Beetroot'],
        name = ['Vegetable Counter'],
        scan = [113323,3434332,2131243,2332783],
        units = [10,15,12,14],
        tax = [0.04,0.03,0.035,0.025],
        itemtype = ['Vegetables'],
        ))
```

9. The output for the `VegeCounter` strategy is as follows:

```
*************Move to Vege Counter*************
*************ABC Megamart*****************
**********-------------------*************
Counter Name:  ['Vegetable Counter']
Onions :  10.4
Tomatoes :  15.45
Cabbage :  12.42
Beetroot :  14.35
Total: 52.620000000000005
**********-------------------*************
*************PAID***********************
```

10. Now, let's test the strategy for the electronics counter by running the pipeline and providing `ElectronicsCounter` as the strategy value:

```
run_pipeline(SuperMarket(STRATEGY = ElectronicsCounter,
                   items =
['television','keyboard','mouse'],
                   name = ['Electronics Counter'],
                   scan = [113323,3434332,2131243],
                   units = [100,16,14],
                   tax = [0.04,0.03,0.035],
                   itemtype = ['Electronics'],
                   ))
```

The output for the `ElectronicsCounter` strategy is as follows:

```
*************Move to Electronics Counter*************
*************ABC Megamart*****************
**********-------------------*************
Counter Name:  ['Electronics Counter']
television :  104.0
keyboard :  16.48
mouse :  14.49
Total: 134.97
**********-------------------*************
*************PAID***********************
```

Now, let's connect the elements of this design pattern with its corresponding objects:

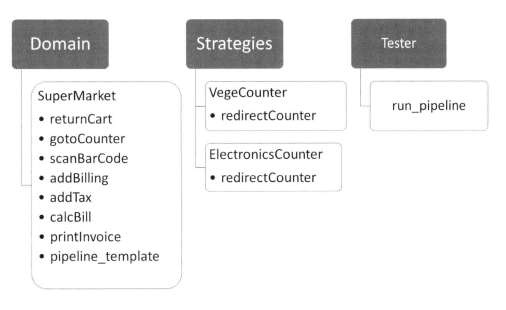

Figure 12.3 – Strategy pattern with classes

With that, we have learned about the strategy design pattern. Now, let's summarize this chapter.

Summary

In this chapter, we learned about behavioral design patterns by applying some of them in Python 3. In particular, we implemented the chain of responsibility, command, and strategy patterns and understood each of their elements.

Similar to the other chapters in this book, this chapter has been split into two parts – this chapter explained design patterns and focused on metaprogramming and its impact on Python code.

In the next chapter, we will continue looking at the concept of design patterns by covering examples of structural and creational design patterns.

13
Applying GOF Design Patterns
– Part 2

In this chapter, we will continue looking at the concept of design patterns in Python 3 and its various categories and their implementation while developing software using Python.

In the previous chapter, we learned how to apply behavioral design patterns with examples. In this chapter, we will continue looking at the remaining two categories – structural and creational design patterns. We will see how they can be applied in Python using our core example of *ABC Megamart*.

In this chapter, we will be looking at the following main topics:

- Understanding structural design patterns
- Understanding creational design patterns

By the end of this chapter, you should be able to understand some of the examples of important structural and creational design patterns and learn how they can be implemented in various applications.

Technical requirements

The code examples shared in this chapter are available on GitHub under the code for this chapter here: `https://github.com/PacktPublishing/Metaprogramming-with-Python/tree/main/Chapter13`.

Exploring structural design patterns

As the name suggests, structural design patterns are used to design the structure of classes and their implementation in such a way that the classes and objects can be extended or reused effectively. In this section, we will be covering three such structural design patterns — bridge, façade, and proxy patterns. We are considering these three design patterns because they are unique and they represent three different aspects of how structural design patterns can be used.

Understanding the bridge pattern

The bridge design pattern is applied to bridge multiple elements or operations of implementation using the concept of abstraction or the abstract method. To explain this further and to implement this design pattern, our code should have the following elements:

- **Abstraction superclass**: The base class with the abstract method to perform a specific action, along with methods to bridge any additional implementation

- **Abstraction subclasses**: One or more subclasses that implement the abstract method from the abstraction superclass to perform their respective action

- **Implementation superclass**: A base that adds an additional implementation or design over the abstraction

- **Implementation subclasses**: Subclasses that inherit the implementation superclass

Let's look at the bridge pattern with an example. In this example, we will look at printing the business card for branch managers that belong to two different supermarkets – *ABC Megamart* and *XYZ Megamart*. Let's see how:

1. To illustrate the design pattern further, let's create an abstraction superclass named `PrintCard`, and add three methods. The `add_name` method adds the name of the supermarket, and the `add_manager` method adds the formatting specific to a manager. The `add_manager` method gets the formatting input from the implementation subclass, which we will discuss later in this section. The third method is the `printcard` method, which is an abstract method and will be defined in the subclasses:

```python
from abc import abstractmethod, ABC
class PrintCard(ABC):
    def add_name(self, name):
        self.name = name
    def add_manager(self, branch):
        self.branch = branch.FORMATTING
    @abstractmethod
    def printcard(self):
        pass
```

2. Let's further create an abstraction subclass named `CardABC`. This class will initialize the logo, name from the super class, and manager from the super class. The `printcard` method will print the logo, the name of the supermarket, and the address of the branch:

```
class CardABC(PrintCard):
    def __init__(self, logo, name, branch):
        self.logo = logo
        super().add_name(name)
        super().add_manager(branch)

    def printcard(self, *args):
        print(self.logo + self.name)
        for arg in args:
            print(self.branch + str(arg))
```

3. Next, create an abstraction subclass named `CardXYZ`. It will initialize the following variables – style, logo, name from super class, and manager from the superclass. The `printcard` method will print the logo, the style for the card, the name of the supermarket, and the address of the branch:

```
class CardXYZ(PrintCard):
    def __init__(self, style, logo, name, branch):
        self.style = style
        self.logo = logo
        super().add_name(name)
        super().add_manager(branch)

    def printcard(self, *args):
        print(self.logo + self.style + self.name)
        for arg in args:
            print(self.branch + str(arg))
```

4. Now, let's create the implementation superclass named `Manager` with a method named `formatting`:

```
class Manager:
    def formatting(self):
        pass
```

5. Next, create an implementation subclass named `Manager_manhattan` to add formatting to the business card, specifically for the branch manager from the Manhattan branch:

```
class Manager_manhattan(Manager):
    def __init__(self):
        self.formatting()


    def formatting(self):
        self.FORMATTING = '\33[7m'
```

6. Let's now create an implementation subclass named `Manager_albany` to add formatting for the business card specifically for the branch manager from the Albany branch:

```
class Manager_albany(Manager):
    def __init__(self):
        self.formatting()


    def formatting(self):
        self.FORMATTING = '\033[94m'
```

7. Next, instantiate `CardABC`, which is an abstraction subclass. The three input parameters for this class are the format of the logo, the name of the supermarket, and the branch from where the formatting will be added to the card:

```
manager_manhattan = CardABC(logo = '\33[43m', name = 'ABC
Megamart', branch = Manager_manhattan())
```

8. And now we will print the card:

```
manager_manhattan.printcard('John M',
            'john.m@abcmegamart.com',
    '40097 5th Main Street',
    'Manhattan',
    'New York City',
    'New York',
    11007)
```

The output is represented as follows, with the formatting as provided in the class instantiation:

```
ABC Megamart
John M
john.m@abcmegamart.com
40097 5th Main Street
Manhattan
New York City
New York
11007
```

9. Let's now instantiate `CardXYZ`, which is an abstraction subclass. The four input parameters for this class are the style, the format of the logo, the name of the supermarket, and the branch from where the formatting will be added to the card:

```
manager_albany = CardXYZ(style = '\33[43m',logo =
'\33[5m', name = 'XYZ Megamart', branch = Manager_
albany())
```

10. Now, let's print the card.

```
manager_albany.printcard('Ron D','ron.d@abcmegamart.
com','123 Main Street','Albany','New York', 12084)
```

The output is represented as follows, with the style and formatting as provided in the class instantiation:

```
XYZ Megamart
Ron D
ron.d@abcmegamart.com
123 Main Street
Albany
New York
12084
```

Let's connect the elements of this design pattern with their corresponding objects in the example with the following graphical representation:

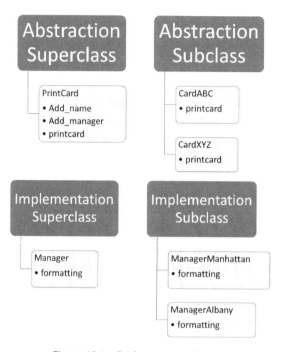

Figure 13.1 – Bridge pattern classes

So, the bridge pattern has been implemented by creating a bridge between the abstraction and the implementation classes. With this understanding, let's look at the facade pattern.

Understanding the facade pattern

In this section, we will look at the facade pattern, where we will design a black box kind of implementation to hide the complexity of a system that handles multiple subsystems from the end user or client. To explain this further and to implement this design/core pattern, our code needs the following elements:

- **Functionality**: The core functionalities that need to be implemented for a system are defined in these functionality classes.

- **Facade**: This is the class that wraps the core functionalities and their implementation from the end users.

- **End user**: The function, method, or class using which the core functionalities of a system are accessed using the facade class.

To understand the facade pattern further, let's create a set of functionalities that starts from adding items to the shopping cart, moving to the counter, scanning bar codes, billing, and finally, printing the invoice:

1. The first functionality class in this series is `Cart`, where items will be added to the shopping cart in the `return_cart` method:

```python
class Cart:
    def __init__(self, items):
        self.items = items
    def return_cart(self):
        cart_items = []
        for i in self.items:
            cart_items.append(i)
        print("Running return_cart...")
        return cart_items
```

2. The second functionality class is the `Counter` class, where the name of the counter is returned in the `goto_counter` method:

```python
class Counter:
    def __init__(self, name):
        self.name = name
    def goto_counter(self):
        countername = self.name
        print("Running goto_counter...")
        return countername
```

3. The third functionality class is the `BarCode` class, where the scanned bar codes are returned in the `scan_bar_code` method:

```python
class BarCode:
    def __init__(self, scan):
        self.scan = scan
    def scan_bar_code(self):
        codes = []
        for i in self.scan:
            codes.append(i)
        print("Running scan_bar_code...")
        return codes
```

4. The fourth functionality is the `Billing` class, where the price is tagged to the bar codes and returned as a dictionary object in the `add_billing` method:

```python
class Billing:
    def __init__(self, codes, units ):
        self.codes = codes
        self.units = units
    def add_billing(self):
        codes = self.codes.scan_bar_code()
        pricetag = []
        for i in self.units:
            pricetag.append(i)
        bill = dict(zip(codes, pricetag))
        print("Running add_billing...")
        return bill
```

5. The next functionality is the `Tax` class, where tax values are returned using the `add_tax` method in the class:

```python
class Tax:
    def __init__(self, tax):
        self.tax = tax
    def add_tax(self):
        taxed = []
        for i in self.tax:
            taxed.append(i)
        print("Running add_tax...")
        return taxed
```

6. The functionality after this is the `FinalBill` class, where we will be calculating the final bill using the `calc_bill` method:

```python
class FinalBill:
    def __init__(self, billing, cart, tax):
        self.billing = billing
        self.cart = cart
        self.tax = tax
    def calc_bill(self):
        bill = self.billing.add_billing()
```

```
            items = []
            cart_items = self.cart.return_cart()
            calc_bill = []
            taxes = self.tax.add_tax()
            for item,tax in zip(bill.items(),taxes):
                items.append(item[1])
                calc_bill.append(item[1] + item[1]*tax)
            finalbill = dict(zip(cart_items, calc_bill))
            print("Running calc_bill...")
            return finalbill
```

7. The final functionality class in the facade pattern is the `Invoice` class, where we will be creating a `print_invoice` method to print the final invoice:

```
class Invoice:
    def __init__(self, finalbill, counter):
        self.finalbill = finalbill
        self.counter = counter
    def print_invoice(self):
        finalbill = self.finalbill.calc_bill()
        final_total = sum(finalbill.values())
        print("Running print_invoice...")
        print('**************ABC
                Megamart*****************')
        print('***********------------------
                **************')
        print('Counter Name: ',
                self.counter.goto_counter())
        for item,price in finalbill.items():
            print(item,": ", price)
        print('Total:',final_total)
        print('***********------------------
                **************')
        print('***************PAID********************
                ****')
```

8. Now, let's create the `Facade` class named `Queue`. It has two functions – the `pipeline` method to explicitly run some of the methods in the functionality classes, and the `pipeline_implicit` method to run the `print_invoice` method from the `Invoice` class, which will in turn call all other methods in the rest of the functionality classes:

```python
class Queue:
    def __init__(self, items, name, scan, units, tax):
        self.cart = Cart(items)
        self.counter = Counter(name)
        self.barcode = BarCode(scan)
        self.billing = Billing(self.barcode, units)
        self.tax = Tax(tax)
        self.finalbill = FinalBill(self.billing,
                        self.cart, self.tax)
        self.invoice = Invoice(self.finalbill,
                        self.counter)
    def pipeline(self):
        self.cart.return_cart()
        self.counter.goto_counter()
        self.barcode.scan_bar_code()
        self.tax.add_tax()
    def pipeline_implicit(self):
        self.invoice.print_invoice()
```

9. Let's create an end user function to run the methods in functionality classes using the `Facade` class by creating an instance for `Queue` and calling the `pipeline` method:

```python
def run_facade():
    queue = Queue(items = ['paperclips','blue
                    pens','stapler','pencils'],
            name = ['Regular Counter'],
            scan = [113323,3434332,2131243,2332783],
            units = [10,15,12,14],
            tax = [0.04,0.03,0.035,0.025],
            )
    queue.pipeline()
```

10. Now, let's call the `run_facade` method to test the design pattern:

```
run_facade()
```

The output for the preceding test is as follows:

```
Running return_cart...
Running goto_counter...
Running scan_bar_code...
Running add_tax...
```

11. Finally, let's create another end user function to run the methods in functionality classes using the `Facade` class by creating an instance for `Queue` and calling the `pipeline_implicit` method:

```
def run_facade_implicit():
    queue = Queue(items = ['paperclips','blue
                    pens','stapler','pencils'],
            name = ['Regular Counter'],
            scan = [113323,3434332,2131243,2332783],
            units = [10,15,12,14],
            tax = [0.04,0.03,0.035,0.025],
            )
        queue.pipeline_implicit()
```

12. Then, let's call the `run_facade_implicit` method to test the design pattern:

```
run_facade_implicit()
```

The output for the preceding test is as follows:

```
Running scan_bar_code...
Running add_billing...
Running return_cart...
Running add_tax...
Running calc_bill...
Running print_invoice...
**************ABC Megamart*****************
***********------------------**************
Running goto_counter...
Counter Name:  ['Regular Counter']
paperclips :  10.4
```

```
blue pens :   15.45
stapler :   12.42
pencils :   14.35
Total: 52.620000000000005
***********-------------------**************
***************PAID***********************
```

Let's connect the elements of this design pattern with their corresponding objects in the example in the following graphical representation:

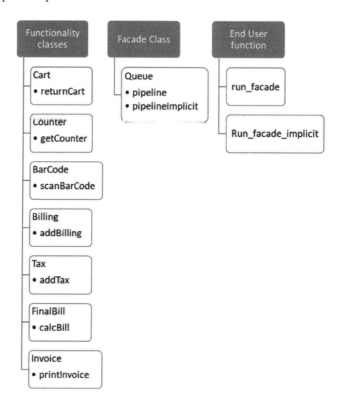

Figure 13.2 – Facade pattern classes

So, the facade pattern has been implemented by creating a black box that provides the end users with an interface to access the functions of a complex system without worrying about the implementation details. Now, let's look at the proxy pattern.

Understanding the proxy pattern

In this section, we will look at the proxy design pattern. As the name implies, the proxy pattern is applied to create a proxy around the actual functionality so that the actual functionality is executed only when the proxy allows it based on certain preconditions. To explain this further and to implement this design pattern, our code needs the following elements:

- **Functionality class**: The base functionalities of the system are designed in this class as methods.

- **Proxy class**: This is a proxy around the `functionality` class and it provides restrictions as to when to execute the base functionalities from the `functionality` class.

In this example, let's consider the NYC branch of *ABC Megamart* and create a class named `NYC`:

1. The `NYC` class is initialized with four empty dictionary parameters named `manager`, `branch`, `product`, and `sales`. Let's also add three methods named `set_parameters` (to set the four dictionary parameters), `get_parameters` (to return the parameters), and `calc_tax_nyc` (to calculate the tax and return the parameters along with selling price data):

```
class NYC:
    def __init__(self):
        self.manager = {}
        self.branch = {}
        self.product = {}
        self.sales = {}
    def set_parameters(self, manager, branch, product,
                       sales):
        self.manager = manager
        self.branch = branch
        self.product = product
        self.sales = sales
    def get_parameters(self):
        return self.manager, self.branch,
               self.product, self.sales
    def calc_tax_nyc(self):
        branch = self.branch
        manager = self.manager
        product = self.product
        sales = self.sales
        pricebeforetax = sales['purchase_price'] +
```

```
                                        sales['purchase_price'] *
                                        sales['profit_margin']
                    finalselling_price = pricebeforetax +
                        (pricebeforetax * (sales['tax_rate'] +
                        sales['local_rate']))
                    sales['selling_price'] = finalselling_price
                    return branch, manager, product, sales
```

2. The next step of the implementation is to create a proxy `ReturnBook` class to call the methods from the NYC class to set parameters, get parameters, and calculate tax:

```
class ReturnBook(NYC):
    def __init__(self, nyc):
        self.nyc = nyc
    def add_book_details(self, state, manager, branch,
                            product, sales):
        if state in ['NY', 'NYC', 'New York']:
            self.nyc.set_parameters(manager, branch,
                                        product, sales)
        else:
            print("There is no branch in the state:",
                    state)
    def show_book_details(self, state):
        if state in ['NY', 'NYC', 'New York']:
            return self.nyc.get_parameters()
        else:
            print(state, "has no data")
    def calc_tax(self, state):
        if state in ['NY', 'NYC', 'New York']:
            return self.nyc.calc_tax_nyc()
        else:
            print("The state", state, "is not
                    supported")
```

3. Let's now instantiate the proxy `ReturnBook` class and provide the NYC functionality class as the input parameter:

```
branch_manhattan = ReturnBook(NYC())
```

4. To set the parameters from the NYC class, we will be calling the `add_book_details` method from the proxy class. The parameters will be set in the NYC class only if the conditions provided in `add_book_details` are successfully met by the input state parameter:

```
branch_manhattan.add_book_details(state = 'NY', manager =
{'regional_manager': 'John M',
  'branch_manager': 'Tom H',
  'sub_branch_id': '2021-01'},
  branch = {'branchID': 2021,
  'branch_street': '40097 5th Main Street',
  'branch_borough': 'Manhattan',
  'branch_city': 'New York City',
  'branch_state': 'New York',
  'branch_zip': 11007},
  product = {'productId': 100002,
  'product_name': 'WashingMachine',
  'product_brand': 'Whirlpool'},
  sales = {'purchase_price': 450,
  'profit_margin': 0.19,
  'tax_rate': 0.4,
  'local_rate': 0.055})
```

5. Let's further call the `show_book_details` method to get the parameters from the NYC class, provided that the state parameter in the input is NY, NYC, or New York:

```
branch_manhattan.show_book_details('NY')
```

The output of the preceding code is as follows:

```
({'regional_manager': 'John M',
  'branch_manager': 'Tom H',
  'sub_branch_id': '2021-01'},
 {'branchID': 2021,
  'branch_street': '40097 5th Main Street',
  'branch_borough': 'Manhattan',
  'branch_city': 'New York City',
  'branch_state': 'New York',
  'branch_zip': 11007},
 {'productId': 100002,
```

```
        'product_name': 'WashingMachine',
        'product_brand': 'Whirlpool'},
      {'purchase_price': 450,
        'profit_margin': 0.19,
        'tax_rate': 0.4,
        'local_rate': 0.055})
```

6. Let's further call the `calc_tax` method from the proxy class to calculate the selling price, provided the state parameters are successful:

```
branch_manhattan.calc_tax('NY')
```

7. Let's test the restrictions in the proxy methods by providing incorrect input to the state parameter:

```
branch_manhattan.add_book_details(state = 'LA', manager =
{'regional_manager': 'John M',
  'branch_manager': 'Tom H',
  'sub_branch_id': '2021-01'},
  branch = {'branchID': 2021,
  'branch_street': '40097 5th Main Street',
  'branch_borough': 'Manhattan',
  'branch_city': 'New York City',
  'branch_state': 'New York',
  'branch_zip': 11007},
  product = {'productId': 100002,
  'product_name': 'WashingMachine',
  'product_brand': 'Whirlpool'},
  sales = {'purchase_price': 450,
  'profit_margin': 0.19,
  'tax_rate': 0.4,
  'local_rate': 0.055})
```

The output of the preceding code is as follows:

```
There is no branch in the state: LA
```

8. Similarly, let's also test the `show_book_details` method:

```
branch_manhattan.show_book_details('LA')
```

The output of the preceding code is as follows:

```
LA has no data
```

9. Finally, let's test the `calc_tax` method from the proxy:

```
branch_manhattan.calc_tax('LA')
```

The output is as follows:

```
The state LA is not supported
```

Let's connect the elements of this design pattern with their corresponding objects in the example in the following graphical representation:

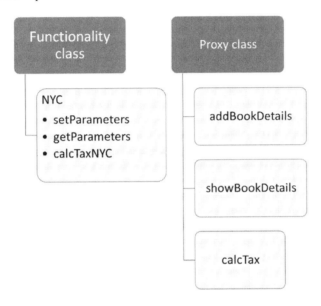

Figure 13.3 – Proxy design pattern classes

So, the proxy pattern has been implemented by creating a proxy class that adds the required conditions to execute the actual functionalities. Next, we're moving on to exploring the creational design patterns.

Exploring creational design patterns

Creational design patterns are various methods to add abstraction in the process of object creation. In this section, we will be looking at three such design patterns, namely the factory method, prototype pattern, and singleton pattern.

Understanding the factory method

The factory design pattern is a method of abstraction where a factory class is created to create an object for the class from the factory class instead of directly instantiating the object. To explain this further and to implement this design pattern, our code needs the following elements:

- **Abstract class**: The abstract class with the abstract methods for functionalities to be defined in the subclasses.

- **Abstraction subclasses**: The subclasses are inherited from the abstract class and overwrite the abstract methods.

- **Factory class**: The class to create objects for the abstraction subclasses.

- **End user method**: The class or method to test or call the factory method.

For this example, let's implement using another scenario from *ABC Megamart*:

1. Let's create an abstract class with two methods, buy_product and maintenance_cost:

    ```python
    from abc import abstractmethod
    class Branch:
        @abstractmethod
        def buy_product(self):
            pass
        @abstractmethod
        def maintenance_cost(self):
            pass
    ```

2. Now, let's create a subclass for the Branch class named Brooklyn and implement the buy_product and maintenance_cost methods:

    ```python
    class Brooklyn(Branch):
        def __init__(self,product,unit_price,quantity,
                     product_type):
            self.product = product
            self.unit_price = unit_price
            self.quantity = quantity
            self.product_type = product_type
        def buy_product(self):
            if (self.product_type == 'FMCG'):
                self.statetax_rate = 0.035
                self.promotiontype = 'Discount'
    ```

```
            self.discount = 0.10
            self.initialprice =
                self.unit_price*self.quantity
            self.salesprice = self.initialprice +
                self.initialprice*self.statetax_rate
            self.finalprice = self.salesprice *
                (1-self.discount)
            return self.salesprice,
                self.product,self.promotiontype
        else:
            return "We don't stock this product"
    def maintenance_cost(self):
        self.coldstorageCost = 100
        if (self.product_type == 'FMCG'):
            self.maintenance_cost = self.quantity *
                0.25 + self.coldstorageCost
            return self.maintenance_cost
        else:
            return "We don't stock this product"
```

3. Similarly, let's create another subclass, named `Manhattan`, which inherits the `Branch` class, as follows:

```
class Manhattan(Branch):
    def __init__(self,product,unit_price,quantity,
                product_type):
        self.product = product
        self.unit_price = unit_price
        self.quantity = quantity
        self.product_type = product_type
```

4. Let's further define a method named `buy_product` to return the product price, product name, and promotion in cases where the product is electronic:

```
    def buy_product(self):
        if (self.product_type == 'Electronics'):
            self.statetax_rate = 0.05
            self.promotiontype = 'Buy 1 Get 1'
```

```
            self.discount = 0.50
            self.initialprice =
                self.unit_price*self.quantity
            self.salesprice = self.initialprice +
                self.initialprice*self.statetax_rate
            self.finalprice = self.salesprice *
                (1-self.discount)
            return self.finalprice,
                self.product,self.promotiontype
        else:
            return "We don't stock this product"
```

5. Let's now define another method to calculate the maintenance cost:

```
    def maintenance_cost(self):
        if (self.product_type == 'Electronics'):
          self.maintenance_cost = self.quantity * 0.05
          return self.maintenance_cost
        else:
          return "We don't stock this product"
```

6. In the next step, let's create a factory class named BranchFactory, which creates the instance for the branch subclasses, Brooklyn or Manhattan:

```
Class BranchFactory:
    def create_branch(self,branch,product,unit_price,
                        quantity,product_type):
        if str.upper(branch) == 'BROOKLYN':
            return Brooklyn(product,unit_price,
                            quantity,product_type)

        elif str.upper(branch) == 'MANHATTAN':
            return Manhattan(product,unit_price,
                            quantity,product_type)
```

7. Now, let's test the factory method by creating a function named test_factory:

```
def test_factory(branch,product,unit_
price,quantity,product_type):
    branchfactory = BranchFactory()
```

```
branchobject = branchfactory.create_branch(branch,
        product,unit_price,quantity,product_type)
print(branchobject)
print(branchobject.buy_product())
print(branchobject.maintenance_cost())
```

8. Let's now call the `test_factory` function with inputs as `Brooklyn`, `Milk`, `10.5`, and FMCG as follows:

```
test_factory('Brooklyn','Milk', 10,5,'FMCG')
```

The output for the preceding code is as follows:

```
<__main__.Brooklyn object at 0x000002101D4569A0>
(51.75, 'Milk', 'Discount')
101.25
```

9. Now, call the `test_factory` function with inputs as `manhattan`, `iPhone`, `1000`, `1`, and `Electronics` as follows:

```
test_factory('manhattan','iPhone', 1000,1,'Electronics')
```

The output for the preceding code is as follows:

```
<__main__.Manhattan object at 0x000002101D456310>
(525.0, 'iPhone', 'Buy 1 Get 1')
0.05
```

Let's connect the elements of this design pattern with their corresponding objects in the example with the following graphical representation:

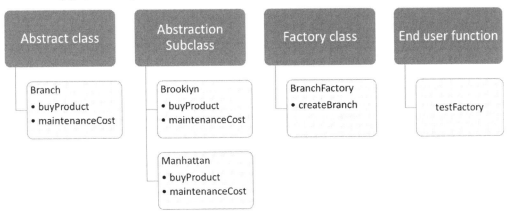

Figure 13.4 – Factory pattern classes

So, the factory pattern has been implemented by creating a factory class that instantiates the `Abstraction` subclasses. With this implementation, we have learned about the creational design pattern with an example.

Understanding the prototype method

The prototype design pattern is also used to implement abstraction during the creation of a Python object. A prototype can be used by the end user to create a copy of an object of a class without the overhead of understanding the detailed implementation behind it. To explain this further and to implement this design pattern, our code needs the following elements:

- **Prototype class**: This class has a method to clone or copy another Python object that has the implementation.

- **Implementation class**: This class has the actual implementation of the functionalities as attributes and methods.

For this example, let's implement using another scenario from *ABC Megamart*:

1. Let's create a class named `Prototype` and define a method named `clone` to copy the Python object provided as input to the method:

    ```python
    class Prototype:
        def __init__(self):
            self.cp = __import__('copy')


        def clone(self, objname):
            return self.cp.deepcopy(objname)
    ```

2. Let's now create an implementation class named FMCG and initialize a set of variables pertaining to the supplier details, and add a method to get the supplier details:

    ```python
    class FMCG:
        def __init__(self,supplier_name,supplier_code,
        supplier_address,supplier_contract_start_date,\
        supplier_contract_end_date,supplier_quality_code):
            self.supplier_name = supplier_name
            self.supplier_code = supplier_code
            self.supplier_address = supplier_address
            self.supplier_contract_start_date =
                supplier_contract_start_date
            self.supplier_contract_end_date =
    ```

```
                    supplier_contract_end_date
        self.supplier_quality_code =
                    supplier_quality_code

    def get_supplier_details(self):
        supplierDetails = {
            'Supplier_name': self.supplier_name,
            'Supplier_code': self.supplier_code,
            'Supplier_address': self.supplier_address,
            'ContractStartDate':
                self.supplier_contract_start_date,
            'ContractEndDate':
                self.supplier_contract_end_date,
            'QualityCode': self.supplier_quality_code
        }
        return supplierDetails
```

3. In the next step, let's create an object named `fmcg_supplier` for the FMCG class:

```
fmcg_supplier = FMCG('Test Supplier','a0015','5093 9th
Main Street, Pasadena,California, 91001', '05/04/2020',
'05/04/2025',1)
```

4. Let's also create an object for the `Prototype` class, named `proto`:

```
proto = Prototype()
```

5. Now, we can directly clone the `fmcg_supplier` object without passing all the attributes of the FMCG class as input. To do this, we will make use of the `clone` method from the `Prototype` class:

```
fmcg_supplier_reuse = proto.clone(fmcg_supplier)
```

6. The `fmcg_supplier_reuse` object is a clone of the `fmcg_supplier` object and it is not the same object itself. This can be verified by looking at the ID of both of these objects:

```
id(fmcg_supplier)
```

The output is as follows:

```
2268233820528
```

7. Similarly, we can also look at the ID of the cloned object:

```
id(fmcg_supplier_reuse)
```

The output is as follows:

```
2268233819616
```

8. Let's also verify that the cloned object can be modified without impacting the actual object:

```
fmcg_supplier_reuse.supplier_name = 'ABC Supplier'
fmcg_supplier_reuse.get_supplier_details()
```

The output is as follows:

```
{'Supplier_name': 'ABC Supplier',
 'Supplier_code': 'a0015',
 'Supplier_address': '5093 9th Main Street,
Pasadena,California, 91001',
 'ContractStartDate': '05/04/2020',
 'ContractEndDate': '05/04/2025',
 'QualityCode': 1}
```

9. In the preceding output, we have modified the cloned object and this should not impact the original object. Let's verify the original object:

```
fmcg_supplier.get_supplier_details()
```

The output is as follows:

```
{'Supplier_name': 'Test Supplier',
 'Supplier_code': 'a0015',
 'Supplier_address': '5093 9th Main Street,
Pasadena,California, 91001',
 'ContractStartDate': '05/04/2020',
 'ContractEndDate': '05/04/2025',
 'QualityCode': 1}
```

So, the prototype pattern has been implemented by creating a `Prototype` class that copies the object of the implementation class. Now that you've understood this, let's look at the singleton design pattern.

Understanding the singleton pattern

As the name suggests, the singleton pattern is a design pattern where we can limit the number of class instances created for a class while initializing the class itself. To explain this further and implement this design pattern, we need to develop the elements of the **singleton class** in our code.

Unlike the other patterns, this pattern has only one element – the singleton class. A singleton class will have a constraint set within its `init` method to limit the number of instances to one.

For this example, let's implement using another scenario from *ABC Megamart*:

1. Let's define a class named `SingletonBilling`. This class will have the attributes required to generate a bill for a product:

    ```python
    class SingletonBilling:
        billing_instance = None
        product_name = 'Dark Chocolate'
        unit_price = 6
        quantity = 4
        tax = 0.054
    ```

2. Let's add a constraint in the `init` method of this class to limit the number of class instances to one:

    ```python
    def __init__(self):
        if SingletonBilling.billing_instance == None:
            SingletonBilling.billing_instance = self
        else:
            print("Billing can have only one
                    instance")
    ```

3. In the next step, let's also add a `generate_bill` method to perform the function of generating a bill for a product based on the class attributes:

    ```python
    def generate_bill(self):
        total = self.unit_price * self.quantity
        final_total = total + total*self.tax
        print('***********-----------------
                **************')
        print('Product:', self.product_name)
    ```

```
print('Total:',final_total)
print('***********------------------
           **************')
```

4. In the next step, we can instantiate the class object for the first time and call its `generate_bill` method:

```
invoice1 = SingletonBilling()
invoice1.generate_bill()
```

The output is displayed as follows:

```
***********--------------------**************
Product: Dark Chocolate
Total: 25.296
***********------  --------------**************
```

5. Let's now test the singleton pattern by instantiating one more instance for the class:

```
invoice2 = SingletonBilling()
```

The second instance could not be created for the class due to its singleton property. The output is as expected:

```
Billing can have only one instance
```

So, the singleton pattern has been implemented by restricting the singleton class from creating more than one instance. With this example, we have covered three types of creational design patterns and their implementation.

Summary

In this chapter, we have learned about the concept of structural and creational design patterns by applying some of these design patterns in Python 3. We implemented the bridge design pattern and understood each of its elements. We understood the facade design pattern and its various elements. We also implemented the proxy design pattern with an example. We also covered creational design patterns such as the factory method, prototype, and singleton patterns with their corresponding examples.

Similar to other chapters covered in this book, this chapter, which explains the second part of design patterns, also focused on metaprogramming and its impact on Python code.

In the next chapter, we will continue the code generation with some examples.

14

Generating Code from AST

In this chapter, we will learn how to use ASTs in Python to generate code for various applications. We will apply these abstract syntax trees to metaprogramming to implement automatic code generated in this chapter.

Automatic code generation is one way of making the life of a programmer easier. An abstract syntax tree is an excellent functionality that can help us generate code in a much simpler way.

The concept of AST is discussed with examples in *Chapter 9* of this book. In this chapter, we will be tapping the advantages of ASTs to generate code automatically. Code generation can be implemented to enable no-code or limited coding while developing applications. In this chapter, we will continue to use the example of *ABC Megamart* to generate code from ASTs.

In this chapter, we will be looking at the following main topics:

- Generating a simple class with a template
- Generating multiple classes from a list
- Generating a class with attributes
- Generating a class with methods
- Defining a custom class factory
- Developing a code generator to generate a simple library

By the end of this chapter, you should be able to understand how to use the existing methods of the `ast` library in Python to enable your application to generate its own code, how to avoid repeating yourself, and how to generate code dynamically.

Technical requirements

The code examples shared in this chapter are available on GitHub under the code for this chapter here: `https://github.com/PacktPublishing/Metaprogramming-with-Python/tree/main/Chapter14`.

Generating a simple class with a template

In this section, we will be looking at how to generate code for a class without actually defining the class itself. We will be creating a string-based template with the structure of a class we want to develop but not the actual code that can be executed. To explain this further, let us look at an example where we will generate a class named VegCounter by parsing a series of strings using the ast module.

The sequence of steps to be followed to generate code for a class is represented in the following flow diagram:

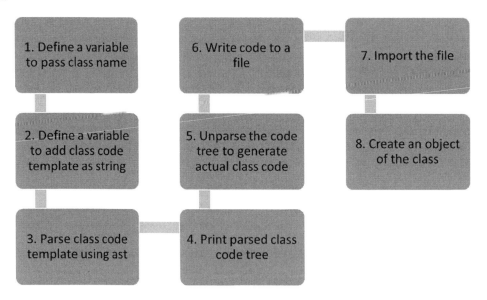

Figure 14.1 – A code generation sequence for a simple class

Let us look at the implementation of this example:

1. We will start by importing the ast library:

    ```
    import ast
    ```

2. Let us now create a variable to pass the class name with which the code needs to be generated:

    ```
    classname = "VegCounter"
    ```

3. We will next define a variable that becomes the template for the class generated in this example:

    ```
    classtemplate = """class """ +classname+ """():pass"""
    ```

4. In the next step, we will parse the class template with the parse method in the `ast` module:

```
print(ast.dump(class_tree, indent = 4))
```

5. The output of the preceding code displays the abstract syntax tree of the class template:

```
Module(
    body=[
        ClassDef(
            name='VegCounter',
            bases=[],
            keywords=[],
            body=[
                Pass()],
            decorator_list=[])],
    type_ignores=[])
```

6. The preceding tree can be compiled and executed as follows:

```
actualclass = compile(class_tree, 'vegctr_tree', 'exec')
actualclass
```

Thus, this leads to the following output:

```
<code object <module> at 0x0000028AAB0D2A80, file
"vegctr_tree", line 1>
```

7. In the next step, we will unparse the tree to generate the actual code for the class:

```
VegCounter.
print(ast.unparse(class_tree))
```

Executing the preceding code leads to the following output:

```
class VegCounter:
    pass
```

8. In the next step, let us write the preceding class code to a file named `classtemplate.py`:

```
code = open("classtemplate.py", "w")
script = code.write(ast.unparse(class_tree))
code.close()
```

9. The `classtemplate` file looks as follows:

```
1  class VegCounter:
2        pass
```

Figure 14.2 – The classtemplate.py file

10. Let us now import the `classtemplate` and create an object:

```
import classtemplate as c
vegc = c.VegCounter()
vegc
```

The output is as follows:

```
<classtemplate.VegCounter at 0x28aab1d6a30>
```

In this section, we have generated a simple class code using the `ast` module. This example helps us in understanding the steps to be followed to generate code for a custom class since it is easier to start understanding code generation by starting simple. With this understanding, let us generate code for multiple classes.

Generating multiple classes from a list

In this section, we will look at generating code for multiple classes dynamically using the `ast` module and its `unparse` method.

Generating the code for more than one class dynamically gives us a direction for implementing code generation for multiple functionalities of an application. The classes need not be for the same functionality and the class code thus generated can later be modified to include additional methods or attributes as required by the application. The skeletal class code will be generated through this example.

To understand this further, we will follow the sequence described in the following flow diagram.

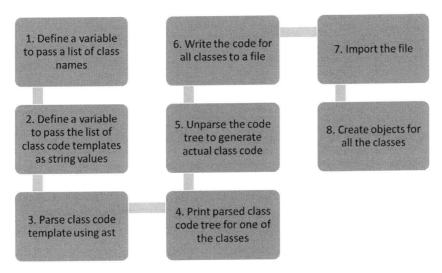

Figure 14.3 – A code generation sequence for multiple classes

Let us now look at how to implement this scenario:

1. We will first define a variable that can be assigned a list of class names as values:

    ```
    classnames = ["VegCounter", "ElectronicsCounter",
    "PasadenaBranch", "VegasBranch"]
    ```

2. In the next step, let us look at generating class templates for each of the class names from the preceding list:

    ```
    classgenerator = []
    for classname in classnames:
        classcode = """class """ +classname+ """():pass"""
        classgenerator.append(classcode)
    classgenerator
    ```

    The class templates are added to another list named classgenerator, and the list is as follows:

    ```
    ['class VegCounter():pass',
     'class ElectronicsCounter():pass',
     'class PasadenaBranch():pass',
     'class VegasBranch():pass']
    ```

3. To parse the string templates from the preceding output and generate their abstract syntax trees, let us create another list named `classtrees` and store the trees:

```
classtrees = []
for i in classgenerator:
    classtree = ast.parse(i)
    classtrees.append(classtree)
classtrees
```

The parsed class trees that are assigned to the `classtrees` list variable are displayed as follows:

```
[<ast.Module at 0x1efa91fde20>,
 <ast.Module at 0x1efa91e6d30>,
 <ast.Module at 0x1efa91e6220>,
 <ast.Module at 0x1efa91e6370>]
```

4. In this step, we will review one of the trees to ensure that the abstract syntax tree is generated for the class as expected:

```
print(ast.dump(classtrees[0], indent = 4))
```

The output is generated as follows:

```
Module(
    body=[
        ClassDef(
            name='VegCounter',
            bases=[],
            keywords=[],
            body=[
                Pass()],
            decorator_list=[])],
    type_ignores=[])
```

5. We can further unparse the `classtrees` variable to generate the code for each class:

```
print(ast.unparse(classtrees[1]))
```

An example output looks as follows:

```
class ElectronicsCounter:
    pass
```

6. Let us further write all the generated classes into a file:

```
code = open("classtemplates.py", "w")
for i in classtrees:
    code.write(ast.unparse(i))
    code.write("\n")
    code.write("\n")
code.close()
```

The generated `classtemplates.py` file looks as follows:

```
1   class VegCounter:
2       pass
3
4   class ElectronicsCounter:
5       pass
6
7   class PasadenaBranch:
8       pass
9
10  class VegasBranch:
11      pass
```

Figure 14.4 – The classtemplates.py file

7. Let us import the file and call an instance of each class to check if it works:

```
import classtemplates as ct
print(ct.ElectronicsCounter())
print(ct.PasadenaBranch())
print(ct.VegasBranch())
print(ct.VegCounter())
```

The output of the preceding code is as follows:

```
<classtemplates.ElectronicsCounter object at
0x00000255C0760FA0>
<classtemplates.PasadenaBranch object at
0x00000255C0760F10>
<classtemplates.VegasBranch object at 0x00000255C0760FA0>
<classtemplates.VegCounter object at 0x00000255C0760F10>
```

In this section, we have generated code for multiple classes using the `ast` module. This example is the next step toward working on automatic code generation for multiple functionalities or modules of an application.

Generating a class with attributes

In this section, we will generate code for a class, along with a list of attributes, that will also be included dynamically in the class. Generating code for a class alone can give the initial skeletal structure for a module, whereas we need to add attributes if we want to make the class more specific. The following flow diagram represents the sequence of steps to be followed for this example:

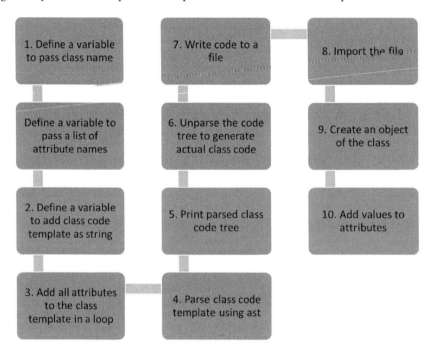

Figure 14.5 – A code generation sequence for a class with multiple attributes

Let us look at the code for this example:

1. We will first define a variable to provide `classname` as input, followed by a `classtemplate` to create the template of the class declaration:

```
classname = "VegCounter"
classtemplate =  '''class ''' +classname+
''':'''+'\n    '
```

2. In the next step, let us define another variable to provide attribute names as input:

```
attributename = ['items', 'countername', 'billamount']
```

3. Let us further update `classtemplate` by providing each of the preceding attributes that are required to generate the class code:

```
for attr in attributename:
    classtemplate = classtemplate + attr +''' =
        None''' + '\n      '
```

4. Let us now parse the `classtemplate` and review the abstract syntax tree:

```
class_tree = ast.parse(classtemplate)
print(ast.dump(class_tree, indent = 4))
```

5. The syntax tree for the preceding class template looks as follows:

```
Module(
    body=[
        ClassDef(
            name='VegCounter',
            bases=[],
            keywords=[],
            body=[
                Assign(
                    targets=[
                        Name(id='items',
                    ctx=Store())],
                    value=Constant(value=None)),
                Assign(
                    targets=[
                        Name(id='countername',
                        ctx=Store())],
                    value=Constant(value=None)),
                Assign(
                    targets=[
                        Name(id='billamount',
                        ctx=Store())],
                    value=Constant(value=None))],
```

```
                    decorator_list=[])],
        type_ignores=[])
```

All three variables – `items`, `countername`, and `billamount` added into the class template – are now part of the syntax tree. If we review the tree in detail, we can look at these variables under `body` | `assign` | `targets` | `name` | `id`.

6.   We can further unparse the tree and look at the code of the class:

```
print(ast.unparse(class_tree))
```

The output looks as follows:

```
class VegCounter:
    items = None
    countername = None
    billamount = None
```

Let us write the code to a file and import it:

```
code = open("classtemplateattr.py", "w")
script = code.write(ast.unparse(class_tree))
code.close()
```

The generated code looks as follows:

```
1  class VegCounter:
2      items = None
3      countername = None
4      billamount = None
```

Figure 14.6 – The classtemplateattr.py file

We can import the `classtemplateattr.py` file and the class can be accessed as follows:

```
import classtemplateattr as c
c.VegCounter()
vegc = c.VegCounter()
vegc.items = ['onions','tomatoes','carrots','lettuce']
vegc.countername = 'Veg Counter'
vegc.billamount = 200
```

The output is displayed as follows, with all the attributes and their corresponding values assigned:

```
['onions', 'tomatoes', 'carrots', 'lettuce']
Veg Counter
200
```

In this section, we have generated a class with multiple attributes without writing the code for the class. Instead, we have defined a template that takes in a class name and a list of attributes as input. With this understanding, we can look at generating a class with methods.

Generating a class with methods

In this section, let us generate code for a class and its methods. Throughout this chapter, our goal is to generate code dynamically for building applications that can solve a specific purpose. Adding methods along with attributes makes the code generation for a class even more application-specific. We can look at two variations of this example:

- Generating a class with an `init` method
- Generating a class with a user-defined method

Let's discuss each in detail.

Generating a class with an init method

In this example, let us generate code for a class and add an `init` method to the class and also initialize attributes. In this example, we will define a class for the vegetable counter of *ABC Megamart*. In the `init` method, let us initialize cart items from the vegetable counter of *ABC Megamart* in this class:

```
classname = "VegCounter"
classtemplate =   '''class ''' +classname+ ''':'''+'\n' +''' def
__init__(self,*items):
        cartItems = []
        for i in items:
            cartItems.append(i)
        self.items = cartItems'''
class_tree = ast.parse(classtemplate)
print(ast.unparse(class_tree))
```

The parsed class template generates the following code:

```
class VegCounter:
    def __init__(self, *items):
        cartItems = []
        for i in items:
            cartItems.append(i)
        self.items = cartItems
```

The abstract syntax tree for this class is generated with the function definition, as represented in the following figure:

```
body=[
    FunctionDef(
        name='__init__',
        args=arguments(
            posonlyargs=[],
            args=[
                arg(arg='self')],
            vararg=arg(arg='items'),
            kwonlyargs=[],
            kw_defaults=[],
            defaults=[]),
```

Figure 14.7 – The function definition of the init method

With this understanding, let us look at one more example of this same class by generating code for a user-defined method.

Generating a class with a user-defined method

In this section, let us look at a variation of the class by creating a template that generates a user-defined method for the class:

```
classname = "VegCounter"
methodname = "returnCart"
classtemplate =   '''class ''' +classname+ ''':'''+'\n' +''' def
'''+methodname+'''(self,*items):
        cartItems = []
        for i in items:
```

```
            cartItems.append(i)
        return cartItems'''
 class_tree = ast.parse(classtemplate)
 print(ast.unparse(class_tree))
```

The parsed `classtemplate` generates the following code:

```
class VegCounter:
    def returnCart(self, *items):
        cartItems = []
        for i in items:
            cartItems.append(i)
        return cartItems
```

The abstract syntax tree for this class is generated with the function definition, as represented in the following figure:

```
body=[
    FunctionDef(
        name='returnCart',
        args=arguments(
            posonlyargs=[],
            args=[
                arg(arg='self')],
            vararg=arg(arg='items'),
            kwonlyargs=[],
            kw_defaults=[],
            defaults=[]),
```

Figure 14.8 – The function definition of the user-defined method

We can either use the `init` method when we want to initialize the cart items at the class level or use the attributes later. By contrast, the user-defined method can be used if we want to keep the attributes specific to the method and perform actions based on the attributes within the method.

With this understanding, let us look at defining a custom class factory.

Defining a custom class factory

In this section, let us define a function named `classgenerator` that generates a custom class, attribute, and method using a class template as follows:

```
def classgenerator(classname, attribute, method):
    classtemplate = '''class ''' +classname+
        ''':'''+'\n     ' +attribute+''' =
        None\n     def '''+method+'''(self,item,status):
      if (status == 'Y'):
          print('Test passed for', item)
      else:
          print('Get another', item)
      '''

    return classtemplate
```

In this section, we are making the code generation more dynamic by creating a function that can generate code with custom values for the class name, attribute name, and method name, respectively. This helps in creating custom code for multiple functionalities in an application.

Let us provide a custom class name, attribute name, and method name as input to the preceding function:

```
class_tree = ast.parse(classgenerator('ElectronicCounter',
'TestItem', 'verifyCart')
actualclass = compile(class_tree, 'elec_tree', 'exec')
print(ast.unparse(class_tree))
```

The generated class code is as follows:

```
class ElectronicCounter:
    TestItem = None
    def verifyCart(self, item, status):
        if status == 'Y':
            print('Test passed for', item)
        else:
            print('Get another', item)
```

We can expand this example further by developing a code generator library in the following section.

Developing a code generator to generate a simple library

In this section, let us develop a simple code generator that generates code for a class with `get`, `set`, and `delete` properties for its custom attributes. The purpose of this section is to generate a complete library through automatic code generation. To fulfill this, let us write the following code:

1. Let us define the code generator as follows:

    ```
    class CodeGenerator:
        def __init__(self, classname, attribute):
            self.classname = classname
            self.attribute = attribute
    ```

2. Let us further define the method to define the class template in the code generator as follows:

    ```
    def generatecode(self):
            classtemplate = '''class ''' +self.
    classname+ ''':'''+'''\n    def __init__(self):''' +
    '\n    '+'''    self._'''+self.attribute+''' = None\
    n\n    @property
        def test'''+self.attribute+'''(self):\n            return
    self.test'''+self.attribute+'''\n\n    @test'''+self.
    attribute+'''.getter
        def test'''+self.
    attribute+'''(self):\n           print("get test'''+self.
    attribute+'''")\n        return self._test'''+self.
    attribute+'''


        @test'''+self.attribute+'''.setter
        def test'''+self.attribute+'''(self, value):
            print("set test'''+self.attribute+'''")
            self._test'''+self.attribute+''' = value


        @test'''+self.attribute+'''.deleter
        def test'''+self.attribute+'''(self):
            print("del test'''+self.attribute+'''")
            del self._test'''+self.attribute+'''
        '''
            class_tree = ast.parse(classtemplate)
            print(ast.unparse(class_tree))
            print('\n')
    ```

3. We will now save the preceding code into a file named `codegenerator.py` and import the file as a library:

```
from codegenerator import CodeGenerator as c
```

4. Let us define a dictionary object and assign multiple class names and their corresponding attribute names as input:

```
classes = {'VegCounter' : 'items',
           'ElectronicCounter' : 'goods',
           'BranchManhattan' : 'Sales',
           'BranchPasadena' : 'Products'
           }
```

5. Let us further define a function named `generatelib` and add `classes` as input parameters. This function takes in the class names and their attribute names as input and generates the code from the class templates of the `codegenerator` library:

```
def generatelib(classes):
    for key, value in classes.items():
        codegen = c(key, value)
        codegen.generatecode()
```

6. In this step, let us write the generated code into a file to generate a custom library that can be used further:

```
from contextlib import redirect_stdout
with open('abcmegamartlib.py', 'w') as code:
    with redirect_stdout(code):
        generatelib(classes)
code.close()
```

7. The generated code is in the following format for each input class:

```
class VegCounter:
    def __init__(self):
        self._items = None
    @property
    def testitems(self):
        return self.testitems
    @testitems.getter
    def testitems(self):
```

```
        print('get testitems')
        return self._testitems
    @testitems.setter
    def testitems(self, value):
        print('set testitems')
        self._testitems = value
    @testitems.deleter
    def testitems(self):
        print('del testitems')
        del self._testitems
```

8. We can further import the generated library and define objects as follows:

```
import abcmegamartlib as abc
abc.BranchManhattan()
```

The preceding code returns the following output:

```
<abcmegamartlib.BranchManhattan at 0x21c4800c7f0>
```

These are various examples of code generation that can be implemented using Python's metaprogramming ast module.

Summary

In this chapter, we have looked at various examples to generate code for a custom class and a class with custom attributes. We have also covered examples of generating code for a custom class with methods and attributes. Finally, we have developed a code generator that can be used to develop a custom library using the concept of abstract syntax trees in Python.

Overall, we have seen various scenarios that can help us utilize the abstract syntax tree within Python's ast module and generate dynamic code using Python metaprogramming.

In the next chapter, we will be discussing a case study to which we can apply all the concepts of metaprogramming that we have covered so far in the book.

15

Implementing a Case Study

In this chapter, we will work on implementing a case study by applying the metaprogramming concepts that we have learned so far. For this case study, we will be using the `Automobile. (1987).UCI Machine Learning Repository` dataset.

In this chapter, we will be looking at the following main topics:

- Explaining the case study
- Defining base classes
- Developing a code generator library
- Generating code
- Designing an execution framework

By the end of this chapter, you should have an understanding of how to use the existing methods of the ast library in Python to enable your application to generate its own code.

Technical requirements

The code examples shared in this chapter are available on GitHub at: `https://github.com/PacktPublishing/Metaprogramming-with-Python/tree/main/Chapter15`.

Explaining the case study

In this section, we will be looking at the details of the case study before we start implementing it. Let's consider a car agency, *ABC Car Agency*, that focuses on sales of new and used cars from multiple brands. This agency would like to build an application that produces customized catalogs for each car displaying the various specifications and features of the car.

We will look at the details available to develop and build the application by applying the concepts that we have learned throughout this book. There are 205 different cars that need to be cataloged and the data used to build this case study is taken from the following dataset: `Automobile. (1987). UCI Machine Learning Repository`.

There are many ways to develop an application that can solve this problem. We are going to look at how to develop a reusable application that uses metaprogramming.

A high-level view of the automobile data is as follows:

symboling	normalized-losses	make	fuel-type	aspiration	num-of-doors	body-style	drive-wheels	engine-location	wheel-base	length	width	height
3	?	alfa-romero	gas	std	two	convertible	rwd	front	88.6	168.8	64.1	48.8
3	?	alfa-romero	gas	std	two	convertible	rwd	front	88.6	168.8	64.1	48.8
1	?	alfa-romero	gas	std	two	hatchback	rwd	front	94.5	171.2	65.5	52.4
2	164	audi	gas	std	four	sedan	fwd	front	99.8	176.6	66.2	54.3
2	164	audi	gas	std	four	sedan	4wd	front	99.4	176.6	66.4	54.3
2	?	audi	gas	std	two	sedan	fwd	front	99.8	177.3	66.3	53.1
1	158	audi	gas	std	four	sedan	fwd	front	105.8	192.7	71.4	55.7
1	?	audi	gas	std	four	wagon	fwd	front	105.8	192.7	71.4	55.7
1	158	audi	gas	turbo	four	sedan	fwd	front	105.8	192.7	71.4	55.9
0	?	audi	gas	turbo	two	hatchback	4wd	front	99.5	178.2	67.9	52
2	192	bmw	gas	std	two	sedan	rwd	front	101.2	176.8	64.8	54.3
0	192	bmw	gas	std	four	sedan	rwd	front	101.2	176.8	64.8	54.3
0	188	bmw	gas	std	two	sedan	rwd	front	101.2	176.8	64.8	54.3
0	188	bmw	gas	std	four	sedan	rwd	front	101.2	176.8	64.8	54.3
1	?	bmw	gas	std	four	sedan	rwd	front	103.5	189	66.9	55.7
0	?	bmw	gas	std	four	sedan	rwd	front	103.5	189	66.9	55.7
0	?	bmw	gas	std	two	sedan	rwd	front	103.5	193.8	67.9	53.7
0	?	bmw	gas	std	four	sedan	rwd	front	110	197	70.9	56.3
2	121	chevrolet	gas	std	two	hatchback	fwd	front	88.4	141.1	60.3	?
1	98	chevrolet	gas	std	two	hatchback	fwd	front	94.5	155.9	63.6	52
0	81	chevrolet	gas	std	four	sedan	fwd	front	94.5	158.8	63.6	52

Figure 15.1 – The Automobile. (1987). UCI Machine Learning Repository dataset

For this case study, we are not going to perform any detailed data processing using the automobile dataset. Instead, we will be using the data available in this dataset to create various components for the application's development. The flow of design for this example will start with developing a code generator library, followed by creating a code generator framework. We will then generate the *ABC Car Agency* library and, finally, create an execution framework. All of these processes will be explained in detail in this section.

The Python scripts that will be developed for this case study will be as follows:

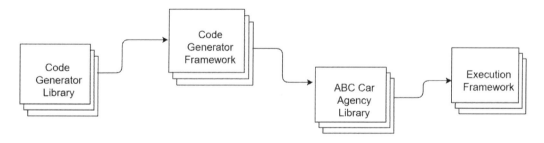

Figure 15.2 – Python scripts for the ABC Car Agency case study

The car sales application will be developed by defining the following classes:

- CarSpecs
- CarMake with its subclasses
- CarCatalogue
- BodyStyle with its subclasses
- SaleType with its subclasses

Each of these classes will be explained in this section.

The overall structure of classes for this application is going to look as follows:

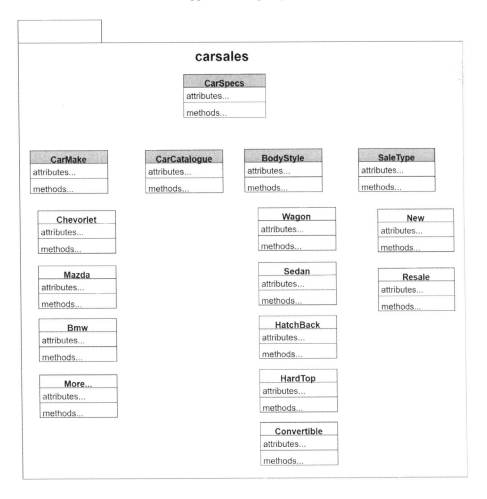

Figure 15.3 – Overview of the car sales application

With this understood, we will look further at the base classes for the application.

Defining base classes

We will now start building the code required for the case study.

Let's start by developing a metaclass named `CarSpecs`. This class will have the following structure:

1. The __new__ of the `CarSpecs` class will perform the following tasks:

    A. If the attribute of the input class is an integer, then add the attribute name in title case as `feature`, the value in string format as `info`, and `type` as numeric.

    B. If the attribute of the input class is a string, then add the attribute name in title case as `feature`, the value in string format as `info`, and `type` as varchar.

    C. If the attribute of the input class is a Boolean, then add the attribute name title case as a `feature`, the value in string format as `info`, and `type` as Boolean.

    D. If not, the actual attribute will be returned as such.

    Let's now look at the definition of `CarSpecs`:

```python
from abc import ABC, abstractmethod
class CarSpecs(type):
    def __new__(classitself, classname, baseclasses,
attributes):
        newattributes = {}
        for attribute, value in attributes.items():
            if attribute.startswith("__"):
                newattributes[attribute] = value
            elif type(value)==int or type(value)==float:
                newattributes[attribute] = {}
                newattributes[attribute]['feature'] =
attribute.title().replace('_', ' ')
                newattributes[attribute]['info'] =
str(value)
                newattributes[attribute]['type'] =
'NUMERIC'
            elif type(value)==str:
                newattributes[attribute] = {}
                newattributes[attribute]['feature'] =
attribute.title().replace('_', ' ')
```

```
                    newattributes[attribute]['info'] = value.
title()
                    newattributes[attribute]['type'] =
'VARCHAR'
            elif type(value)==bool:
                newattributes[attribute] = {}
                newattributes[attribute]['feature'] =
attribute.title().replace('_', ' ')
                newattributes[attribute]['info'] = value.
title()
                newattributes[attribute]['type'] =
'BOOLEAN'

        else:
                newattributes[attribute] = value
        return type.__new__(classitself, classname,
baseclasses, newattributes)
```

2. The next class in this example will be `CarCatalogue` with two abstract methods to define the color and print the catalog:

```
class CarCatalogue(metaclass = CarSpecs):
    @abstractmethod
    def define_color(self):
        pass
    @abstractmethod
    def print_catalogue(self):
        pass
```

3. The next class will be the parent class or superclass that captures the specifications of the car:

```
class CarMake(metaclass = CarSpecs):
    @abstractmethod
    def define_spec(self):
        pass
```

4. Let's create another superclass named `BodyStyle`, which will capture the body style and engine features of the car:

```python
class BodyStyle(metaclass = CarSpecs):
    @abstractmethod
    def body_style_features(self):
        pass
```

5. The next class for this case study will be `SaleType`, in which we will add an abstract method to calculate the price of the car:

```python
class SaleType(metaclass = CarSpecs):
    @abstractmethod
    def calculate_price(self):
        pass
```

6. This class will be a subclass of `SaleType` for calculating the price of new cars:

```python
class New(SaleType, CarCatalogue,   metaclass = CarSpecs):
    def calculate_price(self, classname):
        car = classname()
        price = float(car.price['info'])
        return price
```

7. The next class will be another subclass of `SaleType` for calculating the price of resale cars:

```python
class Resale(SaleType, CarCatalogue,   metaclass =
CarSpecs):
    def calculate_price(self, classname, years):
        car = classname()
        depreciation = years * 0.15
        price = float(car.price['info']) * (1 -
depreciation)
        return price
```

These are the main classes for which we will be creating templates that will be used to generate code in the next section.

Developing a code generator library

In this section, let's look at developing a code generator that will be used to generate code for all the base classes – CarSpecs, CarMake, CarCatalogue, BodyStyle, and SaleType. The detailed steps are as follows:

1. Let's create a file named codegenerator.py and start by defining a class named CodeGenerator:

```
class CodeGenerator:
```

2. Let's define a method that imports the ast library and adds a meta_template attribute that has the string format of the CarSpecs class as a value. The meta_template attribute is further parsed and unparsed into class code:

```
def generate_meta(self):
        ast = __import__('ast')
        meta_template = '''
from abc import ABC, abstractmethod, ABCMeta
class CarSpecs(type, metaclass = ABCMeta):
    def __new__(classitself, classname, baseclasses,
attributes):
            newattributes = {}
            for attribute, value in attributes.items():
                if attribute.startswith("__"):
                    newattributes[attribute] = value
                elif type(value)==int or type(value)==float:
                    newattributes[attribute] = {}
                    newattributes[attribute]['feature'] =
attribute.title().replace('_', ' ')
                    newattributes[attribute]['info'] =
str(value)
                    newattributes[attribute]['type'] =
'NUMERIC'
                elif type(value)==str:
                    newattributes[attribute] = {}
                    newattributes[attribute]['feature'] =
attribute.title().replace('_', ' ')
                    newattributes[attribute]['info'] = value.
title()
```

```
                        newattributes[attribute]['type'] =
'VARCHAR'
                elif type(value)==bool:
                    newattributes[attribute] = {}
                    newattributes[attribute]['feature'] =
attribute.title().replace('_', ' ')
                    newattributes[attribute]['info'] = value.
title()
                    newattributes[attribute]['type'] =
'BOOLEAN'

                else:
                    newattributes[attribute] = value
        return type.__new__(classitself, classname,
baseclasses, newattributes)
    '''

        meta_tree = ast.parse(meta_template)
        print(ast.unparse(meta_tree))
        print('\n')
```

3. Let's now define another method named `generate_car_catalogue` and add the class template for `CarCatalogue`:

```
def generate_car_catalogue(self):
        ast = __import__('ast')
        catalogue_template = '''
class CarCatalogue(metaclass = CarSpecs):
    @abstractmethod
    def define_color(self):
        pass

    @abstractmethod
    def print_catalogue(self):
        pass
    '''
        catalogue_tree = ast.parse(catalogue_template)
        print(ast.unparse(catalogue_tree))
        print('\n')
```

4. The next step is to define a method named `generate_carmake_code` and add the code template for the `CarMake` class:

```
def generate_carmake_code(self):
        ast = __import__('ast')
        carmake_template = '''
class CarMake(metaclass = CarSpecs):
    @abstractmethod
    def define_spec(self):
        pass
        '''
        carmake_tree = ast.parse(carmake_template)
        print(ast.unparse(carmake_tree))
        print('\n')
```

5. In the next code block, we will define another method named `generate_bodystyle_parent` and add the code template for the `BodyStyle` class:

```
def generate_bodystyle_parent(self):
        ast = __import__('ast')
        bodystyle_parent_template = '''
class BodyStyle(metaclass = CarSpecs):
    @abstractmethod
    def body_style_features(self):
        pass
        '''
        bodystyle_parent_tree = ast.parse(bodystyle_parent_template)
        print(ast.unparse(bodystyle_parent_tree))
        print('\n')
```

6. Let's further define the `generate_salestype_code` method, which generates the class code for the `SaleType` class:

```
def generate_salestype_code(self):
        ast = __import__('ast')
        saletype_template = '''
class SaleType(metaclass = CarSpecs):
    @abstractmethod
```

```
    def calculate_price(self):
        pass
    '''

    salestype_tree = ast.parse(saletype_template)
    print(ast.unparse(salestype_tree))
    print('\n')
```

7. In this step, let's define the `generate_newsale_code` method to generate code for the New class:

```
def generate_newsale_code(self):
    ast = __import__('ast')
    newsale_template = '''
class New(SaleType, CarCatalogue,  metaclass = CarSpecs):
    def calculate_price(self, classname):
        car = classname()
        price = float(car.price['info'])
        return price
    '''

    newsale_tree = ast.parse(newsale_template)
    print(ast.unparse(newsale_tree))
    print('\n')
```

8. Let's further define the `generate_resale_code` method, which generates the code for the `Resale` class and has the method for calculating the resale price of the car:

```
    def generate_resale_code(self):
        ast = __import__('ast')
        resale_template = '''
class Resale(SaleType, CarCatalogue,  metaclass =
CarSpecs):
    def calculate_price(self, classname, years):
        car = classname()
        depreciation = years * 0.15
        price = float(car.price['info']) * (1 -
depreciation)
        return price
    '''

        resale_tree = ast.parse(resale_template)
```

```
        print(ast.unparse(resale_tree))
        print('\n')
```

9. In this step, we will define a `generate_car_code` method; it inherits the `CarMake` class, defines the color and specifications for individual car brands, and prints the catalog:

```
def generate_car_code(self, classname, carspecs):
        self.classname = classname
        self.carspecs = carspecs
        ast = __import__('ast')
        car_template = '''
class '''+self.classname+'''(CarMake, CarCatalogue,
metaclass = CarSpecs):
    fuel_type = '''+"'"+self.carspecs['fuel_
type']+"'"+'''
    aspiration = '''+"'"+self.
carspecs['aspiration']+"'"+'''
    num_of_door = '''+"'"+self.carspecs['num_of_
door']+"'"+'''
    drive_wheels = '''+"'"+self.carspecs['drive_
wheels']+"'"+'''
    wheel_base = '''+"'"+self.carspecs['wheel_
base']+"'"+'''
    length = '''+"'"+self.carspecs['length']+"'"+'''
    width = '''+"'"+self.carspecs['width']+"'"+'''
    height = '''+"'"+self.carspecs['height']+"'"+'''
    curb_weight = '''+"'"+self.carspecs['curb_
weight']+"'"+'''
    fuel_system = '''+"'"+self.carspecs['fuel_
system']+"'"+'''
    city_mpg = '''+"'"+self.carspecs['city_mpg']+"'"+'''
    highway_mpg = '''+"'"+self.carspecs['highway_
mpg']+"'"+'''
    price = '''+"'"+self.carspecs['price']+"'"+'''
    def define_color(self):
            BOLD = '\33[5m'
            BLUE = '\033[94m'
            return BOLD + BLUE
    def define_spec(self):
```

```
            specs = [self.fuel_type, self.aspiration,
self.num_of_door, self.drive_wheels,
                    self.wheel_base, self.length, self.
width, self.height, self.curb_weight,
                    self.fuel_system, self.city_mpg,
self.highway_mpg]
            return specs
    def print_catalogue(self):
            for i in self.define_spec():
                print(self.define_color() + i['feature'],
": ", self.define_color() + i['info'])
                '''
        car_tree = ast.parse(car_template)
        print(ast.unparse(car_tree))
        print('\n')
```

10. The last method of this code generator is generate_bodystyle_code, which generates class code for different body styles, such as Sedan and Hatchback, defines the color and features for an individual car body style, and prints the catalog:

```
def generate_bodystyle_code(self, classname,
carfeatures):
        self.classname = classname
        self.carfeatures = carfeatures
        ast = __import__('ast')
        bodystyle_template = '''
class '''+self.classname+'''(BodyStyle, CarCatalogue,
metaclass = CarSpecs):
    engine_location = '''+"'"+self.carfeatures['engine_
location']+"'"+'''
    engine_type = '''+"'"+self.carfeatures['engine_
type']+"'"+'''
    num_of_cylinders = '''+"'"+self.carfeatures['num_of_
cylinders']+"'"+'''
    engine_size = '''+"'"+self.carfeatures['engine_
size']+"'"+'''
    bore = '''+"'"+self.carfeatures['bore']+"'"+'''
    stroke = '''+"'"+self.carfeatures['stroke']+"'"+'''
    compression_ratio = '''+"'"+self.
carfeatures['compression_ratio']+"'"+'''
```

```
        horse_power = '''+"'"+self.carfeatures['horse_
power']+"'"+'''
        peak_rpm = '''+"'"+self.carfeatures['peak_
rpm']+"'"+'''
    def body_style_features(self):
            features = [self.engine_location, self.
engine_type, self.num_of_cylinders, self.engine_size,
                    self.bore, self.stroke, self.
compression_ratio, self.horse_power, self.peak_rpm]
            return features
    def define_color(self):
            BOLD = '\33[5m'
            RED = '\033[31m'
            return BOLD + RED
    def print_catalogue(self):
            for i in self.body_style_features():
                print(self.define_color() + i['feature'],
": ", self.define_color() + i['info'])
                '''
        bodystyle_tree = ast.parse(bodystyle_template)
        print(ast.unparse(bodystyle_tree))
        print('\n')
```

With these methods, we are all set to generate the code required for the ABC Car Agency's catalog.

Now, let's proceed further to develop a code generation framework that generates the hundreds of classes required for our application.

Generating code

In this section, we are going to make use of `codegenerator.py` to generate the base classes and its corresponding subclasses, which maintain and print various catalogs for the ABC Car Agency, as follows:

1. To begin with, let's start using the automobile data to generate the base classes required for this application. For the base data preparation, let's import the `pandas` library, which helps with processing data:

    ```
    import pandas as pd
    ```

2.   Let's load the data and make a copy of it. For this application, we need a unique set of car brands and another unique set of car body styles:

```
auto = pd.read_csv("automobile.csv")
auto_truncated = auto.copy(deep=True)
auto_truncated.drop_duplicates(subset = ['make','body-
style'], inplace = True)
auto_truncated.reset_index(inplace = True, drop = True)
auto_truncated['make'] = auto_truncated['make'].
apply(lambda x: x.title().replace('-',''))
auto_truncated.reset_index(inplace = True)
auto_truncated['index'] = auto_truncated['index'].
astype('str')
auto_truncated['make'] = auto_truncated['make'] + auto_
truncated['index']
auto_truncated['body-style'] = auto_truncated['body-
style'].apply(lambda x: x.title().replace('-',''))
auto_truncated['body-style'] = auto_truncated['body-
style'] + auto_truncated['index']
```

Once the basic data has been processed, let's create two DataFrames that will be used to generate multiple classes using the code generator:

```
auto_specs = auto_truncated[['make', 'fuel-type',
'aspiration', 'num-of-doors', 'drive-wheels', 'wheel-
base', 'length', 'width', 'height', 'curb-weight',
'fuel-system', 'city-mpg', 'highway-mpg', 'price']].
copy(deep = True)
auto_specs.columns = ['classname', 'fuel_type',
'aspiration', 'num_of_door', 'drive_wheels',
'wheel_base', 'length', 'width', 'height', 'curb_weight',
'fuel_system', 'city_mpg', 'highway_mpg', 'price' ]
for col in auto_specs.columns:
    auto_specs[col] = auto_specs[col].astype('str')
auto_features = auto_truncated[['body-style', 'engine-
location', 'engine-type', 'num-of-cylinders', 'engine-
size', 'bore', 'stroke', 'compression-ratio',
'horsepower', 'peak-rpm']].copy(deep = True)
auto_features.columns = ['classname', 'engine_location',
'engine_type', 'num_of_cylinders', 'engine_size', 'bore',
'stroke', 'compression_ratio', 'horse_power', 'peak_rpm']
```

```
for col in auto_features.columns:
    auto_features[col] = auto_features[col].astype('str')
```

3. After processing the data into the format that we need to provide as input to the code generator, the sample data for specifications will be as follows:

	classname	fuel_type	aspiration	num_of_door	drive_wheels	wheel_base	length	width	height	curb_weight
1	AlfaRomero1	gas	std	two	rwd	94.5	171.2	65.5	52.4	2823
24	Mitsubishi24	gas	std	two	fwd	93.7	157.3	64.4	50.8	1918
26	Nissan26	gas	std	two	fwd	94.5	165.3	63.8	54.5	1889
21	MercedesBenz21	diesel	turbo	two	rwd	106.7	187.5	70.3	54.9	3495
9	Dodge9	gas	std	four	fwd	93.7	157.3	63.8	50.6	1989

Figure 15.4 – Sample specifications

4. The sample data for features will be as follows:

	classname	engine_location	engine_type	num_of_cylinders	engine_size	bore	stroke	compression_ratio	horse_power
13	Wagon13	front	ohc	four	92	2.92	3.41	9.2	76
9	Sedan9	front	ohc	four	90	2.97	3.23	9.4	68
16	Sedan16	front	dohc	six	258	3.63	4.17	8.1	176
5	Sedan5	front	ohc	four	108	3.5	2.8	8.8	101
18	Sedan18	front	ohc	four	91	3.03	3.15	9.0	68

Figure 15.5 – Sample features

5. Now that the base data required to generate code is ready, we can start importing the code generator:

```
from codegenerator import CodeGenerator
codegen = CodeGenerator()
```

6. In this step, let's now define a function that generates the library by calling the code to generate each base class in a pipeline followed by generating multiple subclasses for `CarMake` and `BodyStyle`:

```
def generatelib():
    codegen.generate_meta()
    codegen.generate_car_catalogue()
    codegen.generate_carmake_code()
    codegen.generate_bodystyle_parent()
    codegen.generate_salestype_code()
```

```
        codegen.generate_newsale_code()
        codegen.generate_resale_code()
        for index, row in auto_specs.iterrows():
            carspecs = dict(row)
            classname = carspecs['classname']
            del carspecs['classname']
            codegen.generate_car_code(classname = classname,
    carspecs = carspecs)
        for index, row in auto_features.iterrows():
            carfeatures = dict(row)
            classname = carfeatures['classname']
            del carfeatures['classname']
            codegen.generate_bodystyle_code(classname =
    classname, carfeatures = carfeatures)
```

7. Open a Python file named abccaragencylib.py and call a generatelib function to write the code generated for all the required classes:

```
from contextlib import redirect_stdout
with open('abccaragencylib.py', 'w') as code:
    with redirect_stdout(code):
        generatelib()
code.close()
```

8. An example class autogenerated and written into abccaragencylib.py is represented in the following screenshot:

```
 79  class AlfaRomero0(CarMake, CarCatalogue, metaclass=CarSpecs):
 80      fuel_type = 'gas'
 81      aspiration = 'std'
 82      num_of_door = 'two'
 83      drive_wheels = 'rwd'
 84      wheel_base = '88.6'
 85      length = '168.8'
 86      width = '64.1'
 87      height = '48.8'
 88      curb_weight = '2548'
 89      fuel_system = 'mpfi'
 90      city_mpg = '21'
 91      highway_mpg = '27'
 92      price = '13495'
 93
 94      def define_color(self):
 95          BOLD = '\x1b[5m'
 96          BLUE = '\x1b[94m'
 97          return BOLD + BLUE
 98
 99      def define_spec(self):
100          specs = [self.fuel_type, self.aspiration, self.num_of_door, self.drive_wheels, self.wheel_base, self.length, self.width,
    self.height, self.curb_weight, self.fuel_system, self.city_mpg, self.highway_mpg]
101          return specs
102
103      def print_catalogue(self):
104          for i in self.define_spec():
105              print(self.define_color() + i['feature'], ': ', self.define_color() + i['info'])
106
```

Figure 15.6 – An autogenerated class code for a car brand

We have not autogenerated the code required for this example. We will now look at designing an execution framework.

Designing an execution framework

In this section, let's look at the last process of designing the ABC Car Agency application where we will actually run the code generated throughout this case study:

1. Let's start by loading the autogenerated library:

    ```
    import abccaragencylib as carsales
    ```

2. At this stage, we will follow a sequence of steps by implementing a façade design pattern so that we can print the specifications and features for different types of cars:

    ```
    class Queue:
        def __init__(self, makeclass, styleclass, age):
            self.makeclass = makeclass
            self.styleclass = styleclass
            self.make = self.makeclass()
            self.style = self.styleclass()
            self.new = carsales.New()
            self.resale = carsales.Resale()
            self.age = age
        def pipeline(self):
            print('*********ABC Car Agency -
    Catalogue***********')
            self.make.print_catalogue()
            print('\n')
            self.style.print_catalogue()
            print('\n')
            print('New Car Price : ' + str(self.new.
    calculate_price(self.makeclass)))
            print('Resale Price : ' + str(self.resale.
    calculate_price(self.makeclass, self.age)))
    ```

3. Let's define a method to run the façade pattern:

    ```
    def run_facade(makeclass, styleclass, age):
        queue = Queue(makeclass, styleclass, age)
        queue.pipeline()
    ```

4. In this step, we will run one combination of a car brand with a car body style to generate a catalog:

```
run_facade(carsales.AlfaRomero1, carsales.Hatchback28, 3)
```

The output is as follows:

```
*********ABC Car Agency - Catalogue**********
Fuel Type :  Gas
Aspiration :  Std
Num Of Door :  Two
Drive Wheels :  Rwd
Wheel Base :  94.5
Length :  171.2
Width :  65.5
Height :  52.4
Curb Weight :  2823
Fuel System :  Mpfi
City Mpg :  19
Highway Mpg :  26
Engine Location :  Front
Engine Type :  Ohc
Num Of Cylinders :  Four
Engine Size :  97
Bore :  3.15
Stroke :  3.29
Compression Ratio :  9.4
Horse Power :  69
Peak Rpm :  5200

New Car Price : 16500.0
Resale Price : 9075.0
```

There are 56 unique subclasses generated for CarMake and 56 unique subclasses generated for BodyStyle. We can use various combinations of CarMake and BodyStyle to print catalogs for this application.

5. Let's try another combination:

```
run_facade(carsales.Mitsubishi24, carsales.Sedan16, 5)
```

The output generated is as follows:

```
*********ABC Car Agency - Catalogue***********
Fuel Type :  Gas
Aspiration :  Std
Num Of Door :  Two
Drive Wheels :  Fwd
Wheel Base :  93.7
Length :  157.3
Width :  64.4
Height :  50.8
Curb Weight :  1918
Fuel System :  2Bbl
City Mpg :  37
Highway Mpg :  41


Engine Location :  Front
Engine Type :  Dohc
Num Of Cylinders :  Six
Engine Size :  258
Bore :  3.63
Stroke :  4.17
Compression Ratio :  8.1
Horse Power :  176
Peak Rpm :  4750


New Car Price : 5389.0
Resale Price : 1347.25
```

This is the step-by-step process of developing an application by applying metaprogramming methodologies in Python.

Summary

In this chapter, we have learned how to develop an application by applying various techniques of metaprogramming. We started by explaining the case study, and we defined the base classes required for this case study.

We also learned how to develop a code generator and how to generate code using it. We also designed a framework that could be used to execute or test the code generated for the application in this case study.

In the next chapter, we will be looking at some of the best practices that can be followed while designing an application with Python and metaprogramming.

16

Following Best Practices

In this chapter, we will learn some of the best practices from Python programming that we can follow and apply to metaprogramming too. The practices suggested in Python Enhancement Proposal 8 (PEP 8), the style guide for Python code, also apply to metaprogramming.

The concepts behind PEP 8 originated and are explained in detail in the documentation by Guido van Rossum, Barry Warsaw, and Nick Coghlan at `https://peps.python.org/pep-0008/`. This chapter will cover some of the important concepts from PEP 8 with examples using *ABC Megamart* of how they can be implemented in metaprogramming as well as general Python programming.

In this chapter, we will be looking at the following main topics:

- Following PEP 8 standards
- Writing clear comments for debugging and reusability
- Adding documentation strings
- Naming conventions
- Avoiding the reuse of names
- Avoiding metaprogramming where not required

By the end of this chapter, you will know the best practices for performing Python metaprogramming.

Technical requirements

The code examples shared in this chapter are available on GitHub under the code for this chapter at `https://github.com/PacktPublishing/Metaprogramming-with-Python/tree/main/Chapter16`.

Following PEP 8 standards

In this section, we will be looking at the PEP 8 standards that we should follow while coding applications with Python metaprogramming. We will apply these standards from the PEP 8 documentation using our example of *ABC Megamart*.

In this section, rather than looking at whether the coding standards we follow are right, we will consider the difference between coding standards that are easy to maintain in comparison to those that are not.

Indentation

Python is a language that is very sensitive to indentation and can throw many errors when this is not done correctly. Having discipline with the overall indentation of your code helps to avoid errors and also makes the code more readable. In this example, let's look at how we can keep the indentation correct.

To start looking at the indentation, let's begin with an example of a greater-than-10-items counter. We first define a class named `GreaterThan10Counter` with a `return_cart` method to return the cart items:

```
class GreaterThan10Counter():
    def return_cart(self, *items):
        cart_items = []
        for I in items:
            cart_items.append(i)
        return cart_items
```

Let's also create an object instance for the class:

```
greater = GreaterThan10Counter()
```

Next, we create a variable named `cart`, which will store the values returned by the `return_cart` method. Given that the class is for the greater-than-10-items counter, the number of items returned by the cart will be more than 10, hence the code will not be readable.

The following screenshot shows how the code would look in a code editor:

```
cart = greater.return_cart('paper clips','blue pens','stapler','pencils','a4paper','a3paper','chart','
```

Figure 16.1 – The cart variable assignment

Hard to maintain

The code of the `cart` variable in *Figure 16.1* will look as follows if we move the invisible part of the code onto the next line:

```
cart = greater.return_cart('paper clips','blue pens','stapler','pencils','a4paper','a3paper',
'chart','sketch pens','canvas','water color','acrylic colors')
```

Figure 16.2 – The cart variable adjusted without alignment

The preceding code is not incorrect since it will still execute without errors if we run it. The only problem is that it will be difficult to maintain.

Easy to maintain

Let's now change the indentation by aligning the code with symbols to make it readable and easily maintained if another developer needs to take it over for editing. The realigned code looks as follows:

```
cart = greater.return_cart('paper clips','blue pens','stapler','pencils','a4paper','a3paper',
                           'chart','sketch pens','canvas','water color','acrylic colors')
```

Figure 16.3 – The cart variable adjusted with alignment

Now that we understand this, let's look at the next best practice, which is to present code in a neat fashion.

Neat representation

Let's now look at how and where to add white spaces while writing code.

Hard to maintain

Let's look at the following example where we will define a decorator function named signature with no white spaces between operators and their corresponding variables:

```
def signature(branch):
    def footnote(*args):
        LOGO='\33[43m'
        print(LOGO+'ABC Mega Mart')
        return branch(*args)
    return footnote
```

Let's further call the decorator on another function named manager_manhattan without spaces between operators and variables:

```
@signature
def manager_manhattan(*args):
    GREEN='\033[92m'
    SELECT='\33[7m'
```

```
        for arg in args:
            print(SELECT+GREEN+str(arg))
```

Next, let's call the function as follows:

```
manager_manhattan('John M','john.m@abcmegamart.com','40097 5th
Main Street','Manhattan','New York City','New York',11007)
```

The preceding code will still run without errors but the code is not presented neatly nor is it easy to maintain since it is not easy to differentiate between a variable and its operator:

```
ABC Mega Mart
John M
john.m@abcmegamart.com
40097 5th Main Street
Manhattan
New York City
New York
11007
```

Let's add white spaces to this code.

Easy to maintain

Let's add spaces to the `signature` function:

```
def signature(branch):
    def footnote(*args):
        LOGO = '\33[43m'
        print(LOGO + 'ABC Mega Mart')
        return branch(*args)
    return footnote
```

Similarly, let's also add white spaces in the `manager_manhattan` function:

```
@signature
def manager_manhattan(*args):
    GREEN = '\033[92m'
    SELECT = '\33[7m'
    for arg in args:
        print(SELECT + GREEN + str(arg))
```

Let's call the function now:

```
manager_manhattan('John M', 'john.m@abcmegamart.com',
                  '40097 5th Main Street', 'Manhattan', 'New
York City', 'New York',11007)
```

Running the preceding code produces the following output:

```
ABC Mega Mart
John M
john.m@abcmegamart.com
40097 5th Main Street
Manhattan
New York City
New York
11007
```

The preceding code makes it easier to differentiate between variables and their corresponding operators due to the addition of white space.

With this understanding, let's look at the next best practice, which is to add comments in the code.

Writing clear comments for debugging and reusability

Writing inline comments helps us understand why a specific code block is written and we can keep the comments updated as the code changes. We recommend writing comments to make the code easy to debug in the future. However, keep the comments relevant to the code. Let's look at a few examples of inline comments.

Redundant comments

Let's look at the following example where we are creating a meta class and calling the meta class from another class:

```
class ExampleMetaClass1(type):
    def __new__(classitself, *args):
        print("class itself: ", classitself)
        print("Others: ", args)
        return type.__new__(classitself, *args)


class ExampleClass1(metaclass = ExampleMetaClass1):
```

```
int1 = 123                  # int1 is assigned a value of 123
str1 = 'test'
def test():
    print('test')
```

In the preceding code, the comment explains exactly the same thing that is done by the code, which can be easily understood simply by looking at the code. This will not be helpful when we want to debug or modify the code in the future.

Relevant comment

Let's look at the Singleton design pattern and add a relevant comment:

```
class SingletonBilling:             # This code covers an example
of Singleton design pattern
    billing_instance = None
    product_name = 'Dark Chocolate'
    unit_price = 6
    quantity = 4
    tax = 0.054
    def __init__(self):
        if SingletonBilling.billing_instance == None:
            SingletonBilling.billing_instance = self
        else:
            print("Billing can have only one instance")

    def generate_bill(self):
        total = self.unit_price * self.quantity
        final_total = total + total*self.tax
        print('***********-------------------**************')
        print('Product:', self.product_name)
        print('Total:',final_total)
        print('***********-------------------**************')
```

In the preceding code, the comment specifies the purpose of SingletonBilling rather than mentioning the obvious task performed by the code.

With this understanding, let's look at the next best practice, which is to add documentation strings.

Adding documentation strings

Documentation strings are added to provide more information on code that is intended to be imported and used in some other program or application. Documentation strings will provide the end user with information on the code that they are going to call from their programs. This is especially helpful as the end user of the code is not the developer of the library, but a user. Let's look at an example of where to use documentation strings.

Let's start by creating a Python file named `vegcounter.py` and adding the following code:

```
def return_cart(*items):
    '''
    This function returns the list of items added to the cart.
    items: input the cart items. Eg: 'pens', 'pencils'
    '''
    cart_items = []
    for i in items:
        cart_items.append(i)
    return cart_items
```

In the preceding code, we defined the docstring by providing a description of the function and its arguments.

The Python file looks as follows:

```
1  def return_cart(*items):
2      '''
3      This function returns the list of items added to the cart.
4      items: input the cart items. Eg: 'pens', 'pencils'
5      '''
6      cart_items = []
7      for i in items:
8          cart_items.append(i)
9      return cart_items
```

Figure 16.4 – Documentation string added to vegcounter.py

Let's further import `vegcounter.py` into another program as follows:

```
import vegcounter as vc
```

Note that in this program, the code for the functions inside `vegcounter` is not accessible to the end user, but the functions in `vegcounter` can be called by the end user's program.

The following screenshot demonstrates how docstrings provide the information required in this example:

```
import vegcounter as vc
```

```
vc.return_cart()
```

```
                                          ^    +    ✖
    Signature: vc.return_cart(*items)
    Docstring:
    This function returns the list of items added to the cart.
    items: input the cart items. Eg: 'pens', 'pencils'
```

Figure 16.5 – Documentation string example

In this example, the documentation string we added in the Python file provides the end user with information on the function and its corresponding arguments along with an example.

Documentation string for metaprogramming

In this example, let's define a metaclass named `BranchMetaClass` and add a docstring that states that this is a meta class and is not meant to be inherited as a super class or parent class. Save this code into `branch.py`:

```python
class BranchMetaclass(type):
    '''
    This is a meta class for ABC Megamart branch that adds an
additional
    quality to the attributes of branch classes.
    Add this as only a meta class.
    There are no methods to inherit this class as a parent
class or super class.
    '''
    def __new__(classitself, classname, baseclasses,
attributes):
        import inspect
        newattributes = {}
        for attribute, value in attributes.items():
            if attribute.startswith("__"):
                newattributes[attribute] = value
            elif inspect.isfunction(value):
```

```
                    newattributes['branch' + attribute.title()] =
    value
            else:
                newattributes[attribute] = value
        return type.__new__(classitself, classname,
    baseclasses, newattributes)
```

Let's now import the branch and its corresponding meta class as follows:

```
from branch import BranchMetaclass
```

Let's now call `BranchMetaclass` to check the docstring:

```
BranchMetaclass
```

The docstring is displayed in the following screenshot:

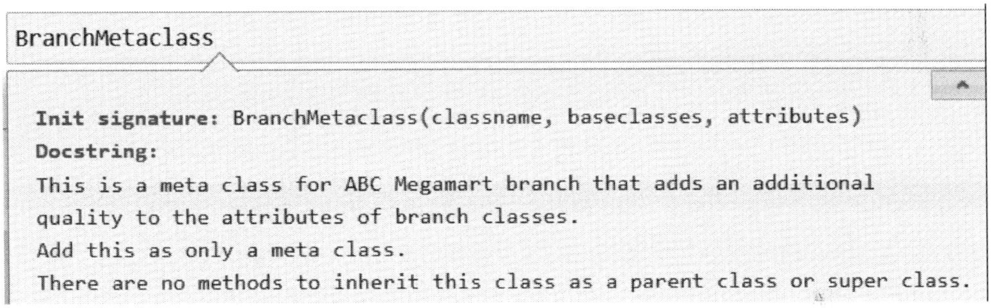

Figure 16.6 – Documentation string for BranchMetaclass

This is an example of how documentation strings should be included as a best practice. Adding documentation strings in the class definition provides end users with the information required to correctly apply a method or a class in their application.

With this understanding, let's further look at the naming conventions to be followed in Python code.

Naming conventions

Naming conventions in Python are recommendations of how various elements in a Python program need to be named to ensure ease of navigation and consistency. Navigating through code, connecting the dots, and understanding the flow are all made easier by following consistent naming conventions throughout the code. This is another important standard that helps in developing maintainable applications.

In this section, we will see how you should ideally name classes, variables, functions, and methods.

Class names

While creating a new class, it is recommended to start the class name with an uppercase letter followed by lowercase letters and capitalize whenever there are words that need differentiation within the class name.

For example, let's define a class for the billing counter.

The following style is not the preferred naming convention:

```
class billing_counter:
    def __init__(self, productname, unitprice, quantity, tax):
        self.productname = productname
        self.unitprice = unitprice
        self.quantity = quantity
        self.tax = tax
```

With the preceding naming convention, we will still be able to execute the code and it will work as expected. But maintaining the class names with one well defined naming style will make future management of the libraries easier. The preferred class naming style is as follows:

```
class BillingCounter:
    def __init__(self, productname, unitprice, quantity, tax):
        self.productname = productname
        self.unitprice = unitprice
        self.quantity = quantity
        self.tax = tax
```

Camel case is used to name classes so that they can be differentiated from variables, methods, and functions. The naming conventions for variables are explained next, followed by methods and functions.

Variables

While creating new variables, it is preferred to use all lowercase letters for variable names followed by numbers, if relevant. When there is more than one word in a variable name, it is a good practice to separate them using an underscore operator. This also helps us to differentiate variables from classes since they follow camel case conventions.

Let's look at an example of how variables should not be named:

```
class BillingCounter:
    def __init__(self, PRODUCTNAME, UnitPrice, Quantity, TaX):
        self.PRODUCTNAME = PRODUCTNAME
```

```
        self.UnitPrice = UnitPrice
        self.Quantity = Quantity
        self.TaX = TaX
```

Let's now look at an example of one preferred method of naming variables:

```
class BillingCounter:
    def __init__(self, product, price, quantity, tax):
        self.product = product
        self.price = price
        self.quantity = quantity
        self.tax = tax
```

Let's further look at another preferred method for naming variables:

```
class BillingCounter:
    def __init__(self, product_name, unit_price, quantity,
tax):
        self.product_name = product_name
        self.unit_price = unit_price
        self.quantity = quantity
        self.tax = tax
```

Functions and methods

Similar to variables, using lowercase for function and method names is the best-practice preference. When there is more than one word in a variable name, it is a good practice to separate them using an underscore operator.

Let's look at an example of how a function or method should not be named:

```
class TypeCheck:
    def Intcheck(self,inputvalue):
        if (type(inputvalue) != int) or (len(str(inputvalue)) >
2):
            return False
        else:
            return True


    def STRINGCHECK(self,inputvalue):
```

```
        if (type(inputvalue) != str) or (len(str(inputvalue)) >
10):
            return False
        else:
            return True
```

Let's now look at an example of the preferred method for naming methods or functions:

```
class TypeCheck:
    def int_check(self,input_value):
        if (type(input_value) != int) or (len(str(input_value))
> 2):
            return False
        else:
            return True

    def string_check(self,input_value):
        if (type(input_value) != str) or (len(str(input_value))
> 10):
            return False
        else:
            return True
```

These naming conventions are recommendations that can be followed while developing new code or a library from scratch. However, if the code has already been developed and is being actively maintained, it is recommended to follow the naming conventions used throughout the code.

Avoiding the reuse of names

In this example, let's look at another best practice of how to use variable or class names such that the reusability aspect of your code is preserved. Sometimes it might seem easy to reuse the same class or variable names while writing code in a sequence. Reusing names will make it difficult to reuse the classes, variables, methods, or functions in your code as calling them in multiple scenarios will be impacted since the same names are reused for different elements.

Let's look at an example to understand the method that is not preferred. Let's define two classes for Branch with a method named maintenance_cost with different definitions.

The first `Branch` class is defined as follows:

```
class Branch:
    def maintenance_cost(self, product_type, quantity):
        self.product_type = product_type
        self.quantity = quantity
        cold_storage_cost = 100
        if (product_type == 'FMCG'):
            maintenance_cost = self.quantity * 0.25 + cold_
storage_cost
            return maintenance_cost
        else:
            return "We don't stock this product"
```

The second `Branch` class is defined as follows:

```
class Branch:
    def maintenance_cost(self, product_type, quantity):
        self.product_type = product_type
        self.quantity = quantity
        if (product_type == 'Electronics'):
            maintenance_cost = self.quantity * 0.05
            return maintenance_cost
        else:
            return "We don't stock this product"
```

In the preceding code, we have two `Branch` classes doing different tasks. Let's now instantiate the `Branch` class, assuming the first `Branch` class needs to be executed at a later point in the code:

```
branch = Branch()
branch.maintenance_cost('FMCG', 1)
```

The preceding code calls the `Branch` class defined last, and thus ends up losing the definition of the first `Branch` class:

```
"We don't stock this product"
```

To avoid such confusion, it is always preferred to provide different names for different elements in code.

Let's look at the preferred method now. We will define a class named `Brooklyn` where FMCG products are stocked as follows:

```python
class Brooklyn:
    def maintenance_cost(self, product_type, quantity):
        self.product_type = product_type
        self.quantity = quantity
        cold_storage_cost = 100
        if (product_type == 'FMCG'):
            maintenance_cost = self.quantity * 0.25 + cold_storage_cost
            return maintenance_cost
        else:
            return "We don't stock this product"
```

We will define another class named `Queens` where electronic products are stocked as follows:

```python
class Queens:
    def maintenance_cost(self, product_type, quantity):
        self.product_type = product_type
        self.quantity = quantity
        if (product_type == 'Electronics'):
            maintenance_cost = self.quantity * 0.05
            return maintenance_cost
        else:
            return "We don't stock this product"
```

We can now call both the classes and their methods without any issues:

```python
brooklyn = Brooklyn()
brooklyn.maintenance_cost('FMCG', 1)
```

The output for `Brooklyn` is as follows:

```
100.25
```

Similarly, we can instantiate the `Queens` class separately:

```python
queens = Queens()
queens.maintenance_cost('Electronics', 1)
```

The output for `Queens` is as follows:

```
0.05
```

Having looked at why we should avoid reusing names, we can further look at where to avoid metaprogramming.

Avoiding metaprogramming where not required

Writing too much metaprogramming just because the feature is available in Python also makes the overall code very complex and hard to handle. The following aspects should be kept in mind while choosing to write a metaprogram for your application:

- Identify your use case and determine the need for metaprogramming based on how frequently you need to modify the code.

- Understand how frequently you need to manipulate your code outside of its core elements such as classes, methods, and variables.

- Check whether your solution can be developed with object-oriented programming alone or whether it depends on elements such as metaclasses, decorators, and code generation.

- Check whether your team has the relevant skills to maintain the metaprogramming features after development.

- Check that you don't have a dependency on earlier versions of Python that do not support some of the metaprogramming features.

These are some of the points to consider when planning to apply metaprogramming techniques during the application design phase.

Summary

In this chapter, we covered various examples to understand the best practices recommended in the PEP 8 standards for Python. We looked at the preferred methods for indentation and the correct use of white spaces. We also looked at how to write useful comments and where to include documentation strings.

We learned the recommended naming conventions through some examples. We also looked at why we need to avoid reusing names and where to avoid metaprogramming.

While the concepts of metaprogramming are advanced and complex, we have tried to explain them with simple, straightforward examples throughout this book to keep it interesting and engaging. Learning Python and its features is a continuous journey. Keep following the future versions of Python and explore the new capabilities it provides for metaprogramming.

Index

Packt.com

Subscribe to our online digital library for full access to over 7,000 books and videos, as well as industry leading tools to help you plan your personal development and advance your career. For more information, please visit our website.

Why subscribe?

- Spend less time learning and more time coding with practical eBooks and Videos from over 4,000 industry professionals

- Improve your learning with Skill Plans built especially for you

- Get a free eBook or video every month

- Fully searchable for easy access to vital information

- Copy and paste, print, and bookmark content

Did you know that Packt offers eBook versions of every book published, with PDF and ePub files available? You can upgrade to the eBook version at packt.com and as a print book customer, you are entitled to a discount on the eBook copy. Get in touch with us at customercare@packtpub.com for more details.

At www.packt.com, you can also read a collection of free technical articles, sign up for a range of free newsletters, and receive exclusive discounts and offers on Packt books and eBooks.

Other Books You May Enjoy

If you enjoyed this book, you may be interested in these other books by Packt:

Learn Python Programming - Third Edition

Fabrizio Romano, Heinrich Kruger

ISBN: 9781801815093

- Get Python up and running on Windows, Mac, and Linux
- Write elegant, reusable, and efficient code in any situation
- Avoid common pitfalls like duplication, complicated design, and over-engineering
- Understand when to use the functional or object-oriented approach to programming
- Build a simple API with FastAPI and program GUI applications with Tkinter
- Get an initial overview of more complex topics such as data persistence and cryptography
- Fetch, clean, and manipulate data, making efficient use of Python's built-in data structures

Mastering Python - Second Edition

Rick van Hattem

ISBN: 9781800207721

- Write beautiful Pythonic code and avoid common Python coding mistakes

- Apply the power of decorators, generators, coroutines, and metaclasses

- Use different testing systems like pytest, unittest, and doctest

- Track and optimize application performance for both memory and CPU usage

- Debug your applications with PDB, Werkzeug, and faulthandler

- Improve your performance through asyncio, multiprocessing, and distributed computing

- Explore popular libraries like Dask, NumPy, SciPy, pandas, TensorFlow, and scikit-learn

- Extend Python's capabilities with C/C++ libraries and system calls

Packt is searching for authors like you

If you're interested in becoming an author for Packt, please visit `authors.packtpub.com` and apply today. We have worked with thousands of developers and tech professionals, just like you, to help them share their insight with the global tech community. You can make a general application, apply for a specific hot topic that we are recruiting an author for, or submit your own idea.

Share Your Thoughts

Now you've finished Metaprogramming with Python, we'd love to hear your thoughts! Scan the QR code below to go straight to the Amazon review page for this book and share your feedback or leave a review on the site that you purchased it from.

`https://packt.link/r/1838554653`

Your review is important to us and the tech community and will help us make sure we're delivering excellent quality content.